Also by Ina Bertrand

FILM CENSORSHIP IN AUSTRALIA

GOVERNMENT AND FILM IN AUSTRALIA (*with Diane Collins*)

CINEMA IN AUSTRALIA: A Documentary History (*edited*)

THE OXFORD COMPANION TO AUSTRALIAN FILMS (*co-edited with Brian McFarlane and Geoff Mayer*)

Also by Peter Hughes

Peter Hughes has contributed chapters to a number of books on documentary film, and is editor of the online journal *Screening the Past*, www.latrobe.edu.au/screeningthepast.

Media Research Methods

Audiences, Institutions, Texts

Ina Bertrand and Peter Hughes

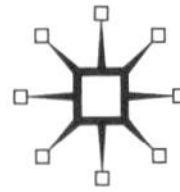

First published 2005 by
PALGRAVE MACMILLAN
Houndmills, Basingstoke, Hampshire RG21 6XS and
175 Fifth Avenue, New York, N.Y. 10010
Companies and representatives throughout the world

PALGRAVE MACMILLAN is the global academic imprint of the Palgrave Macmillan division of St. Martin's Press, LLC and of Palgrave Macmillan Ltd. Macmillan® is a registered trademark in the United States, United Kingdom and other countries. Palgrave is a registered trademark in the European Union and other countries.

ISBN 0–333–96094–7 hardback
ISBN 0–333–96095–5 paperback

This book is printed on paper suitable for recycling and made from fully managed and sustained forest sources.

A catalogue record for this book is available from the British Library.

A catalog record for this book is available from the Library of Congress.
Library of Congress Catalogue Card Number – 2004052830

10 9 8 7 6 5 4 3 2
14 13 12 11 10 09 08 07 06

Printed in China

This book is dedicated to all the authors and colleagues whose work has stimulated our thinking, to all those students whose intellectual curiosity has forced us to refine our research practice and to find new ways to explain our ideas, and to our families who have survived the fallout from this process.

Contents

List of Figures

Acknowledgements

We wish to thank the following people for their invaluable assistance in researching and writing this book. Val Forbes and Eva Fisch, humanities librarians at the Borchardt Library, La Trobe University, Melbourne found books, and provided advice and criticism in relation to library and web-based research. A number of people provided invaluable advice and criticism on different aspects of the theory or practice of research: Tony Barta, Darrel Caulley, Anna Dzenis, John Langer, Ray Lewis, David Gauntlett, Denise Meredyth, Philipa Rothfield, and Terrie Waddell. In relation to archival research we are indebted to: Russell Campbell, Donna Coates, Sue Harper, Roger Horrocks, Harriett Margolis, Janet Moat, Barbara O'Connor, Vincent Porter, Steve Vaughn, Chris Watson. While Graham Bertrand, Claire Hughes and Dinah Partridge provided support of the most practical kind as well as maintaining morale!

Every effort has been made to acknowledge all sources in this book. Owners of uncredited copyright material reproduced here are invited to contact the authors to receive appropriate credit in future editions.

CHAPTER 1

Of Elephants, Definitions and Models: the Context of Media Research

> Five blind men were introduced for the first time to an elephant.
>
> They ran their hands over it, and gave their verdict.
>
> 'Ah', said the first man: 'An elephant is solid and flat, like a wall.'
>
> 'Not so', said the second man: 'An elephant is like the trunk of a young tree, reaching towards the heavens.'
>
> 'No, indeed', said the third man: 'An elephant is like a palm leaf, round and soft and waving in the breeze.'
>
> 'You are all wrong', said the fourth: 'An elephant is like a flexible pipe. The air moves along it with a rushing sound.'
>
> 'No, no', said the fifth man: 'An elephant is like a rope. When you pull on it the heavens open up with rain.'

The lessons to be learned from this parable, which we first heard on a Pete Seeger record from the 1950s and have since come across many times in slightly different written and oral forms, are:

- People are curious: they want to understand their world (what an elephant is).
- They create new understandings in terms of what they already know (elephants in terms of trees or ropes).
- They do not necessarily agree about these new understandings, even after **empirical research** (evidence of the senses).
- It is unwise to jump to conclusions from incomplete data. Even if truth were possible (and not everyone agrees that it is), it is never possible to know with certainty whether you have found it.
- **Research** is an inherently risky business: you might not like what you find.

- Old stories are inherently sexist: women may have reached different conclusions.

Starting a serious text on research methods with a frivolous story also makes the point that research can be intriguing and enjoyable, a mix of dull routine with the excitement and satisfaction of exploring your world and perhaps finding new knowledge.

But it is not only curiosity that takes us to media research. A profound change is occurring in the world: there has been a shift in the developed economies from the manufacture of physical products to the production and exchange of information, a shift from an industrial society to a post-industrial society (Bell 1976; Castells 1997). A series of alliances is being forged between industry and commerce on one hand and the traditional repositories of information on the other: universities are seeking alliances with media companies, libraries are going online, software companies are buying the rights to the electronic dissemination of artworks. We can recognise the post-industrial economy in the dominance of Hollywood products in our lives; in the fact that one of the world's richest men has made his money, not from producing cars and heavy machinery, but from lines of computer code; and from the increasing pace of **convergence** in the telecommunications and entertainment industries. Companies which have been predominantly involved in the creation of communications infrastructure are merging with companies and public organisations which have been involved in the creation of 'content': Time Warner (a major entertainment conglomerate) has merged with America On Line (AOL) which in Europe has links with Bertelsmann (a major media company with a large number of publishing imprints) (Herman and McChesney 1997).

The crucial skills in this post-industrial 'information economy' (Barr 2000; Castells 1997) are those of research and writing: the ability to find information, the ability to synthesise information and the ability to present that information for other people. Such research skills are used in a range of careers: stockbrokers in preparing advice for clients, journalists in writing stories, and civil servants in preparing briefs for ministers or in writing reports. In the media there are broadly three areas of research, that all use these skills:

- Professional research for the media: specialist researchers prepare background material for current affairs and documentary programs on television and radio or do historical research for drama (getting the details right for characters, settings, costumes).
- Commercial research about the media: market research companies conduct **audience** research for television stations or advertising agencies.
- Academic research about the media: students and staff of educational institutions research media audiences, **institutions** and **texts**.

So while this book, intended for the novice researcher, primarily speaks within an academic context, the advice it gives has wider applications. We try not to assume knowledge or experience, and we offer far more alternative methods than any one researcher will ever need. The presentation of the book parallels how we think of the research process – in phases, rather than stages, allowing the various aspects of the research to occur simultaneously, or the researcher to circle back on earlier ideas and aspects of the process. However, we discuss these phases separately and sequentially, merely for convenience.

This book is intended as a first year undergraduate resource which will be carried with you through your later studies, even into postgraduate work, and to which you will refer from time to time in your working life after study.

We begin, in this chapter, with definitions and **models** of the foundation terms (each of which is also defined in the glossary), inviting readers to locate themselves so that they can make informed choices from the alternatives offered in later chapters. Terms which may be new to the reader, or which may need further explanation, are printed in bold type on their first occurrence to remind the reader that a glossary definition is available. Chapter 2 offers advice on developing your research topic and reading around your subject, constantly refining the topic as you go. Then there are three parts, each organised around one of the major streams of media research: audiences, institutions and texts.

Each of these parts begins with an introduction, followed by a chapter reviewing the research on one topic within that research stream: soap opera within audience research (Chapter 3), **censorship** within institutional research (Chapter 6), news within textual research (Chapter 9). Our focus in this book is on research **methodology**, and not on the topics by which we hope to illustrate these methods. So these first chapters within each section provide an example of reading around a subject, but, because we are primarily concerned to survey the models of research to be found in that research stream, they will not cover all aspects of that subject. Our intention is that the novice researcher may be able to locate the research approach that seems most appropriate to them. For Parts I and II, the literature review is followed by chapters (4 and 7 respectively) on gathering data. In each of these, the methods most commonly found in that research stream are given the most detailed treatment: other methods are covered more cursorily and readers referred to other sections of this book or to other reference works. These parts conclude with a chapter (5 and 8 respectively) on the **analysis** and **interpretation** of the data gathered. In the analysis section of these chapters, advice is given on how to systematise data and to start to make inferences from it. In the interpretation section, we discuss the major intellectual **frameworks** through which projects have been built, from the initial selection of a topic right through to the conclusions, leaving you to decide what is useful and/or appropriate in your own case. In Part III, data gathering and analysis are dealt with in Chapter 10 and interpretation in Chapter 11. A final chapter (Chapter 12) discusses how conclusions are reached, how the researcher presents the results, and how the success of the completed project is judged.

In all of these, you will find us using models – conceptual tools that help us to make sense of complex data, by sorting and creating hierarchies. For us, the best models are those that cover the most possibilities and are the most helpful in representing relationships, but a model remains always an abstract representation:

- fallible, because it is based upon assumptions, which may be wrong and will certainly shift over time;
- incomplete, because no one model can ever do it all;
- always context specific, so it will not necessarily remain useful in a different context (though it may be adaptable to other contexts, as you will see from the examples we use).

1.1 Definitions

So, let us move on to consider some of the general **concepts** which construct both the title to this book and its basic purposes.

Media

In **communication theory** a **medium** is, broadly speaking, an intermediary enabling or enhancing communication across time and space. Even between two individual people, communication may require the intervention of a medium – another person (a go-between) or a technology (telephone, letter, fax). Usually, however, we think of the media as those technologies which provide a link between many people, that is, the mass media of radio, television, newspapers, films, the world wide web. These media are also a series of institutions, which are currently undergoing significant structural change.

The academic tradition which studies all these forms has a number of names. In the USA, it is likely to be known as 'communication studies' or 'media literacy'; in the UK and Australia, it may be called 'media studies'. The research methods we discuss in this book apply across all these traditions – to texts, the audiences which consume or make sense of texts, and the institutional contexts within which they are produced and meaning is constructed. At the broadest level this context is **culture**, which needs its own definition.

Culture

Unlike most other animals, humans construct their world by living in it. We have the power to physically change our world (to build houses, to cook food, to kill other people), and also human thought operates upon the world outside our individual minds to create an understanding of it, which we share with other humans through language, the arts and sciences, education, the media – broadly speaking, culture.

This view of culture comes out of the **social sciences**: the **humanities** (particularly **aesthetics**) often use the term much more selectively. What has been called the '**mass culture critique**' (Gans 1974: 3) proposes that popular culture (including – among other things – film, radio and television) is a debased form of culture, because it is mass-produced and aimed at the lowest common denominator – the public as 'mass'. From this position, true 'culture' is high culture: musical and literary classics and the sort of art that is found in public galleries.

In this book we prefer the broader definition of culture, as a whole way of life. It is, however, no longer possible to speak of a single coherent culture – it is more accurate to speak of multiple overlapping cultures (sometimes called subcultures), based on gender and/or sexual preference, ethnic background, **class** positioning, physical location, and many other things. All mass media operate within the context of these multiple cultures and are themselves significant sites of cultural activity, operating as **communication systems**.

Communication

Like most of the important terms we use in this section, the meanings of 'communication' are complex and vary with the field in which it is being used, whether this is media and communication studies, cybernetics, information technology studies, or psychology, and so any definition is merely a beginning of the process of understanding the term. At the simplest level communication is the act of imparting information. This imparting may be conscious and deliberate, or unconscious.

The earliest theoretical models of how human communication operates were by analogy to technology, to telegraphy: A (the transmitter) presses the Morse button to send **signals** (a medium) along a wire (a channel) to B (a receiver). This model demonstrates that the information must be organised: codes (such as Morse) are sets of information organised in another form (in this case into dots and dashes) to enable brevity and security of transmission. The problem with codes is that only those who share them can communicate. If I say to you: 'Setzen Sie sich', you will not understand me unless you speak German, so we cannot share meanings while you are outside the code. Those who wish to communicate have to negotiate meaning. If I add gestures (patting the chair where I wish you to sit) I can use a shared (gestural) code to initiate you into the unshared (linguistic) code. This is how we learn most language, by translating codes we know into those we do not (often visual to verbal). We are surrounded by coded systems, using visual cues: examples are traffic signals (international symbols for go, stop, etc) and tourist symbols (toilets, bus shelters, train stations, etc). When we misread a signal, we may get '**feedback**' (for instance, the reaction of people if we go into the wrong toilet), and that teaches us the code and affects our next behaviour. When we receive communication from others we also give feedback – asking questions, looking puzzled or pleased or angry, doing what is asked of us or not doing it. All these aspects of communication fit together, and can be explained systematically, by constructing a model of communication.

The example so far given comes from the process (or linear) school of communication **theory**. Here the word 'school' refers to a group of people (not necessarily formally related to one another) who share a common approach, or way of understanding the world. This school speaks of the flow of communication, of **messages** passing between **senders** (**encoders**) and **receivers** (**decoders**), producing feedback, which may influence the transmission of the next message. Within this model, 'noise' is whatever interferes between the sender and the receiver, which may be actual sound (for instance a jack hammer in the street below, drowning out speech) or semantic noise (for instance unfamiliarity with a dialect being spoken). If such interference occurs, then the message may be misread (the decoder may misunderstand the encoded meaning), and communication has failed.

The process school of communication theory operates on a model that can be represented (rather simplistically) as shown in Figure 1.1.

In fact, there are many variants on this model, and these have changed over time, becoming much more sophisticated: some allow for stages in the relay of messages, or for the influence of opinion leaders, or the complex effects of feedback. The major models were developed in quite a short period, from Lasswell in 1948 to Gerbner in 1956 (summarised in Fiske 1982: 6–40; or Severin and Tankard 1988: 32–41).

By the 1960s, another family of communication theory was developing – the semiotic school, which uses a different vocabulary and conceptual model. '**Semiotics**' was originally a medical term for the systematic study of symptoms. However, it now has much wider currency, including within communication theory, where it refers to the construction of textual meaning by the process of **signification**, that is the interaction of signs with their referents and with the **readers**/producers who use them.

This school would say that any meaning extracted from a text is never objective or final: it does exist in the text or it could not be read, so there are theoretically only a finite number of potential meanings, but these are always dependent on the reader and so never objective or predictable. This model can be represented (again simplistically) as shown in Figure 1.2.

Source —> Encoder —> Signal —> Decoder —> Destination

Figure 1.1 Model on which the process school of communication theory operates

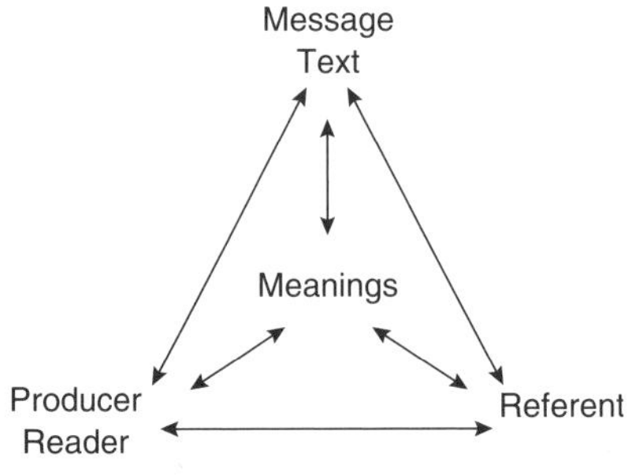

Source: Fiske 1982: 4

Figure 1.2 Semiotic model of communication

From the semiotic perspective, producers (the encoders of the process school) and readers (the decoders of the process school) are not seen as separate: every producer (speaker, writer, television camera operator) also reads (the signs that she produces), and every reader also produces (meaning). Meanings arise from this complex process of interaction, and are exchanged within it. This discussion elides some serious disagreements within the field of semiotics, and again overlooks recent developments, but it will do for the moment. We discuss all this more fully in the third sub-section of section 10.1 in Chapter 10, where we are concerned with the analysis of texts.

To sum up the two schools:

The process school:

- is concerned primarily with acts of communication (messages), with what happens in the process of communicating;
- assumes that meaning is fixed, and inherent in the message, put there by the sender (encoder), and decoded by the receiver (with the possibility of multiple stages along the route, and of feedback from the decoder to the encoder);
- considers that communication can fail as a result of noise (for instance when there is no shared code).

The semiotic school:

- is concerned primarily with works of communication (texts), and with how (as well as what) they mean;
- assumes that meaning is constructed in the process of signification, by the interaction of text and reader/producer within a context, so is always negotiated and never absolute;
- considers that communication always happens, that signification produces meanings, even when the meanings generated are not shared by participants in the communication event.

The definitions of culture and of communication affect how people do their research. Hawkins and Pingree (1982) assume a process (linear) model, that television produces certain effects in viewers (see their diagram p. 244). Lull (1980) discusses similar questions of the relation between media and social reality, but from a semiotic model of communication, using qualitative methodology. In later chapters, we will refer repeatedly to the models of communication in operation as we discuss examples of research.

Research

Although research is central to media studies, the term is absent from most specialist media dictionaries. Simply put, 'research' is the process of asking questions and finding answers. However research is more than this. It involves systematic exploration, guided by well constructed questions, producing new information or reassessing old information. Through the application of **critical** analytical skills to information, the researcher is able to transform it into knowledge, so the researcher needs a way to understand what 'knowledge' is, to recognise and assess knowledge, and to fit new knowledge into old knowledge.

In the chapters in which we review the literature (Chapters 3, 6 and 9), we spend a great deal of time evaluating other people's research, deciding what the strengths and weaknesses are in each case, and hoping to provide readers with standards to apply both to their own reading and to the procedures they follow in their research. Our own value systems must inevitably come into play in such an exercise: we would deny that **objectivity** is ever possible, and would certainly not claim it for ourselves. But we still try to be fair to those other researchers, no matter how different their approaches and methods are from our own. For us, everything we read, from whatever perspective or **paradigm** it emerges, is grist to the mill: we may well learn something from it, and at the very least, it can help us to decide that we prefer our own ways of doing things. We consider it is foolish to close our minds to other possibilities – elephants may, after all, be like trees or walls. At the same time, we need to look carefully at the claims of others, judging for ourselves whether they are convincing. To do that we need to understand the process by which other researchers have come to their conclusions, and this means understanding both their methodologies and the intellectual frameworks within which they have operated. Part of what we want you to take away from this book is enough knowledge of the debates about research to judge what you read for yourselves – including how far you wish to trust or agree with the writers of this book. So it is important both that you understand what a 'framework' is, and that you have at least a nodding acquaintance with the major frameworks that you will come across in your reading.

This is because what we do and what we know are inextricably intertwined. It is not a matter of having a theory and putting it into practice, nor of doing something and deriving a theory from it, but of both theory and practice happening simultaneously and interactively and continuously. Ways of doing things depend upon what we know and believe about the things we do, but we can only find out (can only reach the stage of knowing and believing) by doing. Understanding the range of possible frameworks, and how others have used them, is the first step to understanding your own processes of thought, as well as the material to which you wish to apply the thought.

Even if you are unable to articulate it, you already have an intellectual framework, that governs the way you conceive your world and your own place within it. This framework will shape your research from beginning to end, because it provides the structure within which your choices (including the initial choice of a research subject) are made. Your framework comes partly from the institutional setting within which your research takes place – the position taken by your employers or those who commissioned the research, or by your teachers, by the department within which they work, and by the university/college which employs them. Part of it will come from your personal position, shaped by your previous education, your political and religious beliefs, your gender, sexual preference, race and class affiliations, your personal style. If you already have a fixed position or firm opinions then you may well already be beyond the scope of this book: it is intended for people who either are not yet committed to a position, do not understand what their own position is, or who want to understand how their position fits into a larger picture.

What we have called a framework is sometimes called a paradigm: a framework/paradigm allows some questions to be asked and some research methods to be applied to these questions, while at the same time denying the **validity** of other questions and other methods. Denzin and Lincoln (2000: 157) offer the following useful explanation of how a paradigm shapes our thinking processes:

> A paradigm encompasses four concepts: ethics ... , epistemology, ontology and methodology. Ethics asks, How will I be as a moral person in the world? Epistemology asks, How do I know the world? What is the relationship between the inquirer and the known? Ontology raises basic questions about the nature of reality and the nature of the human being in the world. Methodology focuses on the best means for gaining knowledge about the world.

The paradigm categories proposed by Lincoln and Guba (2000) for **qualitative research** provide a useful model across all forms of media research: **positivism**, **post-positivism**, **critical theory**, **constructivism**, and **participatory action research**.

Positivism was probably the most powerful intellectual framework of the nineteenth and twentieth centuries, across all **disciplines**. It is built upon a realist assumption that the world is out there waiting to be known. It has faith in the **scientific method**, which it sees as leading to the growth of objective and verifiable knowledge (rather than mere superstition and guesswork). The grip of positivism on the scientific world has been weakening over recent decades, as scientific research methodology begins to shift away from the goal of absolute truth, based on claims to objectivity, generalisation and prediction, and find ways to deal with concepts such as 'uncertainty' and 'chaos'. As an indication of this a recent issue of *The Journal of Communication* (LI, no. 3, September 2001) is devoted to 'Uncertainty, evaluation and communication'.

The French writer Auguste Comte (1798–1857) was largely responsible for the extension of the term 'positivism' to cover more than the physical sciences: he proposed that all forms of knowledge (both physical and social) had passed through three stages over the course of human **history** – theological, metaphysical, and scientific. The logical positivists of the Vienna Circle in the 1920s and 1930s required the scientist (including the social scientist) to seek invariable natural laws, which were to be discovered by subjecting empirical data to logical analysis, ideally by a combination of operationalising (turning into quantitative statements) and **verification** (testing on all possible **samples**), though they acknowledged that perfect verification is not possible on data from human **subjects** (Potter 1996: 31). Since then, the definition of positivism has been further expanded, till it may include any sociological approach which operates on the general assumption that the methods of the physical sciences (such as measurement, or the search for general laws) can be carried over into the social sciences (Jary and Jary 1991: 485). Positivism also influences the humanities: there is, for instance, a strand of **historiography** which conceives of history as a science, with covering laws and the capacity to predict from these.

The post-positivist position begins in the middle of the twentieth century, with Karl Popper (1902–1994), who demonstrated that falsification (finding the case that does not fit, and so requires a change in the theory) is a more logically achievable goal than verification. But the term 'post-positivism' is harder to define than positivism. There are, broadly speaking, two families of definition:

- The more limited definition is represented by Lincoln and Guba (2000). They attribute to post-positivism an **ontology** of critical **realism**, an **epistemology** that still seeks knowledge (but admits that verification is not achievable and judges success on Popper's principles and the search for relative objectivity through the critical community of scholars), and a methodology more open to qualitative methods and the **grounded theory** arising from these. This is a relatively precise definition, making post-positivism a slightly softer, revised, version of positivism. It places positivism and post-positivism on one side of the debate (seeking objectivity, even though, in the case of post-positivists, acknowledging that it is out of reach), and critical theory, constructivism and participatory action research on the opposite side of the debate (acknowledging, and to different degrees celebrating, the inherent **subjectivity** of research and relativity of knowledge). This makes critical theory in particular a kind of grab-bag term, covering all sorts of positions that won't fit into the three other more precise categories.
- A more inclusive definition proposes post-positivism as the covering term for all the intellectual frameworks which have positioned themselves against positivism. Lather (1991: 7) breaks this field, not in relation to attitudes to objectivity/subjectivity, but in relation to goals (to understand/to emancipate/to deconstruct). This allows her to acknowledge that all the categories positioned against positivism (including Lincoln and Guba's post-positivism) see the research process to some degree as circular or spiral or cumulative (rather than linear and sequential), prefer qualitative over quantitative methods of research, and apply hermeneutic and contextual explanatory systems within a constructivist epistemology.

Because positivism was more openly acknowledged within the social sciences than within the humanities, it is primarily in these fields (particularly sociology, education and psychology) that the debate between positivism and post-positivism has developed: within the humanities (literary studies, history), opposition to positivism tends to use a slightly different vocabulary (see Chapters 8 and 11). Such debates about terminology clearly demonstrate how important definitions are in the research process. In this book we will (as we would advise you to do in your own research) adopt the terminology that is most useful to us: we will limit the use of post-positivism as Lincoln and Guba do, and use '**non-positivist**' when we wish to refer to all those categories positioned against positivism (Lather's post-positivism).

If you feel as if you are now drowning in terminology, be reassured. Most of these terms will become clearer as you read on, and part of the confusion is not your responsibility – it arises because research theorists (and practitioners) are still struggling with the definitions, redefining them in use, while the categories themselves are shifting as a result of such struggles.

That is why it is so difficult to distinguish among those non-positivist categories. One method is to watch them in action: for instance, for critical theory see Kincheloe and McLaren (2000), for constructivism see Charmaz (2000), for participatory action research see Kemmis and McTaggart (2000).

Another way is to look at the history of the categories, and the changing relations among them. Denzin and Lincoln (2000) introduce their impressive *Handbook of Qualitative Methodology* with such a history, in what they call seven 'moments': we recommend you read their discussion. Our version of this history is a continuum, with over-lapping categories of research, that can probably be divided into three:

- the unchallenged dominance of positivism;
- the challenges to positivism, both from within (producing post-positivism) and from outside (from various interpretive perspectives);
- the challenge of **post-modernism** (producing a breaking down of boundaries and an interest in alternate forms, both of enquiry and of writing).

In such a terminological quicksand, a model can be a useful lifeline. We recommend the model offered by Lincoln and Guba (2000: 168), which we reproduce here as Figure 1.3, repeating the warning that models are **heuristic** devices, not exact representations of any reality.

All these frameworks can be found in media research, as we will demonstrate in later chapters. The number crunching of the **ratings** game comes straight out of the positivist paradigm, as do some of the **effects studies**, some early **uses and gratifications studies**, and some early content analyses of texts. But more recent effects and/or uses and gratifications studies have sometimes been post-positivist, and certainly **ethnomethodology** and other **cultural studies** approaches to media research have come from a perspective beyond or even hostile to positivist assumptions, perhaps constructivism or critical theory. We have not yet found any participatory action research on media: that may be our ignorance, or it may be just too early for this to have filtered through.

Issue	Positivism	Post-positivism	Critical theory et al.	Constructivism	Participatory action research
Ontology	Naïve realism – real reality but apprehendable	Critical realism – 'real' reality, but only imperfectly and probabilistically apprehendable	Historical realism – virtual reality shaped by social, political, cultural, economic, ethnic, and gender values crystallised over time	Relativism – local and specific constructed realities	Participative reality – subjective-objective reality, co-created by mind and given cosmos
Epistemology	Dualistic-objectivist; findings true	Modified dualist/objectivist; critical tradition/community; findings probably true	Transactional/subjectivist; value-mediated findings	Transactional/subjectivist; created findings	Critical subjectivity in participatory transaction with cosmos; extended epistemology of experiential, propositional, and practical knowing; co-created findings
Methodology	Experimental/manipulative; verification of hypotheses; chiefly quantitative methods	Modified experimental/manipulative; critical multiplism; falsification of hypotheses; may include qualitative methods	Dialogic/dialectic	Hermeneutic/dialectic	Political participation in collaborative action inquiry; primacy of the practical; use of language grounded in shared experiential context

Source: Yvonna S. Lincoln and Egon G Guba, 'Paradigmatic Controversies, Contradictions, and Emerging Confluences', in *Handbook of Qualitative Research*, ed. Norman K. Denzin and Yvonna S. Lincoln p. 168 © 2000 (Sage Publications). Reprinted by permission of Sage Publications

Figure 1.3 Research frameworks

We agree with Denzin and Lincoln's proposition that 'the borders and boundary lines separating these paradigms and perspectives have begun to blur' (2000: 157). If you espouse positivism rigidly (and it is becoming harder and harder to find anyone who does), the boundaries are absolute – there is 'real' science, and there is 'woolly thinking' which cannot enrich the pool of human knowledge at all. Beyond that positivist paradigm, all kinds of possibilities open up. In this book, we propose that there is no need to choose between a social science and a humanities approach, or between quantitative and qualitative methods: once you have decided what your question or **hypothesis** is, any method which is appropriate is acceptable.

Increasingly, the boundaries between the two major academic and intellectual traditions that study the media (the social sciences and the humanities) are weakening. It was once possible to define each academic 'discipline' in terms of its research paradigm, built upon a specific ontology and epistemology: the fields of 'mathematics' or 'physics' or 'biology' or 'history' or 'literature' or 'classics' recognised boundaries not only of what was appropriate for the discipline to know but of how the appropriate knowledge could be obtained. But now, not only are many frameworks operating simultaneously, but they are also operating across disciplines. That is where this book positions itself – on the boundary between the humanities and the social sciences: we believe that good media research can come out of both these academic traditions, and from all intellectual positions past rigid positivism.

A model like that of Lincoln and Guba acknowledges the necessary connection between our processes of thought and our actions. It also allows us to see not only that methods can cross discipline boundaries, but that both the social sciences and the humanities share common frameworks. Though some variants of each framework may be incompatible with some variants of another, it is not uncommon to find that individual researchers subscribe to more than one framework at a time, and move about among them (and among variants within them) over the course of their research career.

Till quite recently, it was considered both unwise and unprofessional to articulate your framework in a research report. However, as the positivist paradigm, with its claim to objectivity and its assumption that research must be value-free, has been increasingly challenged, more researchers feel free, or even obliged, to express their position openly. Janet Staiger, for instance, usually leaves the reader to infer her position from her text, but in one article (Staiger and Barker 2000) she locates herself as a Marxist, associating **psychoanalysis** and critical Marxist sociology, under the heading of critical theory, and accepting that cognitive psychology and functional sociology also help to explain audiences. Patti Lather (1991) identifies herself with neo-**Marxism**, **feminism** and **post-structuralism**: her research is also a good example of empirical research from a non-positivist perspective, demonstrating that the two are not incompatible.

We cannot be completely comprehensive in this book – there is not enough space, and we do not claim sufficient expertise across all the alternatives. In each section we discuss only some of the frameworks that have contributed significantly to that stream of research, and in some cases the same framework will appear again later. We do not propose that all these frameworks are equal, or even equally valid: only that all are currently in use, so you are likely to find them represented in the reading you do, and you are likely to have absorbed some at least of this into your own ways of thinking. We hope here to provide you with a map of the terrain – a way of understanding how all these various elements (the general philosophical frameworks, the fundamental methodological approaches, and the practical methods within each) relate to each other. With this knowledge, we hope you will be empowered to understand your own framework(s) and so to select your methodology wisely – choosing those methods that are appropriate for your project, and understanding the implications of your choices. We give you enough information to structure a research plan, some advice on the more commonly used methods, and information on where to find other texts that will provide you with the detail to carry your project through to a successful conclusion. The novice researcher can expect to be engaged in small scale research at first, but the principles you learn there can be applied later to larger scale research.

In the above discussion of research we have not explored one of the terms used by Lincoln and Guba in their grid – **ethics**. They may be correct to link ethics with spirituality, which they suggest will in future be increasingly recognised within the research process but we are taking a more pragmatic approach to ethics, as the moral judgments that researchers must make within their own work as well as about the research of others.

1.2 Ethics

Lincoln and Guba (2000: 170) note on their grid that the positivist sees ethical problems as extrinsic to (outside) the research process, leaving the researcher to decide what is ethical, for instance whether or not to deceive participants: if the goal is a worthy one (the increase of human knowledge) then the end justifies the means (deception is acceptable). The post-positivist will probably agree with the positivist in principle, though she may in practice accept more responsibility for the effects of the research on research subjects.

Other non-positivists, however, take a fundamentally different position, seeing the moral dimension of the research as intrinsic – a necessary part of the decisions they must make. Lincoln and Guba suggest that the critical theorist will always try to act morally (so protecting the participants from harm), while the constructivist and the participatory researcher will have involved participants all along, so moral decisions will have become a necessary aspect of the process itself.

This model makes clear that ethical issues are a part of the research from beginning to end, shaped by the intellectual framework in which the researcher is operating. But ethical decisions may not be entirely up to you. Universities and colleges usually have an ethics policy and standard procedures to protect all parties:

- to protect the right of the researcher to conduct the research;
- to ensure that the research subjects are not placed at any risk of physical, emotional or financial harm;
- to reduce the likelihood of legal action by research subjects against researchers or their institution.

The ethics policy of your institution should be scrupulously adhered to, for your own protection as well as for the protection of your research subjects. This will probably involve making an application to an ethical standards committee, which should be seen as an opportunity, to be taken advantage of, rather than as a burden, to be circumvented. It is important both to your own peace of mind, and to the quality of your research, that you have confidence in your moral position and your capacity to put it into practice. Before you begin, it is worth reading some of the thoughtful approaches to complex ethical issues provided in (for instance) Miles and Huberman (1994: 288–97), Christians (2000), or Olesen (2000). You can start to work out your own position, by considering the ethical/moral dimension of the web of relationships in which you are enmeshed:

(i) Relationship to the profession
As a media researcher (or aspiring researcher), you have a responsibility to your colleagues, to uphold the good name of the profession. This will require you to:

- meet high standards, both in your behaviour during the research and in the quality of the work you produce;
- behave in such a fashion that others will have no difficulty in entering the field after you.

Professional organisations now have voluntary codes of conduct which help to protect ethical standards within the profession, but such organisations are distant and impersonal. You would be wise to have someone (a lecturer; your thesis supervisor; a departmental head) to whom you can immediately turn, if ethical problems arise.

(ii) Relationship to funding/commissioning bodies
This raises ethical issues that are not likely to concern students, but which remain significant for the field as a whole. Is it possible to accept funding for media and communications research without:

- losing credibility with your peers (can you, for instance, ethically accept money from advertising agencies for research on the effects of products advertised, such as cigarettes?);

- compromising your own moral position (for instance, seeing your research used to justify selling cigarettes to minors)?

(iii) Relationship to sources
Whether your sources are real people, or just the documents and other evidence they leave behind, relationships with sources produce more ethical dilemmas than other relationships. You need to decide both how far you wish to protect your sources and how strictly you will implement your policy. If you consider that the end justifies the means, then you have no problem. Anything less than this will involve accepting responsibility for (in ascending order):

- protecting subjects from physical, financial or emotional harm;
- protecting subjects from invasion of privacy (new laws to protect privacy have been introduced recently in some jurisdictions);
- providing subjects with information about the research process;
- providing subjects with access to the research process and its results;
- involving subjects in the research process and its results.

Once again, how far you go will depend upon your intellectual framework. The post-positivist will certainly accept the first of these responsibilities, and probably the first three; the participatory action researcher will accept at least the fourth of these, and probably the fifth.

Once you have decided what your ethical goals are, you can decide how to implement them. Clearly, doing this will take time, but no matter how irritating it all is, there is no excuse for researchers not behaving ethically. If you are in a position to reward participants (either by gifts or outright payment for their time and effort), your ethical responsibility is not diminished.

(iii a) Use of documents and images
You need first to decide who 'owns' the information you turn up – you or your sources? This is of particular sensitivity when you are studying a culture different from your own, with different standards concerning the 'ownership' and use of information. Some cultures are particularly sensitive about the use of images: for instance, in Australian indigenous culture it is unacceptable to show an image of a deceased person.

You will always need to be sensitive to the feelings of the subject of any text, and to use the text in ways that do not hurt or offend. Library and archival research may turn up incriminating or embarrassing private documents, or institutional records. If these have caveats in place on their use, you must obey these (no matter how disappointing this is), and if they do not you still have the responsibility of dealing fairly and honestly (that is, ethically) with them. Fair dealing provides considerable leeway, but does not absolve you from considering the feelings of the person(s) implicated, or (if the person is already dead) of their family. Perhaps you may feel that you have a larger responsibility to the community, particularly when disclosure might result in re-shaping public opinion or future action. If so, consider first the legal implications, and take legal advice if there is the slightest possibility of action against you for slander or libel.

(iii b) Selection of human subjects (for instance, for **interview**)

- Some subjects may be more vulnerable than others: for instance it would be unfair to test the effect of road safety advertisements on people who have been recently bereaved as the result of a road accident.
- Some subjects may not be capable of fully understanding the implications of your project: for instance, you may need to use interpreters when explaining to people of different linguistic background to your own, or advocates or counsellors if you wish to interview intellectually disabled people.
- Children are a special case. You will need to get the cooperation of parents, and you should consider carefully both how vulnerable children are (to suggestion or manipulation) and that they may not fully understand what you plan to do.

(iii c) Deception

This was recognised as an ethical minefield from very early in the history of social research, and a great deal has been written about it, for instance about whether **covert research** (research on subjects without their knowledge or consent) is ever ethical. Fortunately, there are not many media research projects where deception may become an issue, or where subjects might refuse consent. A possible exception is those areas of institutional research which might expose institutions or individuals to public criticism or be interpreted as commercial espionage.

A researcher must also be aware that subjects may deceive in **questionnaires** and interviews. For a post-positivist, this is a problem requiring the development of strategies, both in the data gathering phase and in interpretation. For a constructivist, it is simply a part of the research process: if all knowledge is constructed through interpretation, then lies (once recognised) are simply another form of data, requiring appropriate interpretation and inviting attention to the phenomenon of lying itself.

(iii d) Informed consent

This is the process (within post-positivist, critical, or constructivist research frameworks) of informing research subjects of their rights, and obtaining their consent to the research. If you are administering a questionnaire, it is enough that the questionnaire contain a statement of the intentions of the research and the level of confidentiality that is promised: provided this gives sufficient information, simply filling in the form can be taken to constitute consent.

Signing an 'informed consent' document (most institutions have standard forms) protects research subjects:

- There should be provision to withdraw (up to an agreed final date) at any time, even if that inconveniences the researcher.
- There should be information on the format in which data will be collected (for instance, by written questionnaire or by telephone or by personal interview) and recorded (for instance on audiotape or videotape).
- There should be information about how and where the research data will be stored, for how long this will be kept, and who will have access to it.
- There should be information about the use to which the research will be put, to whom and when the research report will be made and where and when it is likely to be published.
- There should be a guarantee of confidentiality and option for the subject to remain anonymous at all times.
- There should be information about the procedure to follow if the subject wishes to make a complaint.

If you wish to work within an institution (such as a school, hospital or workplace), you will need the approval of the management (the principal of a school, the board or director of a hospital, the managing director of a business), but such approval does not excuse you from also obtaining informed consent from individual subjects.

After the data is collected, you should follow the procedures indicated on the informed consent form, remembering that a promise of anonymity means that there is no way that subjects can be identified, including through details of their cases, even where their names have been changed. Complaints procedures, and in the last resort laws against libel and slander, can be invoked if your research subjects are not satisfied that you have done what you promised. Caulley (1998) provides some examples of informed consent, and Burgess (1993: 203–7) describes some of the problems that can arise in attempting to protect the anonymity of research subjects.

(iii e) Involving the subjects in the research

From some positions (obviously positivism, but also possibly post-positivism, critical theory and constructivism), it is unwise for the researcher to get personally involved. This does not necessarily entail a claim to objectivity of research position (which would be unacceptable to some of the above positions), but is rather a practical matter of protecting yourself from claims against you (emotional, financial, or legal), and of protecting those who are contributing to your research from any bad advice you might give or interference you may attempt.

However, from all the non-positivist positions, it may be advisable (and in the case of participatory action research it is obligatory) that you involve research subjects actively in the research. This can take many forms (again, in ascending order):

- written feedback questionnaires at various stages within the research and/or at the end;
- formal and informal consultation in person, at various stages and/or at the end;
- providing the subjects with an active role within the research (administering questionnaires, interviewing other subjects);
- setting up the project in such a way as to make the subjects also the researchers.

These strategies all acknowledge that the research process sets up power relationships, which have ethical aspects. It is in the attempt to redress power imbalances that some writers advise that an interviewer should be of the same gender as and similar age to the interviewee. However, this is not always practicable, and even when it is possible, a power imbalance will still remain, while one is in the position of providing information and the other of soliciting it. Each research project has its own particular ethical dilemmas. For instance, case studies are often done on media institutions, sometimes with the knowledge and co-operation of the institution, even perhaps commissioned, and therefore funded, by them. This means that the researcher may well have freer access to documents and people, but might also have more constraints on using the information in any report. Some of these constraints are formal, for instance, the commissioning institution requiring that it approve of any report before publication. Sometimes ethical problems arise informally out of the relationship that develops between a researcher and the people with whom she is working over an extended period of time. If your ethical position is clear before you start, you will be able to deal with any such problems quickly and consistently, as they arise.

To sum up: develop and implement your own ethical position, making sure you treat all research subjects with respect.

1.3 Conclusion

In this chapter we have provided alternative definitions of key terms ('media', 'culture', 'communication', 'research') and an introduction to some of the major intellectual frameworks that have shaped media research. As you engage in the process of research, you will be locating yourself within these alternatives: over time, you may find your position changing as your own ideas develop and as the field mutates around you. This process of locating yourself begins with the selection of a topic and 'reading around' it: as you read what others have done and said you can make judgments about which other researchers see the world as you do. If you can find a position you can comfortably share (with an individual or a group or a school of thought), you can ease yourself into the field by initially modelling your own research on other research from that position. Fortunately, no two people are identical, and no two research projects are ever quite the same: you will soon find yourself branching off on your own, developing your own unique approach.

Research is exciting! Like a good detective mystery, it confronts you with the unknown and constantly challenges you with problems needing solutions. Though the procedural detail of research may be tedious and repetitive, the outcomes can be very satisfying. But, let us begin at the beginning, by discussing the selection of a research topic, and the reading that shapes your thinking about this.

CHAPTER 2

Getting Started

2.1 Choosing and refining a topic

Your research starts with choosing a topic: at the undergraduate level this may be assigned by your teachers, but at postgraduate level you usually choose your own. Our advice is:

- Choose a field that can sustain your interest over a long period – something that you can find infinite variety within or are truly passionate about. Too many postgraduate students find they run out of steam before the end, and their research either becomes grindingly tedious or they abandon it altogether.
- Choose a topic that is intrinsically worthwhile – something that you can feel some pride in, and that outsiders will appreciate the significance of. Of course, everyone has different ideas of what is 'worthwhile'...
- Check what has been done or said about the topic by others. Your goal is not to avoid a topic already researched, but to find a niche for your own particular approach to this subject.

In practice, you will begin your research within a broad field of study, from which you will choose a 'topic'. As you read around that topic, your aim is to refine it into a specific question or problem. Eventually you should be able to state to others (such as librarians assisting you) just what your research is about, in a short sentence or question. It is a circular process – reading, that shifts your thinking, that sends you to more reading, that further shifts your thinking.

Develop the ability to think critically about your own work. Ask yourself: 'What, exactly, am I trying to find out about my topic?' While your broad topic may be censorship, there has already been a great deal written about this 'field', so what are you trying to find out about censorship and why do you want to find it out? For example, are you interested in the past or the present? Do you want to restrict yourself to a single country or jurisdiction or do you want to make comparisons between several? Do you want to restrict yourself to a particular period, or compare more than one? Do you want to confine yourself to one particular medium, or deal with censorship across a number of media? Is your main interest in describing the process or arguing about the political or ethical implications of censorship? Are you interested in an issue which seemed 'settled', but has arisen again with the development of the internet? This is how a 'topic' emerges from within a 'field'. As you read around your subject, you will also be constantly returning to the topic and refining it, so that your 'topic' becomes a 'question' that can guide your research.

2.2 Using print and electronic resources

All research is cumulative in some way. Through print and electronic resources found in the library and resources found on the internet you encounter the previous work upon which you are going to build, or against which you are seeking to argue. You will use these resources:

- to acquire a sound grasp of your topic, including finding out what has already been done;
- to acquire knowledge of how previous research has been conducted, and the strengths and weaknesses of the various methodologies.

Traditionally libraries have been storehouses of knowledge, with comprehensive collections of books, journals, government publications, newspapers and magazines, and more recently audiovisual collections. The cost of this has become prohibitive, so while some specialist libraries and archives remain, many libraries now position themselves as gateways to information rather than as comprehensive storehouses. The library as a distributed information environment may no longer be concentrated in one building, or even on one campus, so a good researcher needs to become even more knowledgeable about and skilful in using catalogues, databases, indices and abstracts and other resources found on the internet.

The new electronic library resources offer a number of advantages:

- accessibility: because catalogues and databases can be accessed via the web they can be retrievable from computers located anywhere;
- ease of distribution: abstracts and full texts can be read through the web interface;
- integration: hypertext links seem to integrate all sites seamlessly on the web into one massive archive, linking the electronic resources of the library with the wider horizons of cyberspace.

However increasingly libraries do not hold the books and journals you may be after and you will rely on electronic delivery of articles, which may involve expenditure, or interlibrary loans of paper copies of articles or books, with consequent frustrating waits, except where electronic delivery is available.

The library catalogue

The library catalogue is always the place to begin: it allows you to gain some familiarity with your field of research even before you take a book off the shelves.

Unlike much on the world wide web, library catalogues and databases are collections of systematically evaluated information. Librarians are 'gatekeepers' whose job is to anticipate what information users will want and to provide that information in the most accessible manner – usually through catalogues organised by standardised fields such as author's name, title, place of publication, date of publication.

The catalogue is usually accessible and searchable through a computer, often using a world wide web style of interface, though some more specialised libraries and archives may use different interfaces, and some catalogues (particularly for older collections) may still be card-based. Web-based catalogues usually also provide hypertext links from one catalogue entry to another, across authors' names or across keywords or descriptors.

In searching the catalogue, or indeed in searching indices (whether print or electronic) you should:

- keep meticulous records of all your searches, including the keywords (and combinations of keywords) used, whether the search was successful or not, and the catalogues and databases to which each was applied. This saves repeating work because of a lack of records of previous searches;
- be systematic, in your search procedures, and your record keeping. For instance note the names of media organisations that should be further researched, or of authors whose names keep recurring. But also allow for serendipity. Browse the shelves of the library, or check hyperlinks in the catalogue allowing you to view the records of books with adjacent call numbers;
- build a 'thesaurus' of keywords and search terms which you have found useful: different catalogues and indices tend to use different descriptors (some refer to 'cinema' others to 'moving pictures' for example), and don't forget the differences between US and English spelling, which can be significant in descriptors;
- be aware that when keywords (or descriptors) are hypertext-linked, clicking on the keywords can bring up other titles, but can also provide further keywords which may prove valuable, and should be added to your own personal 'thesaurus';
- be prepared to revisit some resources after you've gathered new information.

You could begin to search through library catalogues totally at random, but you will find it much more productive to be systematic. For electronic databases this involves constructing a search statement, which can also help you to clarify your research question. Many reference librarians suggest the use of a grid, identifying at least two different concepts in your topic:

Concept A: Censorship and Concept B: Internet [and Concept C: This will often be a modifier such as an historical period, a geographical domain, a medium or some other way of narrowing the topic].

Under each concept, write any possible alternative terms (there may not be one) separated by the word 'or', and using a truncation symbol where appropriate. Truncation allows you to use only part of a word to search for all variations of the concept: for instance, by using the truncated form 'censor*' you can simultaneously search for 'censors', 'censorship', and 'censoring'. In this case the asterisk is the symbol for truncation, but some databases use other symbols. Remember to include your original concept term (see Figure 2.1).

In this case we do not offer alternatives for concept C, but that would be necessary if your research concerned a comparison of internet censorship regimes in two countries (Australia and the USA for example).

Reading off this grid you can now write out a search statement, in which alternative terms for a particular concept will be 'nested' within brackets: concept A and (concept B1 or concept B2) and concept C. Many catalogues, databases and some search engines are able to interpret such 'nested' terms as alternatives to be searched for. The terms in each of the spaces in the statement then become your 'keywords' or 'descriptors' (a list which will grow as you search). If you get no result with your first search then you modify the search by adding keywords or recombining them. If, on the other hand, you get too many 'hits' you need to choose a narrower term (for example 'television' rather than 'media').

This process of constructing a search statement is a valuable exercise as it helps you understand exactly what it is you are trying to find out – and move from a vague topic (such as 'censorship') to a specific question.

A good search statement is invaluable when using online databases, which are commonly accessible through the library online catalogue or the library's web page. The databases are not accessible through search engines such as Google as they are not part of 'the internet', although they are accessed through your web browser. They provide searchable listings of journal articles, newspaper and magazine articles and other research resources many of which can be downloaded as 'full text' files through subscribing libraries: your library home page will link you directly to the databases and electronically accessible journals to which they subscribe. One advantage of material available through

Concept A	**Concept B**	**Concept C**
censor* or classification or	internet or world wide web or	Australia or [United States] or

Figure 2.1 Constructing a search statement

these databases is that it has been through a process of gatekeeping: articles in refereed journals have been checked by at least two 'referees' considered knowledgeable in the relevant field.

Searching on the internet

The internet is becoming an increasingly useful tool for research, and can be valuable in developing your literature review. The internet is not a single homogenous medium, but a series of technologies and protocols, of varying usefulness to a researcher. You should be familiar at least with the world wide web, email listservs and possibly news groups. Because of the scale of the internet, in contrast to library catalogues and databases, it is not possible for human gatekeepers such as librarians to catalogue its content. This service is being partly performed by search engines. However, unlike catalogues and databases, information on the web is not usually indexed into separate searchable fields (author, title, date of publication, etc) presented consistently: a web search is usually a full text search, through entire documents.

The world wide web will not necessarily be useful in obtaining a systematic overview of a field, nor in searching for key documents in a field when you do not actually know what those documents are.

The web is most useful:

- early in your research, for initial exploration;
- for basic information, when you are in a hurry and/or feeling lazy;
- when you are searching for a specific document, person, or organisation, details of which you already know, or have a reasonable 'hunch' about.

Learn the strengths and weaknesses of search engines and directory services available on the web: however, their ownership, policies and methodologies change constantly. The web site Search Engine Watch is useful (www.searchenginewatch.com).

Email listservs

As your knowledge of your research field improves, it can be useful to join one of the many discussion lists (or listservs) which deal with aspects of the media, from film and television through to new media, or more specific cultural issues.

Advantages:

- the chance to make personal contact with other researchers in the field;
- the opportunity to see what other people are researching, along with their theoretical perspectives and methodologies.

When such lists work well (and that does not always happen) they can act as a form of 'virtual' conversation between scholars, allowing you to obtain information, and even test some of your own ideas. However, you should not use listservs as a way of avoiding your groundwork. The following question was posted to the discussion list 'Film theory':

> Hello, my name is ... I am a film student at the University of California at Santa Barbara. I am writing a theoretical paper on Jean Mitry, and I want to ask if there are any particular articles that you might recommend. Thank you.

The problem here is not the appeal for assistance, nor the need for some indication of the relative importance of what has been published, but the lack of groundwork. Pertinent questions might be: What are you wanting to say about Jean Mitry in the 'theoretical paper'? Is this to be an evaluation of Mitry's work? If so, an evaluation in terms of what criteria (influence on later film theorists? the extent to which Mitry's insights are still valid?) Is the paper seeking to evaluate the determinants of Mitry's theoretical work – the influences on him? Is it seeking to place him within a particular theoretical tradition?

A listserv conversation is most useful after you have done enough groundwork yourself to be able to make your questions specific as well as concise.

2.3 Managing information

How do you keep the bibliographic information you collect from library catalogues, electronic databases and the internet? The traditional method has been to use a card file system, which has some advantages:

- They are more portable: you can carry around just the cards you are using at any time (plus some spares for new notes).
- They are sortable.
- You do not need to spend time turning on card files just to check one detail.

However computer databases (such as *EndNote*) have significant advantages:

- They are searchable.
- They are still sortable.
- You can download bibliographic records from library catalogues, which saves time, increases accuracy of records, and may provide abstracts and other information.
- They can be linked to your word processor for ease of **citation** while writing.
- They can output references in widely used styles (eg: MLA, Chicago, Harvard, Cambridge).

Alternatively you can use simpler databases such as *Filemaker* or *Access* but these lack some of the above features.

Databases use 'records' (the equivalent of 'cards'), each of which contains 'fields': you create a field for each piece of standardised information you collect (such as author, or title, or publisher), as well as a larger field for general comments (your annotation). Make sure that you only enter one type of information in each field, or you lose the ability to search and sort fields effectively.

Your system is only as good as the information you record, so be accurate and consistent in collecting your data in a standardised format:

- Record accurately and in detail all the information available about books, journal articles, government reports, films and videos, radio programs, television programs, CD-ROMs, and any other sources you are using in your research.
- Include a field into which you can place such information as where you obtained the reference being cited, and (if relevant) where it was cited. If you are unable to find the reference, you can then go back to the original citation and make sure that you have not made a copying error.
- Do not assume you can go back to the catalogue and get missing information later: this wastes time and is not always possible.

Detailed records are particularly important when citing the often ephemeral material found on the world wide web. Do not expect to be able to go back to a site weeks or months later and get missing citation details: the site may no longer exist and finding a cached version on Google is not always possible. If a site is important to your work, it is useful to print off the relevant pages, making sure that when you do so the author, title, date and URL (Universal Resource Locator, such as www.latrobe.edu.au/screeningthepast) are inserted into the headers and footers of the printout.

Citation

As a researcher you have a range of tools at your disposal. Some of these are physical tools like your computer, while others are intellectual tools, discussed for instance in Turabian (1996) or Strunk and White (2000). One important intellectual tool is the system of citation you choose. Consistent and accurate adherence to a coherent system of citation is not merely pedantry.

Why cite sources?

- It adds credibility to your research, by providing evidence that you have consulted other sources: slipshod citation implies slipshod research.
- It enables you to share your research with other researchers. The citations of others have provided valuable sources of information to you, and your

citations are part of a reciprocal system of information exchange: this can be seen as an ethical (perhaps even a political) imperative.

- Correct and accurate citation ensures that you cannot be accused of plagiarism, and a rigorous determination to acknowledge sources creates a mindset which will make you less likely to commit plagiarism accidentally. Plagiarism is the unacknowledged passing off of someone else's words or ideas as your own without proper acknowledgement of your sources. It is considered at best to be unethical, and at worst to be an offence leading to the sacking of the offender. In some celebrated cases it has led to professional ruin for the researcher(s) concerned. The best way to avoid plagiarism is through rigorous and accurate record keeping and citation.

You should collect at least the following information:

Books:

- full names of all authors (or editors or compilers if an edited collection) accurately and completely, even if later you will abbreviate to 'et al.';
- all names of authors of any section of the book, such as chapters;
- names of any translators of works or parts of works;
- full and absolutely accurate title of any part of the book, and of the complete work in which the parts are located;
- the edition used, and the number(s) of the volume(s) used;
- the name of the publisher (not the printer), the year of publication, and the city of publication.

It is not enough to record the country (such as United Kingdom, United States), but it is sometimes the case that the state is recorded along with the city. This convention often applies to US publishers, especially when there is also a city of the same name in the UK, for example Cambridge (Massachusetts or England). If you are in doubt about the place of publication or the publisher, you can clarify by checking a library catalogue.

Each edition of the book may have subtle (or significant) differences which may be important in your research, so make sure you record the details of the actual copy of the book you used, as you are using it.

Journal articles:
Record complete and accurate details of author (s), article title, journal title, volume and issue number, the page range of the article, and (as with books) the page numbers of any quotations or paraphrases you will use.

Web sites:
Many web sites do not conform to academic convention, and citation conventions for the web are still being developed. If you cannot find all the information normally expected in an academic citation, provide as much as possible. Where no individual author is named for a site, or a page at a site, you may need to treat the organisation which created the site as a 'corporate author'. You should always look for a date of upload, and, if relevant, any dates on

which the page was modified (but not all sites include this information) and you should include, as part of your citation, the date on which you visited the site. This is especially important if the site is undated. Academic sites, such as online journals, are much better at providing citation details than most sites: see, for example *Screening the Past* (www.latrobe.edu.au/screeningthepast) and *First Monday* (www.firstmonday.org).

However frustrating it can be seeking citation details on a web page, it is never enough to simply provide the URL: that would be like citing an article in the *New York Times* with a citation which simply read: *New York Times*!

Systems of citation

Systems of citation have developed to meet the need to provide as much information as possible as succinctly and concisely as possible. Citation systems use conventions which act as a form of shorthand: for example, the order in which details are provided will indicate the class of information. Take the following citation:

Altheide, D. L. 'The news media, the problem frame, and the production of fear', *The Sociological Quarterly* XXXVIII, no. 4 (1997) 647–68.

This means that the article is in volume XXXVIII (38), issue 4: if the same information was supplied, but in reverse order it would indicate volume 4, issue 38. Citation relies on conventions of placement and abbreviation which only work if used accurately and consistently. As one of your main tools, it is your responsibility to learn to cite properly. Choosing a system is sometimes not up to you. The university department in which you are working, or the journal or publisher for which you are writing may specify a particular system, in which case you need to follow that system accurately and consistently. Whether you are following direction, or choosing for yourself, you are strongly advised to consult the manual: for APA consult American Psychological Association (2001) or Gelfland and Walker (1991); for MLA consult Gibaldi (1999), for Chicago style consult University of Chicago Press (1993). However, when you do have a choice of system, a number of factors may shape your decision.

Briefly, citation can be divided into systems which use notes (either endnotes at the end of a section or the document, or footnotes at the foot of a page) or in-text systems (also known as 'author-date' systems or 'parenthetical systems', which usually involve inserting a brief citation directly into the text which then refers to an item in a bibliography or reference list at the end of the document).

In-text systems were developed before the days of word processing programs, when the use of footnotes in particular made it difficult to lay out pages.

The advantages of in-text systems are:

- They are simple to use and save the reader having to turn to the foot of the page or the end of the section to see the citation.
- When drafting your work, if you move a section of the document to another location the citation also moves in its entirety.

Disadvantages of such systems are:

- They do not eliminate the need for notes when making incidental comments or qualifying points. In such cases you will finish up with both notes and in-text citations.
- Some readers find in-text citations more distracting as they read, particularly when citations (such as web sites or archival references) are complex or cumbersome. In such cases, you will be tempted to use a note instead, thereby introducing inconsistency.

Note systems allow you to use either footnotes or endnotes and these are catered for very well by modern word processing software, which can convert one into the other or move the whole note when the word to which it is attached is moved.

The advantages of note systems are:

- They impose minimal distractions for the reader, as the reference mark is very small.
- They are completely consistent: citations and comments and qualifications all appear in notes, in the order in which they are relevant in the text.
- You can make each note as brief or as long as you like, so complex or cumbersome citations are less of a problem.
- They can be simplified through use of abbreviations such as 'ibid'.

Disadvantages of such systems are:

- Some readers find them more distracting because of the need to go to the foot of the page or the end of the document to see if the note is a simple citation or a comment or qualification.
- When drafting a document, and moving sections of text around, you are strongly advised not to use abbreviations. If you create a note which simply says 'ibid., p. 21' and move it elsewhere in the text you will lose the connection to the previous citation to which 'ibid.' is linked. The effect of this, particularly if you are working over an extended period of time, is that when the document is completed your citations may no longer be at all coherent and by this stage you may not be able to reassemble the citations yourself. If you plan to use abbreviations, wait until the final draft before replacing the full citation with an abbreviation.

2.4 Evaluating sources and reading critically

Before you read, evaluation has begun with the 'gatekeeping' process for library purchases and cataloguing. Similarly, academic articles and books are sent out for 'peer review' before publication: 'referees' who are considered to be experts in the particular field make comments, which may lead to the article being rejected by the publisher or sent back to the author for clarification of arguments or further rewriting before publication. Your search of the library catalogue, of electronic databases and indices, or the world wide web initiates your own 'gatekeeping' process: it brings up more titles than you can immediately deal with, so your first step is to decide which references are likely to be of immediate use to you. Then you start to read and take notes (on your cards, or in the comments section of your bibliographic database). There are three kinds of notes that may be useful:

- those that judge the value of the reference to your project (comments such as that this book may be worth re-visiting at a later stage of the research, or that its title led you to expect it would be valuable but it turned out to be largely irrelevant);
- those that summarise the content of the reference (in our experience, the most common form of note-taking, especially by students);
- those that comment on the methods and approaches of the text.

The last of these is the least common. As you become more familiar with the various intellectual frameworks that operate in your field, you will be better equipped to identify these in your reading. Gene Wise proposes that every reading is a 'strategic journey' (Wise 1980: 363), and that readers can understand this journey better if they have tools for questioning the writer's purposes. To this end, he offers a schedule of questions, concerning the 'constructed world inside the text', 'worlds and lives outside the text', and 'from the context outside back into the text again' (Wise 1980: 364–8). This is a very practical approach to your reading, and one that can be applied across all areas of research. It is time-consuming, but the time would be well spent, particularly on those references which are likely to have a key role in shaping your own understanding. The exercise is also likely to point up how you agree or disagree with the writer, and therefore to help you to locate your own reading/writing position.

When using books and articles you will make your own personal evaluation, assessing the argument being put, the evidence provided, the basis for that evidence, and the authority of the writer. Internet resources can be evaluated with similar criteria, particularly when (as with online journals, government reports, or reports of academic research) they have been through a gate-keeping process analogous to that for printed books.

There are however, a vast majority of internet sites where this is not the case. This does not necessarily mean that those sites have no value, but their value may well be of a different order: a site which is highly polemical, and tenders no evidence for an argument, can still have value for demonstrating strands of popular opinion on a topic at a particular moment. There are several other issues which distinguish material on the web from printed material, and may make the appraisal of internet sources different, including the sheer number of sites and the difficulty in identifying information with which to judge the sites' currency (up-to-dateness), **authority** (credibility and point of view) and accuracy. When searching for information on the web you often go directly to an individual page within a site: this is rather like finding a newspaper cutting, or a page from a person's diary, or a few pages from a photograph album.

When assessing the value of a printed journal article you may take into account the reputation of the journal in which it is published, and perhaps even the credibility of the source which directed you there in the first place: you need to do the same with web sites and individual web pages. Ask yourself: how did you find the site? (search engine? linked to a site you were already at? cited by an author you have been reading?) What is the credibility of the author or site which directed you there in the first place? What is the 'status' of the publisher of the site? In the case of a book or a journal this is recorded on the opening pages, but it may not be so easy to locate the publisher of a web site. The domain at which the site was found will be a clue: for example domains such as edu., com., org indicate an educational site, a commercial site, an organisation.

If you have come to a page through a search engine or by simply 'surfing' you need to determine if the page is part of a larger site: there may be a 'return' button which takes you to the home page, which in turn might provide information to assist in determining the credibility of the site. Is it produced by a body with a 'real world' existence (indicated by a postal address for example)? Is there an author cited for the page, and are her qualifications indicated and are these relevant? How current is the site (is it possible to determine this)? Is there evidence that material on the site might be accurate and reliable – for example is there an indication that material is peer reviewed, or has been edited by a professional editor, or does it appear amateurish and slipshod? (Although to be fair an amateurish appearance does not always indicate lack of quality: under pressure from universities to create a more public profile, many academics have created web sites, some of which conform to high academic standards but still appear amateurish! Nevertheless you should expect that on such pages there will be proper citation, correct spelling, a clear argument well supported by evidence.) The lack of any such 'cues' should alert you to be sceptical of the material on the site.

2.5 A note on 'backing up'

As you will have realised, research is becoming increasingly dependent on computers, so having your computer 'crash' can be devastating. You should 'back up' your data regularly, and you can never be too paranoid or too meticulous about this.

Backing up is making a copy of all your files to another medium.

- Keep all those drafts which you print from time to time – you could retype or scan your work into the computer again.
- Save copies of your files to floppy disks, zip disks, tape backups, or even a CD-ROM; or
- regularly download a copy of your files on a remote server.
- Keep your backups in a different location (remote server, locked filing cabinet in a different home/office) in case of theft of your computer or fire.
- When you delete significant parts of your work, keep the old version in case you want to go back: to avoid overwriting earlier versions, save copies with different names.

If your university provides automatic backup at night make sure that you use this service, however, do not be too complacent: servers can crash too, and private companies such as internet service providers sometimes have limits to the amount of data you can store and have been known to erase files when a predetermined quota has been filled.

Backing up meticulously may seem a nuisance, but it may also save you from a disaster, as well as encouraging you to keep accurate and detailed records, which are 'marketable skills' in a world in which the computer is one of the main tools of the researcher.

2.6 Conclusion

By this stage, you have selected a topic and set up systems for locating and managing information from the library and the web. As you read, you need to develop a 'map of the field' in your head, which will help you to locate yourself within it and also to better understand and use what you read. Later sections of this book take up the research process at this point – dividing the field according to whether your research is primarily concerned with audiences, institutions or texts. We start with audiences, and particularly with how the field of audience research has been conceptualised by the authors you will meet in your reading.

PART I

RESEARCH ON AUDIENCES

We begin with 'audiences', because that is where mass media research began, and where much of it is still focused. This apparently simple term has been applied differently over time and in different circumstances (see Barker 1998; Fiske 1989; Hartley 1987; Nightingale 1986). If we are speaking about mass media – press, film, radio and television – then the simplest definition of the audience is the receiver or consumer of a text. We admit from the start that 'the audience' as a collectivity does not exist independently of the research: 'The audience exists nowhere; it inhabits no real space, only positions within analytic discourses' (Allor 1988: 228).

Audiences, institutions and texts are never really separate: research always addresses part of that complex interaction between audience and text, audience and industry, and audience and medium (Nightingale 1994). However, before these relationships can be researched, the terms must be understood separately, and working definitions constructed for each. Research usually then focuses primarily on one of these aspects, while acknowledging the influence of the others: in Part I, we focus on the audience, while acknowledging the interaction of audience with text and/or institution.

Audience research can be divided, 'between the voluntarism of a conception of the full human subject as agent of meaning making and the determinism of a conception of the individual as the object of socialization' (Allor 1988: 217). As discussed in section 1.3 in Chapter 1, the former grows out of the semiotic school of communication (concerned with the circulation of meanings), the latter out of the process school of communication (concerned with the transmission of messages).

The simplest audience research counts consumers (listeners/viewers/readers), and assigns individuals to demographic categories. This is easier to do in a public place (such as a concert venue or a cinema) than when the audience is dispersed and private, for instance listening to the radio in a car. However, simply counting the audience will not help us to find out how the communication process operates, so audience research seldom stays at that level.

Jensen and Rosengren (1990) is a good starting point for a discussion of the various ways of researching audiences, providing a 'map of the field' which we find very useful, and on which we have built Figure I.1 at the end of this introduction. We have linked Jensen and Rosengren's categories of audience research with Fiske's categories of linear and semiotic theories of communication. The approaches on the left of the diagram come from the social sciences, and depend upon scientific method: quantitative methods are accepted but so too are qualitative methods, empirical methods are common but interpretive methods are not excluded, and linear communication theory is usually (though not exclusively) applied. The approaches on the right of this table come from the humanities: although some do not rule out empirical and quantitative methods, most employ qualitative methods and require informed contemplation and interpretation, and most (though not all) adopt the semiotic model of communication.

Some social scientists are inclined to dismiss the humanities scholars as woolly thinkers and some humanities scholars are inclined to dismiss the social scientists as mechanical empiricists. Those in the centre of the diagram prefer to avoid such extremes: though they seldom express it in these terms, in practice they are working towards a reconciliation between social science and the humanities, using methods appropriate to their research questions, whichever approach these methods come from.

At the far left of the table is 'effects studies'. As each new mass medium has been introduced (books, journals, newspapers, film, radio, television), and as each technological development has made these more accessible to wider sections of the public (recently through cable, satellite, video, and the internet), there have been a series of moral panics about their effects on the community, and so science was called upon to identify these effects, so that the harm could be minimised. An early example of the search for media effects is the Payne Fund studies of 'Motion Pictures and Youth', their conclusions summarised in Charters (1933). These studies (and many others that followed them) employed a linear model of communication – the 'hypodermic model', which identified effects as direct and immediate, and used already-recognised scientific procedures to determine and measure these effects. The research methods used in these came increasingly under intense criticism, and in recent years this strand of research has been fundamentally rethought and has come closer methodologically to the next approach – uses and gratifications studies.

The uses and gratifications approach seeks to discover how audiences use the media, asking not only who consumes mass media but also why individuals do so and in what social context. The methods used for such research – interviewing audience members and observing audience behaviour – have been refined over many years, but the relationship of these methods to traditional ethnographic research methods is still a matter for debate.

At the far right of the table is literary criticism, which pre-dates all the social scientific approaches. Early analysis of literary texts was by analogy to the analysis of the Bible, and the first methods of interpretation of such texts copied the **hermeneutic** methods of biblical scholars, in which the major focus is on the text, and on the intentions of its author rather than on the audience. However, the audience is understood to be the consumer of the text, the person to whom the text is addressed, the person to be influenced by the text.

In this way, this approach harks back even further, to the pre-Christian forms of communication study with which Jensen and Rosengren begin their article: the scholars of oratory, **rhetoric** and poetics such as Aristotle, Cicero, Quintilian. They, too, were concerned with how texts can influence readers/listeners. It was only when printing made texts available to the mass of people that we had the possibility of mass communication, and so the possibility of applying the skills of rhetoric and oratory in ways that can influence whole populations.

These two strands, then (literary criticism/hermeneutics and classical oratory/rhetoric/poetics) share a belief in the audience as passive, acted-upon, rather like the audience of the effects studies. But this is not necessarily seen as a 'bad' thing: from these positions, the capacity of a text to influence – its power over readers – is a measure of the skill of the text's producer, not of the weakness and vulnerability of the reader. Jensen and Rosengren describe several strands of literary research that do take notice of the audience, though in these strands individual readers are usually more important than the social conditions of reception of texts.

At this point we diverge slightly from Jensen and Rosengren's categories, by turning what they consider just a part of a category into a complete category in its own right: **reader-response studies**. This is because that strand of literary criticism *does* place major emphasis on the audience, not just as an object of study but as an active player in the game of constructing meaning. Where for traditional literary criticism the audience is acted upon by the text (similar to **rhetorical analysis** or effects studies), in reader-response theory the reader acts upon the text to actively construct it in the process of reading (similar to the active audiences of uses and gratifications studies). It is therefore theoretically possible to study that process of meaning-construction from the point-of-view of the reader just as much as from the point-of-view of the text. However, in practice, empirical studies of how readers construct meaning are not common.

This leaves the last two of Jensen and Rosengren's categories, which we consider to have been converging so rapidly that the distinction is becoming difficult to sustain. Both are concerned with how texts are read within culture. The differences between them are only matters of emphasis: cultural studies places primary focus on the cultural context, **reception analysis** on the variant readings of texts. So, we will discuss them separately as Jensen and Rosengren do, but we place them close together in our diagram – cultural studies closer to the social sciences end and reception analysis closer to the humanities end.

Cultural studies employ the social science (particularly anthropological) definition of culture as 'a whole way of life', rather than the definition (from the humanities, particularly aesthetics) of culture as 'the best of artistic expressions'. Cultural studies share social science's interest in the social contexts of human behaviour or 'practices', considered as meaningful social activities (Williams 1977). The Marxist leanings of the Birmingham School, where 'British Cultural Studies' originated, ensured that the field always paid attention to how social and economic power was distributed, and how communication was imbricated in these power relations.

Reception studies are more likely to address written texts, though they are also likely to define this broadly, to include popular forms (such as Harlequin romances). Their interest in audiences is as readers of texts, selectively interpreting what they read, choosing meanings from the text's **polysemy** (its potentially multiple meanings). They explain this process in terms of social and cultural positioning – particularly gender and race (class is usually less important than it is within cultural studies). Reception analysts are eclectic in their methodology – using both **quantitative** and qualitative methods, and often combining the insights of both the social sciences and the humanities.

The differences between our interpretation and that of Jensen and Rosengren are minor compared to the areas of agreement. We agree with them

Concepts of 'audience'	Mass audience passively acted upon by media	Socially differentiated mass audience(s) using media actively	Individuals and social groups engaged in meaning construction within cultural contexts	Individual readers activating texts within parameters established by the creative artist	Individual readers constructed by the text (narratively or ideologically) or passive consumers
Types of audience research (after Jensen and Rosengren 1990)	Effects studies	Uses and gratifications studies	Cultural/Reception studies/analysis	Reader-response analysis	Literary criticism. Little interest in audience, except perhaps historical studies of taste
Basic model of communication (after Fiske 1982)	LINEAR		SEMIOTIC		LINEAR

Figure I.1 Map of the field of audience research

that over the years we have seen increasing autonomy given to audiences – the recognition that audiences are active and selective. There has also been increasing recognition of the importance of the social context in which the reading takes place. And, finally, there has been a shift also in the methodologies applied within the research, leading to a combination and interaction of empirical and interpretive methods.

To sum up the different approaches, we suggest some basic questions that each approach might pose in attempting to understand media audiences:

- Ratings studies: How large is the audience and what is its demographic composition?
- Effects studies: What do the media do to audiences?
- Uses and gratifications studies: What do audiences do with the media?
- Literary critical studies: How do texts construct an audience?
- Reader-response studies: How do individual readers construct texts?
- Cultural studies: How does culture operate to produce socially differentiated readings of texts?
- Reception analysis: How do socially differentiated readers produce readings of texts within a cultural context?

CHAPTER 3

Researching Audiences

In this historical survey of audience research we have taken our examples from soap opera research, first radio soap opera and later television soaps. The term 'soap opera' was first applied to daytime radio serials funded by soap manufacturers: television soap opera developed in new directions, for instance into prime-time. Within television theory a soap opera is a series with an infinite number of episodes, and (unless the writers are given warning of the impending end of their story and so shift into serial mode) a lack of closure. Aesthetic discourse has not been kind to soap opera (see Allen 1985: 12–18), but the popularity of the form, and hence its importance to advertisers, has made soap opera a frequent subject for audience research, well-represented right across all research categories.

3.1 Ratings

Ratings – simply, the counting of the audience – were the earliest form of mass media research. Newspapers now proudly announce their circulation on their banner, and radio and television stations and networks compete to head the ratings tables, so they fund the research that produces ratings information. Ratings research companies such as AC Nielsen now collect information on the internet.

The function of ratings varies among the different groups who use them:

- Media owners/operators measure their position against their competitors, and determine what they will charge advertisers.
- Advertisers (through advertising agencies) decide whether to advertise within a certain programme and how much to pay for this privilege.
- Programme makers decide whether to continue to make a programme and in what **narrative** or ideological direction to take the programme in the future.

- Network schedulers decide whether to retain a programme and how much to pay for the right to do so.
- Academic researchers use ratings to formulate research questions for future study.

For television, ratings are now measured by the 'people meter'. A meter-box is hard-wired into the television set, to record every second, provided that any programme has been watched for a minimum time (perhaps 15 or 30 seconds). Every regular viewer in the household has their own handheld device (rather like a remote control), on which they are required to press a button when they start or stop viewing and whenever an automatic message on the television screen reminds them. Additional meters are provided for guests. The data is transferred to the ratings company by a daily automated phone call. Management of this system has changed hands occasionally (for Britain see Sharot 1994), but the principle remains, except to make provision for technological change (such as the change from analog to digital broadcasting).

Ratings measure popularity, and 'soap opera' has always been extremely popular. Ratings, and their accompanying demographic data, have been able to demonstrate that the early audience for soap opera was overwhelmingly female. The BBC publishes annual reports on research based upon ratings data, including one on soap operas (Hemming 1989), and one more broadly on women's viewing patterns (Beere 1991).

The strengths of current ratings research are:

- Sampling procedures are reliable enough that confident generalisations about the popularity of individual programmes can be made from the data.
- Demographic data enable relationships between viewing habits and types of viewers to be considered.
- The raw data can be used to develop research hypotheses, for later exploration by other research methods.

The weaknesses are:

- No method has yet been found to ensure the absolute **reliability** of data collected.
- The types of conclusions that can be drawn from ratings are limited to issues of popularity (what is being watched, and when).

However, questions of the response of audiences to the texts they listen to or watch have always been of intense interest to social scientists, and can even be of value to broadcasters and programme makers, in providing information on which to make decisions about the future. This has led to research that starts with gathering ratings information, but extends more broadly into research on audience responses.

J. M. Wober and S. Fazal were working for the Independent Television Commission in Britain when they surveyed 'a nationally representative television opinion panel' (Wober and Fazal 1994: 79) about their appreciation of the imported soap operas *Neighbours* and *Home and Away*. The research was aimed at understanding the popularity of these programmes in Britain:

> The panel consisted of over 4000 individuals aged 12 and over, each in a separate household, recruited at the end of a 'daily survey' carried out on a quota sampled group of 1000 respondents who were then asked if they agree to be on the panel. The panel was sent, each week, two booklets: one containing a complete list of all programmes shown with the request to show the degree of appreciation for each programme viewed (the 'diary') and a separate booklet carrying sets of questions either about particular episodes seen, or about programmes, broadcasting issues and everything relevant to them. Those who responded to each set of questions had their answers weighted so they again represent the known proportions in the population of people of each sex, age and social class. Respondents also gave their general weight of viewing as part of their personal characteristics. (Wober and Fazal 1994: 80)

The questionnaires that respondents completed required first an appreciation of each programme on a six-point scale, then answers to descriptive questions similar to those used in an earlier study of the British soap, *Coronation Street*. The results were collated, analysed statistically, and reported in both tables and descriptive prose. The researchers concluded that in general the local programme was more popular than the imported soaps, but that *Neighbours* and *Home and Away* both had a particular following among younger people. The Australian programmes were seen as moral tales and the Australian lifestyle depicted in them was often very important to the British viewers.

The strengths of such research are:

- Sampling procedures (including the weighting of samples) can be rigorous enough to make conclusions reasonably reliable and therefore generalisable.
- Numerical results can be manipulated by sophisticated statistical procedures.
- Difficult questions (of why audiences watch and what they take from a programme) can be asked.
- Like simple ratings, the results can point up issues for further study.

However, some problems of reliability remain, and – more importantly – once you leave behind the simple questions of fact ('How many times did you watch *Neighbours* last week?'), a more important problem arises, of defining terms sufficiently rigorously to avoid misunderstanding, and to produce answers which are sufficiently comparable to be manipulated statistically. It was this problem of definition that largely contributed to the difference of opinion in the 1930s between Paul Lazarsfeld (see the first sub-section of section 5.2 in Chapter 5) and Theodor Adorno over the value of **survey** research concerning radio audiences (see the second sub-section): Lazarsfeld was concerned to develop quantitative measures of the influence of radio on listeners, Adorno preferred qualitative research on questions of preference and **pleasure**.

3.2 Effects studies

Soap opera – our chosen field for this chapter – attracted the attention of effects researchers very early, because it was assumed that such a disdained form could only have bad effects on any audience. Robert C. Allen describes some early research by Louis Berg, a New York psychiatrist. In March 1942, when soap opera was still exclusively a radio **genre**, Berg

> told the Buffalo Advertising Club that listening to soap operas caused 'acute anxiety state, tachycardia, arrhythmias, increase in blood pressure, profuse perspiration, tremors, vasomotor instability, nocturnal frights, vertigo, and gastro-intestinal disturbances'. Berg charged that at a time when radio programming ought to be contributing to the war effort, broadcasters proffered a surfeit of daytime fare that 'pandered to perversity' and played out 'destructive conflicts'. 'These serials furnish the same release for the emotionally distorted that is supplied to those who desire satisfaction from a lynching bee, lick their lips at the salacious scandals of the *crime passionel*, who in the unregretted past cried out in ecstasy at a witch burning.' (Allen 1985: 21–2)

It is the methods of the research that concern us here – physiological tests on himself while he was watching soap operas. This research was fundamentally flawed:

- His sample (one person) is too small to be representative of anything, and therefore his conclusions cannot be generalised. There are ways of using such data productively within a paradigm that does not claim **generalisability**, but Berg was implying that his conclusions were valid across the whole **population** of soap opera viewers.
- He makes a completely unsupportable jump from physiological effects to psychological and ultimately moral ones.

Laboratory techniques had already been used in the Payne Fund studies in the 1930s, for instance Dysinger and Ruckmick worked with a galvanometer to measure galvanic responses and with the pneumo-cardiograph to measure changes in the circulatory system (Charters 1933: 25), from which were inferred the effects of film on young people. These researchers used a larger sample than Berg, but still made unsupportable inferences about the causes of the measured physical effects.

Such research is based on the model of scientific experiment on the physical world, in which a pre-test establishes a stable benchmark of 'dependent **variables**' (in Berg's case, physiological measures of the audience). Then an 'independent variable' is introduced, that is the variable that is under the control of the researcher (in Berg's case the application of a behaviour stimulus – viewing a soap opera). Finally, a post-test is administered, and it is assumed that any variation from the bench mark is a measure of the influence of the independent variable. Experimental procedures have been developed to deal with the effect of an 'intervening variable' (a variable which changes the relationship between the independent or dependent variable, for instance if some of a sample were interviewed separately, some in a focus group), or a 'confounding variable' (a variable which is not part of the research design but which might be causing an observed outcome, for instance if some of the sample have read books about popular culture and are reading the soap opera ironically). Statistical procedures have also been developed to measure the significance of the extent of any variation discovered.

However, experimental research is inherently difficult in the social sciences:

- It is almost impossible to establish an experimental situation involving human subjects where a benchmark accurately measures every possible relevant variable present in the pre-test situation.
- It is difficult to isolate any variable for introduction, or to define that variable accurately enough, to ensure that the influence of it, and only it, can be identified in the post-test.
- It is therefore difficult to attribute any difference between the pre- and post-test accurately to a single variable, and therefore almost impossible to identify a causal relationship between the stimulus variable and later behaviour.

We consider these difficulties to be overwhelming, so we do not recommend laboratory studies of audiences, and do not provide advice in later chapters on conducting these. Market research operates by survey rather than experiment, but it still depends on the same linear model of communication as Berg, and still belongs to the category of 'effects studies': it assumes that the effects of advertising strategies can be identified by measuring attitudes (to products) and surveying (buying/consuming) behaviours. Over many years, market research has become more effective and reliable, as improved sampling procedures were used, and advances were made in establishing definitions and collecting data. More general questions about the composition and preferences of the audience have been included, facilitating changes in television programming: the research of Wober and Fazal (discussed above) is an example of research that bridges marketing and broader issues of social influence.

In addition to research commissioned by the broadcasters, there is a strong thread of effects research which is not directly instrumental. In the early days, even social scientists assumed that the television audience behaved as a mass, in response to what were presented as undifferentiated stimuli such as 'violence', considered as a single category. More recently, in an effort to understand human behaviour (rather than to develop ways of changing it), theories have developed that accommodate the idea of differentiated stimuli acting differentially on socially situated audiences, and more sophisticated research methods have been developed.

Perhaps the best-known of these is the Cultural Indicators (CI) programme developed by George Gerbner and his colleagues (starting with Gerbner 1969). One aspect of CI is '**cultivation analysis**'. Shanahan and Morgan (1999: 5) explain that 'Cultivation is about the implications of stable, repetitive, pervasive and virtually inescapable patterns of images and ideologies that television (especially dramatic, fictional entertainment) provides.' Within this framework, researchers are usually concerned with how heavy viewers of television perceive the world around them differently from those who view less television: the issue most discussed from this perspective has been violence on television, and its contribution to viewers' perceptions that the world outside television is a violent and dangerous place.

The methodology starts with **content analysis** to establish recurrent patterns of behaviour within television programmes. From this data, questions are formulated which can be posed in surveys of television viewers, to measure beliefs, opinions, attitudes or behaviours (Morgan and Signorielli in Signorielli and Morgan 1990: 19), and the responses of heavy and light viewers are compared. Because of the ubiquity of television, it is assumed that even small differences are significant, and that these are indicators of the cultivation effect. Variations on the basis of gender, age, family structure, and real-life experience are also considered, in an effort to establish which types of people are more vulnerable to cultivation effects and why.

This is a form of experimental research, in that it is attempting to identify the influence of variables. However, instead of an objective pre-test of audience behaviour, it establishes benchmarks by surveys of aspects of the real world and of the level of television viewing among the sample: this has the advantage of not trying to manipulate the behaviour of research subjects, but the disadvantage of relying on their honesty in replying to surveys and their capacity to answer. The fierce debate among communication scholars in the late 1970s about the value of cultivation theory and the refinements in the methods that this debate produced is well summed up by Shanahan and Morgan (1999).

Those studying the cultivation effect are not usually concerned with a specific genre, such as soap opera. However, Buerkel-Rothfuss and Mayes (1981) did ask the question 'What types of effects could we reasonably expect from repeated exposure to soap opera content?', hypothesising that heavy viewers would have a distorted perception of the real world. They first established some benchmarks in the real world against which a content analysis of soap operas could be measured on matters such as the gender distribution of the professions, or the rate of divorce and single parenthood. They then surveyed 290 students in an introductory communications class at the University of Kentucky, asking them about themselves (to establish demographic data such as gender, age, class standing, and 'self-concept'), their soap opera viewing habits (to establish a group of viewers and a group of non-viewers), and their perceptions of the social world (their estimates of the number of professional women in the general population, the number having extra-marital affairs, etc, to enable comparison with both data about the real world and data about the world of soap opera). They found that those who regularly viewed soap operas made higher estimates of most categories in the real world – both higher than those of non-viewers and higher than actually existed in the real world. They also found these results statistically significant, even when controlled for demographic data.

To sum up the strengths of current effects studies:

- They are concerned with real people living in the real world.
- They employ their chosen methodology with rigour, taking great care to maximise reliability and validity.
- They are endeavouring to accommodate changing theories and methodologies. Though their methods are basically quantitative, they are increasingly recognising the value of qualitative research, if only for small pre-tests to set up hypotheses to be later tested quantitatively.

The major weaknesses of effects studies are:

- They are limited by the (basically linear) communication model on which they depend, which still assumes a passive audience acted upon by the media, no matter how much scope they give (in more recent examples) for audience resistance.
- They are limited by the (basically quantitative) methods they employ, and so by the definitions they create to establish categories for quantification.
- They claim (scientific) objectivity, but they are researching in a field (human behaviour) where subjects cannot be manipulated like objects in the physical world, and where they are themselves implicated (as television watchers).

For more detailed discussion of weaknesses in effects studies see Gauntlett (1998).Classical effects studies continue (Gunter 2000), however other effects studies research has been moving ever closer to uses and gratifications studies (for example, Kim and Rubin 1997; Lindlof 1987).

3.3 Uses and gratifications studies

Among the earliest systematic studies of radio soap opera were several which asked how such a critically despised form could secure and maintain such a huge and loyal audience, that is, what gratifications the audience received from listening. Though some (notably Arnheim 1944, see the first sub-section of section 9.1 in Chapter 9) inferred behavioural effects from textual meanings established by content analysis, even some of the very early examples

(Herzog 1941, 1944; Kaufman 1944) studied real audiences. Rosengren et al. (1985) provide a very useful summary of the stages of development of uses and gratifications research, and Jensen and Rosengren (1990: 210) follow their four-phase schema.

For soap opera research, an early example of the first phase ('prima facie descriptions') is a 1944 article by Herta Herzog. She started out in classic scientific research mode, seeing the researcher (herself, or the others who contributed) as outside the problem to be addressed, separate and different from the subjects of the research – radio serial listeners. She then made informed guesses, which she turned into hypotheses: that, in comparison with non-listeners, habitual listeners might be more isolated and less socially active, of lower-than-average intellect and so with poor powers of discrimination, concerned with their own problems rather than with politics or current affairs, unhappy and low achieving and so seeking compensation for their own limitations, or perhaps just more habitual radio listeners in general, so their soap opera habits might be determined more by their radio listening habits than vice versa.

She tested these hypotheses by reference to data from four large surveys done in different ways (some written questionnaires, some interviews) and on different samples (a national sample of non-farm women, a cross-section of the Iowa population and of the population of Erie County, Ohio, and a sample of women in Syracuse, Memphis and Minneapolis). The survey data was manipulated statistically, so she could provide (for instance) comparisons of the social activities of 'listeners' and 'non-listeners' (groups established from demographic data). The descriptive data was used as an illustration of some of her broader claims, which she was careful to couch always in less absolute terms than the statistics.

To this point, her approach was similar to the Cultural Indicators researchers, but she phrased her conclusions in terms of uses and gratifications, rather than in terms of effects. To test her first hypothesis that habitual serial listeners would be more isolated and less socially active than non-listeners, she compared the answers of the two groups to questions about attendance at church, or movies or other social gatherings during the previous week. She found that her expectations of a difference were not met: non-listeners attended slightly more church affairs, slightly more other social gatherings and slightly fewer movies than listeners, but in no case was the difference great enough to be considered statistically significant. What is happening here is a shift from 'prima facie descriptions' to 'typological efforts building on systematic operationalisations of central variables' (Jensen and Rosengren 1990: 210), trying to systematise relationships between categories: between 'listeners' and 'non-listeners', and between both of these and measures of social participation, range of intellectual interests, concern with public affairs, personality characteristics (which she measured, with some caution, on a five-point rating scale), and media practices and preferences. She found less systematic variation than anticipated: the only measure which seemed to be consistently different between the two groups was the extent of formal education.

We have discussed this 1944 article first because it so clearly belongs to the first two groups of research categories in Jensen and Rosengren's list – 'prima facie description' and 'systematic operationalisations'. Herzog's article goes on to sum up some of her conclusions from what was actually an earlier study, but one which fits into Jensen and Rosengren's third category: efforts at explanation.

The 1941 article, 'On borrowed experience', reports on a study aimed at finding out what radio serials mean to their listeners. The researchers interviewed one hundred women living in Greater New York. The first twenty interviews were wide-ranging and open-ended, and from the responses to these a questionnaire (attached to the article as an appendix) was drawn up for the second part of the sample.

Herzog found that listeners described the basic story-line of the soap operas as 'getting into trouble and out again', and that they selected their favourite programmes according to how well the stories matched their own experience. But then she offered an explanation of this behaviour, in terms of different kinds of gratifications experienced by the viewers:

> Basically the various stories mean the same thing to all the listeners. They appeal to their insecurity and provide them in one way or another with remedies of a substitute character. This occurs in, roughly, three types of reactions, which are differentiated as modes of experience but not in terms of their function.
>
> 1. Listening to the stories offers an emotional release.
> 2. Listening to the stories allows for a wishful remodelling of the listener's 'drudgery'.
> 3. Listening provides an ideology and recipes for adjustment. (Herzog 1941: 69)

Herzog's research remains germinal in the field. Its strengths are:

- It researched real people.
- It addressed the issue(s) systematically, and selected appropriate ways of doing this (questionnaires and interviews).
- Its sampling techniques are sensible and appropriate.
- It recognised that listeners are not totally blank pages on which the media write, but active participants in an exchange, from which they obtain 'gratifications'.

However, it also has its weaknesses:

- It sets out to find systematic differences between 'listeners' and 'non-listeners', terms which are defined in use, not independent of context.
- There are several slippages from simply reporting on what respondents said and finding relationships among such reports, to interpreting what respondents said through Herzog's own intellectual framework, for instance her conjectures about women without formal education.

- Similarly, but in a broader vein, Herzog did not recognise her own biases (and particularly her linear model of communication and behaviourist model of social/psychological explanation) so she could not recognise how the research design shaped and predetermined the results. Terms like 'psychological mass education' or 'stultifying tales' are pejorative, but were not recognised as such by Herzog or others at the time.

Despite these weaknesses, this was ground-breaking research. The way that Herzog discovered systematised relationships among responses and organised these into groupings to explain the relationships, has been the model for many audience studies from that time forward. Data manipulation techniques have become more sophisticated, particularly since the development of **factor analysis** for quantitative data, and, more recently still, sophisticated computer programmes for the analysis of qualitative data such as interview transcripts. These developments are obvious from other research reports on gratifications of daytime television serial viewers, for instance Compesi (1980).

All uses and gratifications studies, however, share certain problems:

- Problems of audience responses: they assume that it is possible for audience members to recognise their own conscious and subconscious motivations and to describe the uses to which they put each programme, as distinct from the gratification they obtain from television viewing generally. They also underestimate the difficulty of explaining responses to whole programmes when different characters/plot elements/settings/ images may be providing different (possibly even conflicting) uses and gratifications for a viewer.
- Problems of terminology: they are dependent upon the use of very slippery terms ('satisfaction' or 'need', or even 'use' and 'gratification'), which are defined in use. But they usually apply these terms as if their meaning is self-evident.
- Problems of measurement: they assume that responses from different people measure the same thing and therefore can be treated statistically (added, factor analysed and interpreted).
- Logical problems: they assume that the given responses exhaust all the possibilities.
- Problems of context: they question audiences about texts, assuming that texts are self-evident in their meaning, independent of viewing context (see Ellis 1992; Hill and McLoone 1996; Morley 1989: 34). They find explanations ultimately in social and psychological differences among individual viewers, rather than addressing the broader social context of viewing.

Despite these problems, uses and gratifications studies continue, and are now in a fourth stage: attempts at systematic theory building. This brings these (basically sociological) studies ever closer to the (originally more humanities-inclined) cultural studies approach (see section 3.5).

3.4 Literary and historical analyses and reader-response studies

We started on the left of the model on page 40, with the social science tradition, because that is where the academic study of real audiences has been most prolific. Nevertheless, we need to look at the little that has come directly out of the humanities about real people as media audiences. There have been attempts to locate the historical audience, but the difficulties of such research have limited its frequency. One example is Docherty et al. (1987), who used early social survey research (such as that produced by Hutton Research 1949, or the Gallup polls) to trace the history of cinema attendance in Britain from 1946 to 1987, then did their own survey in 1986–7. Just as they used other people's research to trace early audiences, so their 1987 data can be used now as historical evidence for later researchers. We know of no comparable studies of the historical audience for television soap opera, though theoretically the data produced by so many previous studies of soap opera audience could be mined for use in **meta-analysis** within an historical project.

Within literary studies, traditional (hermeneutic) literary critics had (and still have) little interest in real readers. Reader-response theory was the first literary theory to formally recognise and explore the concept of 'the reader', but this exploration was likely to be textual – the potential reader as constructed within the text rather than the real-life reader in a social context. Allen (1985: 78) recognises the limitations of the position within reader-response theory from which he, himself, speaks when he says:

> 'Actual' readers have entered my discussion much more obliquely: as extrapolations from demographic and ratings data or from my own experience as a reader of soap operas. The implicit challenge is to relate these constructed reader positions to the experiences of actual soap opera readers. It is a challenge I fully admit to not having taken up. (Allen 1985: 182)

So, Allen's very useful book on soap operas concentrates on the meaning of the text, and how the text constructs a position for the implied reader. Other researchers, however, from both the humanities and social sciences, *are* interested in real people as well as in the social world they occupy.

3.5 Cultural studies and reception studies

From the seventies onwards the semiotic model of communication became increasingly powerful, and in a grey area between the social sciences and the humanities 'cultural studies' began carving out a niche. Its brief history is complex (see Frow and Morris 2000), but the various claimants to the label share a concern with the interaction between texts and contexts, within culture(s).

They accept culture as a 'whole way of life', so they study popular textual forms such as comics and music video as well as written texts. Their interest in any specific 'audience' is directed to enhancing the understanding of social processes.

There is a similar complexity within reception studies. It has been proposed (for example, Corner 1991: 268; 1998: 110–11) that reception studies have split into two streams – the 'public knowledge' project focusing (as the Birmingham Media Group do) on news and current affairs and conceptualising the viewer as citizen, and the 'popular culture' project focusing (as do feminist studies of soap opera) on fiction and conceptualising the viewer as the **consumer** of entertainment. For the 'public knowledge' project, the main questions concern agency – who has power over the dissemination of information within society? For the 'popular culture' project, the main questions concern pleasure – how is taste formed and desire satisfied by a commercial media **industry**? For both projects, the interest is in how cognitive processes (individual psychology) shape readings of texts, within a cultural context (Höijer 1998).

We see the differences between cultural studies and reception studies as minor – a matter of emphasis. Pertti Alasuutari (1999) similarly links cultural studies with reception studies, identifying three stages: a linguistic turn (starting with Stuart Hall), followed by 'audience **ethnography**', followed by a constructionist view.

Hall led some of the earliest practitioners of what is now called cultural studies, within the Birmingham Media Group. Hall (1984, first published as an occasional paper, 1974) conceived communication as a (basically linear) flow between unequal elements, recognising stages in the process of moving from encoding to decoding and asking, how and why do audiences decode differentially? He concluded that the message is a structured polysemy, with a preferred meaning: at both the encoding and decoding stages, meaning can be read semiotically. Assuming that social class would be the basic determinant, Hall proposed that audiences read from one of three hypothetical positions (based on Parkin 1973): the dominant-hegemonic position (where the communication is read from a position similar to the one from which it has been spoken), the negotiated position (where the basic structures may be accepted, but the details may be challenged and negotiated), and the oppositional position (where the message is decoded entirely from within a different framework).

Morley tested this proposition in research on audiences of the current affairs television programme *Nationwide*, first providing a content analysis of the programme (Brunsdon and Morley 1978), then looking specifically at the audience (Morley 1980). For the latter, 29 focus groups, each of five to ten members, were gathered in their educational or occupational context and shown two episodes of *Nationwide*. Their responses were codified and compared, both statistically and descriptively, with sample **profiles**. Morley then discussed which groups inhabited dominant, negotiated or oppositional codes, and connected this discussion to the social class of the groups, finding much less of a match of reading with class position than expected. His conclusion was that we can get away from both the textually produced **spectator** (of the 'lit. crit.' end of the research spectrum) and the socially determined audience (of the effects studies end of the research spectrum): he proposed that readings occur through socially produced discourses, within limits imposed by texts.

The strengths of this research are:

- It builds upon (testing and adapting) earlier research (Hall's).
- It links textual and audience research productively, without reading one unproblematically from the other.
- The sample (chosen by work and education) is appropriate for the issues under examination (relationship between social class and viewing practices).

Weaknesses identified by Morley's critics were:

- His 'audience' is a construct from the research, not independent of it.
- He does not observe people, but relies on what they choose to tell (they might lie) and on what they are able to tell (what they can articulate about their preferences and choices).
- He concentrates on meaning, leaving no room to consider pleasure.
- The research was conducted in artificial contexts, rather than in people's living rooms, which is where they usually view.
- He did not distinguish between habitual viewers and those who did not usually watch television.
- He treats the groups as representative of their social class, without defining what he means by class, or explaining how individuals were assigned to class groups such as 'skilled upper working class'. At the same time, he misses the opportunity to investigate the social dynamics of the focus groups themselves.

As all good researchers should do, Morley took these criticisms into account in his later research, and was influential in establishing what Alasuutari (1999: 4) identifies as the second stage of reception studies – audience ethnography. Morley (1988) interviewed eighteen families in their homes in South London, analysing their use of domestic space and how the television fitted into the family structure, again finding use clearly differentiated according to gender. This addressed the criticism that his earlier project took viewing out of its domestic context, but he still chose not to observe people, but rather to rely on what they said. His defence was that even observed behaviour has to be interpreted, which still leaves an (admittedly different) margin for **error**: so, 'should you wish to understand what I am doing it would probably be as well to ask me' (Morley 1988: 46).

However, this research, too, has been criticised, both directly and through other research projects taking a different approach. The BFI Audience Tracking Study was a longitudinal study, tracking its sample over five years. It used a larger sample than Morley's (about 500 respondents at first although over five years that number shrank) who filled in open diary questionnaires. The study sought to 'ascertain the relationship between media and everyday life' (Gauntlett and Hill 1999: 3). Their study incorporated the 'life analysis' approach which 'assumes that through close study of people's everyday lives over time, we will acquire a picture of broader changes in society which are having an impact at the individual level' (Gauntlett and Hill 1999: 18). In doing so they sought to avoid the overdetermined 'explanations of things which people said [in their diaries] by referring to their demographic characteristics or background' (Gauntlett and Hill 1999: 19). As a result of their research Gauntlett and Hill argue that Morley presents a too polarised view of gender relations with respect to television and especially the use of the remote control: 'whilst previous studies have suggested that men have dominated control over the television, our evidence indicates that in the 1990s this is relatively rare' (Gauntlett and Hill 1999: 245).

Nevertheless, Morley's body of research has been germinal in the field of television audience studies, and his methods place him (in terms of the Jensen and Rosengren model) in the central 'cultural studies' category, approached from the social science end of the spectrum. Approaching from the humanities end produces a rather different kind of research, closer to what Jensen and Rosengren call 'reception analysis', but still within what Alasuutari identifies as the second stage of cultural studies/reception studies.

Soap opera was among the first media forms (along with its related form, the romance novel: see Radway 1984) to be researched using reception studies, partly because feminists were interested in those media forms which were popular with women. So, these researchers start with the question: 'What is it about these texts, which are universally despised as aesthetic objects, that makes audiences (particularly female audiences) love them so much?' This question cannot be answered by looking only at the audience, or only at the text: studying reception requires studying the interaction between text and reader.

Dorothy Hobson (1982) researched the audience for *Crossroads* by visiting women in their homes, observing them and talking with them as they watched television while preparing the evening meal. This was a project clearly based in the social sciences, sharing some of its methodology with researchers such as Morley. But other researchers, still wanting to ask very much the same question, started from a humanities rather than a social science perspective. Carol Lopate, for instance, considered soap opera as part of the broader vista of daytime television. She concluded:

> For the woman confined to her house, daytime television fills out the empty spaces of the long day when she is home alone, channels her fantasies toward love and family dramas, and promises her that the life she is in can fulfil her needs. But it does not call to her attention her aloneness and isolation, and it does not suggest to her that it is precisely in her solitude that she has the possibility for gaining a self. (Lopate 1977: 51)

This was a reference to real women, confined in their houses, but (unlike Hobson) Lopate inferred the audience from a reading of the text: she did not go out into the community where presumably these women could be found, and ask them if that was, indeed, how they read the soap operas they watch.

Tania Modleski (1982: 85–109) started her report with a content analysis of soap opera, not based on empirical research on the social science model, but on intuition after much informal viewing. Like Lopate, Modleski referred frequently to the reader, whom she called (from the tradition of psychoanalytic criticism, see the second sub-section in section 11.2 in Chapter 11) the 'spectator/subject', and claimed to be constructed by the text. But in later parts of the chapter Modleski addressed directly the issue of the pleasure(s) obtained from soap operas by real 'viewers' (as distinct from constructed 'spectators'). There are obvious parallels here with the questions of pleasure raised by the uses and gratifications approach, but (unlike Hobson) Modleski reaches her conclusions by speculation, not by experiment or direct **observation**. She asks why the narrative form of soap opera has special appeal to women, and provides two inter-locking explanations. The psychological/psychoanalytic explanation links film critic Marsha Kinder's claim that the 'open-ended, slow paced, multi-climaxed' **structure** of soap opera is 'in tune with patterns of female sexuality' (Kinder 1974–5) with the endless and circular narrative form of soaps (Modleski 1982: 98). The institutional explanation links the complex rhythms of work of a housewife with the cyclical form of the soap opera, suggesting that soap opera provides the female viewer with models of how to do everything at once.

In addition, she suggests (Modleski 1983) that the decentred and fragmented form of the soap opera and its programming mirrors the decentred and fragmented form of the housewife's own life, so the form may be seen as a distinctly *female* form of representation: one that can be posited against the centred, unified form of the classical narrative film viewed in a state of intense concentration in a cinema. She concludes that soaps mirror the desires of their audience, desires which are never satisfied more than temporarily.

Modleski's work, too, has been criticised. Seiter et al. (1989) point out that Modleski does not recognise her own white middle-class social position: in their own research, Seiter et al. admit that they are, as researchers, still inside the culture they are observing, as they adapt Morley's concept of 'preferred reading' to cope with the shift from non-fiction (current affairs) to fiction (soap opera). Liesbet van Zoonen (1994: 40) critiqued the view of soap opera as 'women's culture' for having too fixed a view of gender, a view shared by Gauntlett and Hill (1999: 226) who argued that no gender division in relation to soap opera was evident in the Audience Tracking Study.

The early work of Ien Ang (1985) is very different from Modleski's, in that she is concerned (like Seiter and other social science researchers already discussed) with real readers, members of the social audience, and she approaches these people directly rather than inferring them from analysis of the text. But she does it in a far less formal and structured way than those other researchers.

Intrigued by the phenomenal success of the American soap opera *Dallas* in Holland, she put an advertisement in a Dutch newspaper asking people who had strong feelings about the serial to write to her, and then analysed the 42 responses. This sample is self-selecting, and the researcher denies having set out with an hypothesis to test. Ang does not claim to be objective and outside the research: her invitation was framed as starting from her own pleasure in the text and her curiosity about other people's responses. Unsurprisingly, she found that some of the people who responded liked the programme and some did not. What was more surprising was the frequency with which *both* groups explained their feelings in terms of 'realism', and even sometimes referred to the same characters or plot developments in defence of their contradictory judgments.

Ang explained this dependence on realism as a result of the 'mass culture critique' (Gans 1974: 3): the view that popular culture (including television) is a debased form of culture, mass-produced and aimed at the lowest common denominator – the public as 'mass'. This view sees 'realism' as the primary criterion for discriminating between mass culture and high culture, and treats this very slippery term as if it has only one generally agreed meaning, transcending context (see the first sub-section in section 11.2 in Chapter 11). Ang coins two terms to differentiate those viewing experiences which match our experience of the real world (her 'empirical realism') and those which match rather our feelings about that real world (her 'emotional realism'). She can then explain those divergent responses as being based upon either empirical realism (so *Dallas* is found wanting because the viewer has no experience of that kind of lifestyle against which to judge the programme, or because the viewer does judge it and finds it inadequate) or emotional realism (so *Dallas* is considered to represent realistically the emotional world of its characters). In a more recent article on soap opera, Ang and Stratton (1995) explain how the realistic effect of the standard soap opera comes from the 'unstated naturalisation of the moral order'. They also describe another kind of soap opera based upon 'post-realism' which they identify as a response to post-modernism.

In her original research the evidence Ang used in support of her findings was quotations from readers' letters, so the report looks very like those social scientific studies that quote extensively from survey or interview data. But she was not looking for ways of sorting these responses into categories which can provide covering explanations: rather she was looking for insights which the responses could give into the experience of individual viewers, and particularly what pleased or displeased them. She accounted for direct dislike of the programme as the result of adoption of the mass culture critique, or of the perverse pleasure of watching ironically, enjoying their own superiority. So she concluded that, though the mass culture argument dominated the rational consciousness of most respondents, populist aesthetics continued to dominate their practice, because this allowed for pleasure which the mass culture argument continued to denigrate or ignore.

Hobson, Modleski, Ang, Gauntlett and Hill, and Seiter et al. all ask the question which we have suggested is appropriate for reception analysis: how do socially differentiated readers produce readings of texts within a cultural context? Their concern is primarily with the reader, and with explaining readers' pleasure. This contrasts with Morley, whom we placed within cultural studies, looking at readings to understand culture and cultural positioning. All these projects have specific strengths and weaknesses, but we propose to discuss them all together. Frow and Morris (2000: 329) admit that cultural studies now overlap in significant ways (both in object of study and in methodology) with **anthropology**, sociology of culture, social and cultural history, critical geography and literary studies. One methodology all these approaches share is ethnography, though some of the researchers we have discussed would challenge the application of the term to their projects. Ann Gray (1992), for example, argues that there are very few real ethnographies, but sees her study of the role of VCRs in women's lives as having 'ethnographic intentions' because 'it insists that we must locate subjects in their social and historical contexts and develop ways of researching "real" viewers' (Gray 1992: 32).

'Ethnography' is derived from the Greek *ethnos* (nation) and *graphe* (writing), so it means 'writing about nations' (cultures, ways of life, people). The most serious problems of ethnographic research are:

- Examining a culture in depth requires the presence of researchers, observing and asking questions: but this presence then necessarily becomes a part of the situation being observed, and the effect of this is impossible to measure.
- The ethnographer may attempt to stand outside the culture, to avoid contaminating behaviour or allowing her own biases to affect results, but:
    - this is extremely difficult to do (some say impossible), and it is certainly never possible to know for certain how far you have succeeded;
    - there is always the possibility of an outsider misunderstanding the culture, as the more complex it is, the more an insider understands it differently from even an impartial observer (assuming that impartiality is possible);
    - it is impossible for an outsider researcher to know for certain how reliable her informants are.
- The ethnographer may attempt to become an insider, to empathise with the culture, or even to socialise within it as a full participant, but:
    - this is still difficult to do, and it is still never possible to know for certain if you have understood correctly;
    - attempting to see from inside can still lead to misunderstandings, and can still produce false information, as those who are more long-standing members of the culture resist the intrusion of an outsider;
    - the researcher is at risk of 'going native', of taking the insider position so thoroughly that it distorts both the research process and the results.

Ethnographic research methodology was developed for the study of unfamiliar and exotic cultures. It was almost inevitable that the result was to set these up as strange, in opposition to (as the Other of) the culture of the researcher. In recent years, the power differential that this establishes has been subject to critique (both ideological and methodological), and as a result the attention of ethnographers has turned towards the more unfamiliar and exotic aspects of their own culture. However, for middle class educated researchers to study football hooliganism or drug addiction is simply to create a different kind of Other, with similar power differentials still in operation. Even interviewers sympathetic to the behaviour being studied (like watching soap operas) can find themselves in difficulties, as discussed at length in Seiter (1990).

All of these problems have led ethnographers away from the post-positivist framework, towards critical theory or constructivist or participatory action frameworks (see section 1.4 in Chapter 1), and to new ways of writing research reports (see section 12.3 in Chapter 12).

Meanwhile, the term 'ethnography' has been applied to those studies of media audiences which closely observe the actual behaviour of audiences while they interact with media (for instance while watching television), and later question the audience about this behaviour, in contrast for example to Modleski who does not ask the audience, and Ang who asks only by mail, without actually meeting her research subjects.

But this kind of media research on audiences has all the problems of traditional ethnography, plus a few new ones (see Hermes 2000; Lotz 2000; Seiter et al. 1989: 227):

- Traditional ethnography is long-term and in-depth, but most audience studies observe for short periods (sometimes less than an hour, at most up to a few days), and might better be called '**participant observation**' (Lotz 2000: 450–1).
- Ethnography examines culture as a whole, but audience studies isolate one aspect of culture (television viewing), and seldom consider it within a larger context (although see both Gray (1992) and Schlesinger et al. (1992) for two studies which sought to study how women make sense of their media experiences within their social context). When they do compare and contrast audience behaviour, preferences and understandings across different cultures, this may be compounding the problem rather than helping to solve it.
- Ethnography examines a culture from outside (whether objectively or sympathetically), but television audiences are often from the same culture (including the same television culture) as the researcher.

Soap opera is a good example of the difficulties of employing ethnographic methods to study media audiences (Lotz 2000). At first, soap opera audiences were selected for study precisely because they were seen as odd, different from the social ideal and certainly from the social positioning of the researchers who were studying them. After many years, the **ideology** behind such study came into question. Researching a critically denigrated form such as soap opera might well identify what pleasure and profit a predominantly female audience might obtain from the form, but it did not change society's judgment of the moral and aesthetic value of the form, nor the assumption that the audience were somehow inferior. Even when the researcher was seeking to defend the form, the research methodology still positioned the (mainly female) subjects in subordination to the researchers (both male and female). Hermes (2000) describes her surprise that her interviewees refused to accept that detective fiction (like soap opera) occupies a lowly cultural position: she had simply assumed that they would adopt the cultural cringe of the mass-culture-critique position, but they were proud of their favourite form and confident about their own pleasure in it.

Alasuutari's third category, the 'constructionist view' (1999: 6), grows out of audience ethnography, taking into account the complexities of the insider/outsider debate, being more reflexive, and moving from audience psychology to sociology (Alasuutari 1999: 8–9). This opens up for debate the area of how audiences have been conceptualised within different worldviews, as well as how specific audiences have read texts. It leads to discussion of where audiences fit in a post-modern world (Tulloch 2000: 19).

3.6 Conclusion

In this chapter we have concentrated on studies of soap opera audiences to provide a degree of coherence and unity to our discussion. This does, however, mean that we have not dealt with other studies which have used innovative approaches to audience study, and which we commend to those seeking to study audience behaviour. Here we include studies such as Annette Hill's study of 'the reactive mechanisms associated with viewing violent movies' (1997: 5) and her more recent research into audience responses to popular factual entertainment (2002). Jane Roscoe's research into the television documentary *An Immigrant Nation* used a range of methodologies to study production of the documentary, its textual discourses and audience interpretations of the programme (1999), while a number of projects at the Bournemouth Media School (2003) are using a variety of production based and creative techniques to study young people's interaction with media.

The various projects discussed in this chapter should not be considered as exemplifying discrete and sequential research approaches, but rather as interwoven layers, a matrix with each new development building upon and incorporating aspects of earlier research. Change can take place in any of the layers, and this means that experienced researchers need to monitor all the potential sites of change, or be in danger of re-inventing someone else's wheel. Beginners can be forgiven for using other people's maps to guide them, such as provided in this chapter, and in works such as Jensen and Rosengren (1985), Ang (1996), Alasuutari (1999), Denzin and Lincoln (2000), Tulloch (2000). The nearer our examples are to the present day, the less likely they are to present a 'pure' example of any particular research approach or methodology. More and more nowadays researchers are acknowledging that, provided they are not absolutely incompatible, different methods can be mixed and matched, to ask more interesting questions and offer more compelling conclusions. As a result, much of what was once taken for granted about audience research, is being fundamentally re-thought, for instance by the contributors to Hay et al. (1996) and Alasuutari (1999).

Currently it is becoming more difficult than ever to keep the audience and the text separate. This is acknowledged, for instance, in Baym (2000), which explores the interpretations of soap opera shared within an audience community on an internet newsgroup. We will, in later chapters, return to audiences incidentally as we discuss texts and the institutions that produce them. But, before then we need to talk in more detail about the many techniques used in the process of gathering data about audiences, and the principles in operation when that data is analysed and interpreted.

Chapter 4

Gathering Data on Audiences

You may have decided to structure your research project around data collected by others (such as ratings data), but if you decide to gather your own data you will probably seek out documents, or use observation (of individuals or groups), or surveys (from documents or by tests, questionnaires or interviews), or a combination of these. Remember to have an ethics policy in place before you start (see section 1.5 in Chapter 1).

4.1 Selecting subjects

You will not examine every possible member of every possible audience: you will need to understand why you include some individuals or groups and exclude others. Remember that you may well need different methods of selection for different aspects of a research project.

Generalisability – populations and profiles

From a positivist or post-positivist position, you will wish to generalise from your examples to a wider group of people, so you will start with a 'population'. Each country has a periodic census, which counts every member of the population, and asks questions about gender, age, education, racial or ethnic background, place of birth and so on. This can be collated into a 'profile', a summary description of that population.

Within your own research, the population is the total number of people in the group about which you hope to draw conclusions. This may be very large ('all soap opera viewers'), or much smaller ('all soap opera viewers in a [named] town' or 'all viewers of [a named soap opera]'), but in positivist research and most post-positivist research it is inappropriate to examine a single case ('my aunt who watches *Neighbours* regularly'). The demographic composition of your research 'population' can then be compared to census data, to measure how far the population being studied matches (represents) the wider community.

When selecting a research population:

- Choose a population relevant to the question being asked, small enough to be practically manageable and large enough to provide the sort of data you need, within your budget and at the necessary level of discrimination.
- Define your population carefully, to include only those that are relevant to the question you are asking. For instance, if your project is to compare the popularity of television news and soap operas among regular television viewers, it would be inappropriate to include in your population anyone who answered 0 (zero) to the question of how many hours of television they viewed each week.

When establishing a profile:

- Collect the descriptive data early so that gaps and skews can be addressed.
- Collate this descriptive data early, so that hypotheses can be modified to suit the population.
- Make sure that the descriptive data collected is relevant to the question being addressed. For media audiences, appropriate measures might be age, gender, employment, education level, first language, or ethnic origin. Taste in breakfast foods may be significant in a marketing project, but is not likely to be helpful in research on soap opera preferences.
- The more homogeneous a group is on any measure, the smaller the range required in any profile category. For instance, if the age of your population ranges from 10 to 50, it may be appropriate to ensure that each decade is represented, but if they are all in their twenties then you may need to divide the range into years.

Remember that any 'population' is a construct, created by assuming that the qualities and experiences of individuals can be added together.

Transferability – cases and instances

From a critical theory, constructivist or participatory action approach, you will not be aiming at making generalisations. Rather you will be seeking to understand individual cases, or considering examples from defined groups, or looking at instances of a process:

> Every instance of a case or process bears the stamp of the general class of phenomena to which it belongs. However, any given instance is likely to be particular and unique. Thus, for example, any given classroom is like all classrooms, but no two classrooms are the same. (Denzin and Lincoln 2000: 370)

Similarly, any given television audience is like all television audiences, but no two audiences are the same.

You may hope that your conclusions may be transferable in some degree, even if generalisation is not possible. However, even **transferability** is irrelevant to the 'method of instances', which 'takes each instance of a phenomenon as an occurrence that evidences the operation of a set of cultural understandings currently available for use by cultural members' (Denzin and Lincoln 2000: 370). A media example might be that every television programme is evidence of the operation of a set of conventions available to the viewer, or every audience viewing is an example of the application of conventions of reading to a particular programme. The research can address any aspect of this instance, seeking to understand the process.

For cases and instances you do not need to define a population: but you do still need to understand the rationale behind your selection of the particular case(s) or instance(s).

4.2 Sampling and selecting

'Sampling' is a positivist term for selecting a smaller group to represent a larger group, allowing generalisation from the results. However, the term 'sampling' is also used less rigorously, to describe any process of selecting subjects for study, including cases and instances, where there is no intention to generalise. So, the sampling procedures developed within a positivist framework have been adapted for use in non-positivist social science research (see, for instance, Miles and Huberman 1994: 27–34). Humanities research does not usually talk about 'sampling': however, the subjects for humanities research still need to be selected, in ways that can be demonstrated to be relevant and appropriate to the question being addressed.

Size of the sample

If you are not aiming at generalisability, there are no rules on sample size: depending on your purpose, in some cases a large sample will be wise, and in others a single case, provided it is information-rich, is sufficient.

If you are aiming at generalisability (even, possibly, prediction) you will require that your sample be highly representative of the total population: however, large sample size does not guarantee representativeness. A 1936 pre-poll survey of voting intentions in the US presidential elections received 2,500,000 responses to a survey sent to 12,000,000 persons selected from telephone directories and automobile registration lists, but failed to predict the success of Roosevelt, because those who owned cars and telephones did not accurately represent the voting population.

Since then, polling organisations have refined their techniques, till a quite small sample can predict with remarkable accuracy: the projections of major opinion polls, such as those we see reported in the newspapers, are made on fewer than 2000 respondents. There are now tables that provide optimum sample sizes for achieving a representative sample from populations of varying sizes, and for varying levels of confidence (for instance, Grosof and Sardy 1985: 183–4).

You may still need to adapt your sample size by reference to:

- the time and money available to you (smaller samples are cheaper and take less time);
- what you already know about the population, and hence how confident you can be of identifying a representative sample (so stratified sampling requires a smaller sample for the same level of accuracy as simple random sampling);
- how many variables you are measuring (in general, the more variables, the larger the sample size);
- for questionnaires and surveys, the expected level of non-response (a high level requires a larger sample).

You may also need to conduct a pilot study on a small sample before you decide just how large your main sample will need to be.

Methods of sampling

When choosing a sampling/selection method, take into account:

- accessibility of subjects (how easy it will be to find suitable people);
- costs (unless your research is funded, you may find even bus fares or telephone charges difficult to meet);
- how generalisable or transferable you wish your conclusions to be, and therefore how much sampling error you are willing to tolerate ('sampling error' is the degree to which the sample is not representative of the population);
- how appropriate different kinds of sampling or selection procedures are to the question you are asking.

There are two broad families of sampling/selection procedures and each includes a number of sampling/selection techniques. Consult statistical texts (such as Agresti and Finlay 1986: Chapter 2; Levin and Fox 1997: Chapter 6) for details of the implementation of each of these, and research methods handbooks (such as Grosof and Sardy 1985: Chapter 8; Miles and Huberman 1994: 27–34; Patton 1990) for additional ways of sampling, beyond those listed below.

Probability sampling

Probability sampling methods produce a sample which is statistically representative of a larger population, allowing generalisation from the sample to the population, on the assumption that repeated sampling would produce similar results, and sampling error can be measured.

You start with a 'sampling frame', that is a complete list of the whole population from which the sample will be chosen (such as an electoral roll, or a register of schools). You then establish a profile of the population for comparison with the sample: Hemming (1989), for instance, provides census information for the entire British population on age, gender and 'social grade'. Personal profiles may be useful for some forms of research (particularly those on small populations), but group profiles, accumulating data about all members, are more common in audience research.

Forms of probability sampling:

- Simple random sampling: define a population (for instance, people listed on a census return or in a telephone book), give each member of the population a unique number starting from one, generate a list of random numbers (for instance on a computer, or by randomly selecting numbered balls) or find such a list on the web, select every person from the sampling frame whose number matches the random list.
- Systematic sampling: define a population, give each member of the population a unique number starting from one, divide the total number of the population by the number you have decided to use as a sample (this gives your 'periodicity'), select randomly a number less than the periodicity and, starting at that number on the list, select every nth person systematically from the list.
- Stratified sampling: define the population, define subgroups within the population (for instance by gender or age range), use random or systematic sampling within each subgroup.
- Cluster sampling: define the population, select a cluster, for instance by geographical proximity or by institutional affiliation, then use the whole of the cluster as a sample of the population, or use random or systematic sampling within it.
- Multi-stage sampling: define the population, select a cluster, select a smaller cluster from within the first cluster (and so on, till the optimum number sample size is reached).

Non-probability sampling

Non-probability sampling methods produce a sample which bears no known relationship to any population: there is no way to know whether any other sample would produce similar results, nor to measure sampling error. Non-probability samples can be used within a positivist or post-positivist framework, for exploratory research before hypotheses are developed for more rigorous testing, or within non-positivist, qualitative research where the results are not intended to be generalised to a whole population.

Forms of non-probability sampling:

- Purposive sampling: on the basis of earlier experience, select a sample as a test, that may be deliberately extreme or deviant, or information-rich, or meeting certain predetermined criteria. A variant of this occurs during field work, as you recognise what might be confirming or disconfirming cases, which then become a purposive sample.
- Quota sampling: define the population, select a sample that appears to match what is already known of the population. This requires foreknowledge of the general characteristics of the whole population, but not with the same rigour as for probability sampling.
- Convenience or availability sampling: use what comes to hand, knowing that it is not representative. 'Snowball' sampling is a variant on this: you find one person, who directs you to another, who in turn directs you to still others. This allows you to tap into kinship and friendship networks, which may be part of what you are studying. Another variant is sometimes called 'opportunistic sampling', taking advantage of new opportunities that arise after the study (usually fieldwork interviews or participant observation) has already begun. These methods may raise privacy issues (see section 1.5 in Chapter 1).

4.3 Survey methods

Surveys are systematic collections of data, which can then be used for:

- collating descriptive information (for instance, on the soap opera viewing habits of teenage girls);
- making comparisons between groups of people (for instance, comparing the soap opera viewing habits of teenage girls and teenage boys, or of teenage girls and housewives);
- exploring relationships between variables (for instance, exploring the relationship between soap opera viewing and level of formal education).

In media and communications research on audiences, surveys might be done by:

- document analysis;
- questionnaires and forms (administered face-to-face, or by mail or phone);
- interviews (structured, semi-structured or unstructured).

Documents

Documents have long been the preferred data for humanities researchers, perhaps because so many have been trained in the document methods required by historical and literary research (see the first sub-section of section 8.1 in Chapter 8). Social science, on the other hand, has traditionally preferred to set up controlled situations for experiment or observation, but documents have now become more acceptable as social science data. The methods for finding documents are discussed more fully in the second sub-section of section 7.1 in Chapter 7, however some document sources provide data specific to audience research.

Ratings measure audience preferences and produce quantitative data, for statistical analysis. In addition, individual audience members record discursively what they think about programmes, or actors, or network programming policy in the form of letters to the editors of journals and newspapers, or contributions to online chat and newsgroup discussions.

Programme guides can be a rich source of data on audiences. Remember that there may be regional variants of these: at one stage there were 26 variants of the journal *TV Week* being published to cover the whole of Australia.

The internet has become a major clearing house for all kinds of information about and responses to media programmes. In the case of soap opera, there are the official sites maintained by the networks (for instance www.homeandaway.org), but there are also newsgroups and sites maintained by individuals and groups of fans (for instance, www.summerbayweb.com/menu.htm).

Questionnaires

Questionnaires are an efficient way of reaching a large number of respondents at relatively low cost, and are often used in social research. For detailed advice on how to construct, test and implement a questionnaire, consult Cox (1996).

Questionnaires can be appropriate to media research for:

- demographic surveys (questions about soap opera viewers: age, gender, family structure, class, education);
- ratings surveys (questions about hours viewed, soap opera programmes selected);
- attitude and opinion surveys (questions about likes and dislikes among individual soap operas or stars, or opinions about issues such as media censorship or violence on television);
- surveys of behaviour (questions about viewing context, how programmes are selected, who controls the on/off switch, whether viewers copy the behaviour or dress of favourite characters).

They share certain problems:

- They provide simple answers to simple questions, so they cannot help to establish **thick description** or to understand process or social context.

- They depend upon the capacity of the researcher to ask unambiguous questions dependent on clear definitions, but in social and cultural research definitions are always influenced by the context.
- They depend upon the capacity of the respondent to answer, and their willingness to do so honestly, so questionnaire answers are always inherently unreliable.
- The simpler the questions, the less chance for misunderstanding, but also the more chance that respondents will assume that the questionnaire is not important and will not give it serious attention.
- There will always be a proportion of non-response or incomplete response: taking a larger sample than strictly necessary helps to reduce the effect of this, but may exacerbate bias.

There are several ways in which questionnaires can be administered:

- In institutional settings like a classroom or a workplace, questionnaires can be administered to a complete population or a controlled sample. This saves time and money, but some participants may be reluctant and may produce incomplete or inaccurate responses.
- Questionnaires delivered by mail can be sent to a carefully selected sample, allowing a large sample over a widespread geographic area to be reached relatively cheaply, and reaching people who are not home when interviewers call. However, time must be allowed for their return, and they usually produce a low response rate, which can skew results.
- Administering a questionnaire by telephone saves time but is expensive, and (like a mail survey) usually results in a lower response rate. It also opens the possibility of respondents withdrawing before the interview is complete, producing incomplete data, and it limits respondents to those who have telephones, which can introduce bias into the sample.

An effective questionnaire will:

- be short enough for respondents to complete in a reasonable time;
- use language simple enough to avoid misunderstandings;
- have concise and clear instructions;
- ask questions clearly:
  - without ambiguous wording, jargon, technical language, and complicated and confusing wording ('Place a tick against the boxes for those items which you do not watch');
  - asking one thing at a time, avoiding double-barrelled questions ('When and why did you watch your first soap opera?');
- avoid leading questions ('What soap operas do you watch?' assumes that the respondent watches at least one soap opera);
- be logical:
  - asking questions in logical order;

    - providing simple pathways for respondents to see which questions apply to them and which do not;
- provide for all possible answers including 'zero' and 'not applicable';
- give a visual impression that is uncluttered and not intimidating;
- produce data in a form that is easily processed, either by people or by machine.

Question types

Closed questions are those which limit possible responses. These can be very useful:

- They are generally simpler to answer and the answers are easier to process (including manipulate statistically) than those for open questions.
- They are appropriate when the researcher can reasonably anticipate the range of likely answers and when approximate answers are all that is needed.
- When sensitive information is being sought, closed questions are usually more acceptable to respondents, and more likely to be honestly answered.

On the other hand:

- They are difficult to word accurately and effectively.
- It may be advisable to do some interviewing before devising the questionnaire, so that the concepts raised in the interviews can be incorporated into the questionnaire, rather than coming entirely out of the preconceptions of the researcher.
- They usually require pre-testing (sometimes more than once), to identify and correct the flaws.
- If there are a large number of similar questions (particularly lists of statements to be rated), the respondent may answer all similarly in an effort to hurry.
- They may still be difficult to interpret:
    - different respondents may interpret the questions or the rating scales differently;
    - expressions of attitude may not be an accurate measure of actual behaviour.

Some possible types of closed question are:

- Limited choice (requiring one answer from two mutually exclusive alternatives):

  Have you ever watched *Neighbours*? (circle one) Yes/No

- Multiple choice (requiring one answer from a range of responses):

  When did your household most recently buy a television set? (tick one):
  1. Never
  2. 2000 or before
  3. 2001 or later
- Checklist questions (allowing respondents to choose more than one of a range of possibilities):

  Have you ever watched any of the following (tick those applicable):
  1. *Dallas*
  2. *Days of Our Lives*
  3. *Coronation Street*
  4. *Home and Away*
  5. *Neighbours*
- Partially closed questions (providing a set of responses where the last is 'Other' and provision is allowed for an explanation of the meaning of this response):

  The types of television programmes that I regularly watch are (tick those applicable):
  ○ Soap operas
  ○ News and current affairs
  ○ Comedy
  ○ Sport
  ○ Other (please specify)________________________
- Attitudinal questions (providing a scale on which a respondent may indicate the level of agreement or disagreement with a statement):

  Circle a number on a scale of 1–5, where 1 is 'strongly disagree' and 5 is 'strongly agree':
  The acting on *Neighbours* is generally convincing:
  1 2 3 4 5

Open questions are those which allow the respondent to answer in their own words. These are most appropriate when:

- the researcher cannot reasonably anticipate the range of likely answers;
- more extensive or more exact information is being sought;
- the information being sought is not sensitive.

They also have their problems:

- They are still difficult to design well, to avoid misunderstanding, and to allow respondents to answer 'No' or 'Zero' or 'Not applicable'.
- It is important to provide enough space for respondents to answer each question.

- They are more difficult to answer, taking more time and effort from the respondent. If there are a large number of questions requiring discursive answers, respondents may answer only cursorily, in an effort to hurry.
- They are more difficult to process:
  - Questions requiring exact answers produce a wider range of information, which can still be manipulated statistically but only after considerably more work.
  - Discursive answers to questions are much more difficult to interpret.
  - Handwriting can be difficult to read.

There are many different kinds of open question. Some examples are:

- Opener questions (broad, expansive, inviting a general response):

  What is the place of television in your everyday life?
- Followup questions (asking for detail, or to enlarge on what has already been said):

  What do you do in your spare time when the television breaks down?
  How many minutes of television did you watch yesterday?
- 'Grand tour' questions (Spradley 1979: 86–8), inviting a large but structured response:

  Describe the activities of an ordinary day and how television fits into these.
- Suggestions questions:

  How would you like television programmes to be improved?
- Argument questions:

  What are the arguments against watching soap opera?
- Reasons why questions:

  Why do you think that is so?
- Opinions/values questions:

  Who is your favourite character on *Neighbours*?
- Feeling/behaviour questions:

  Have you or your friends ever copied the clothing or behaviour of soap opera characters? If so, which characters and which clothing/behaviour?

For a sample questionnaire, see Brown (1994: 188–91). For a taxonomy of ethnographic questions, see Spradley (1979: 223). It is wise to be sceptical of any survey results you find in research reports, and cautious about the reliability of questionnaires used in the research. When they are presented as part of the data you should examine the questionnaires and their results analytically, but it is unnecessarily pedantic to assume that the questions have been manipulated to achieve the desired results. Similarly, it is necessary to be very careful if you use such techniques yourself, although it is foolish to avoid such techniques in fear of their innate unreliability.

Interviewing

Interviewing is purposive conversation. The interviewer is always a part of the interview process, and is also always an observer of the process, so interviewing is clearly related to participant observation (see section 7.4 in Chapter 7). Interviewing can be done individually or in groups, in a structured, semi-structured or unstructured format. Interviewing in the field is the standard method for ethnography, and many texts have been written giving advice on how to do it well, for instance Spradley (1979), or Fontana and Frey (2000).

The value of interviews is that:

- They provide opportunities for interviewees to respond in their own terms, through their own linguistic structures.
- Verbal answers can be longer and more complex, and so more rich and interesting, than written answers.
- Simply observing may not provide the information sought or may provide only ambiguous data: asking the person helps to clarify what has been observed.

But care still needs to be taken:

- The interviewing process is never totally objective, as the interviewer is always implicated in the interview situation.
- There may be difficulties with how respondents engage with the interviewer:
  - Respondents may not be able to articulate what they think/believe/feel.
  - Respondents may misinterpret the interviewer's questions.
  - Respondents may deliberately lie, either to protect themselves from what they see as intrusion or to make themselves look better to the interviewer.
  - Respondents may give answers that they assume to be those the interviewer wants to hear. This is a particular risk in cultures that protect 'face', or where it is impolite to disagree directly with another person.
- Interview data is necessarily discursive, which makes it difficult to interpret.
- Interviewing involves the exercise of a power differential, usually with the interviewee less powerful than the interviewer. At the very least, the interviewer assumes the right to ask questions and to expect answers from the interviewee (Holstein and Gubrium 1997: 115).
- Interview data is often assumed to be a 'window onto the world' of the interviewee. However, it is wiser to think of it as 'the rhetoric of socially situated speakers, *not* an objective report of thoughts, feelings or things out in the world' (Lindlof 1995: 165).

Some basic advice about all interviewing:

- Prepare thoroughly. Know your subject-matter as well as the personal and cultural circumstances of the interviewee before you begin the interview.
- Establish rapport. The success of the interview, and so the quality (usefulness) of the data gathered, will depend upon your willingness to listen attentively but without judgement, and to make the interviewee feel completely comfortable.
- If you are audio- or videotaping, be familiar with your recording equipment. Before you enter the interview situation, test that the equipment is in working order, that all batteries are charged, and that you also have spare batteries. Identify the tape both on the container and in audio on the tape itself, and have a second tape on hand, also identified.
- Before you turn on any tape, check that taping is acceptable to the interviewee (and be ready to switch to taking notes if it is not), and explain any consent procedure which you will be employing.
- Both on the tape and on any notes, always start by identifying the person being interviewed, the name of the interviewer, and the date and place of the interview.
- Ask simple questions at first, to allow everyone time to settle down.
- Keep a low profile, and never badger an interviewee. Audience research is not investigative journalism: you are not trying to trick the person into a confession.
- Remember to get any 'informed consent' form signed before you leave.
- Always end by thanking the interviewee, and always send a written acknowledgement and thanks a few days after the interview.

See also the second sub-section of section 7.3 in Chapter 7.

Choosing your recording medium

(i) Written notes have some value:

- There is less equipment to go wrong (but don't forget to take spare pens or pencils).
- Taking written notes may be the best you can do, if your interviewee is reluctant to be taped or finds the recording apparatus intimidating.
- Even if you are recording electronically, written notes can be helpful in keeping a record of the spelling of names (people and places), or of events that the tape does not record (body language, other people entering or leaving the room, and so on).

Disadvantages of written notes:

- If you cannot write fast enough, you can destroy the momentum of the interview by asking people to slow down or repeat what they have said.
- It is difficult to write notes (even if you are skilled in shorthand) and to attend at the same time to what is happening and being said in the interview.

(ii) Audiotaping is the most commonly used interview recording medium. It can be done face-to-face, or (provided you follow ethical and legal protocols) you can tape telephone interviews. Its advantages are:

- It records everything, allowing the researcher to decide later how much and what needs to be transcribed.
- It can be set going at the beginning of the session and left running, so the interviewer can concentrate on keeping the interview flowing. (But remember to watch for when the tape needs to be turned over or replaced with a second cassette.)
- It is (compared to videotaping) relatively inexpensive.

Disadvantages of audiotaping are:

- You must obtain permission before taping, and some interviewees are reluctant to be taped.
- Speakers are not identified automatically. If the only people present are the interviewer and the interviewee this is not usually a problem, but it can become a problem in a group interview. You can overcome this by keeping a written record of the initials of each speaker as the interview proceeds, to match up later as you listen to changes of voice on the tape.

(iii) Videotaping has some advantages over audiotaping:

- It provides visual information (such as the interaction between group members) that is not evident from audiotape.
- There is not usually the problem of identification of speakers that can occur with audiotape.

However:

- It is more expensive, and requires two people to attend, one as interviewer and one to operate the camera.
- It is more intrusive. The interviewee(s) may refuse to be videotaped, and in any case is/are more likely to feel self-conscious in front of a camera than in front of a microphone.

- The speech can be transcribed, but if that is all that is done, why not use the cheaper audiotape? If the visual element is to be analysed and interpreted, than sophisticated methods of content or semiotic or **discourse analysis** are required (see Chapters 10 and 11).

(iv) A relatively new interviewing medium is the internet (see Chen and Hinton 1999; Schonlau et al. 2002). Its advantages are:

- It allows interviews with people from far away, without travel costs for either party.
- It immediately stores the data in written form, saving time and money on transcription.
- It can be done in the form of a questionnaire, or in 'chat' format.

However:

- It limits interviewers and interviewees to those who have internet access, and the time and skills necessary to use it. This is a limitation that will progressively diminish over time.
- Like telephone interviewing, it eliminates data that is available only when the interviewer and interviewee are both physically present (body language, gesture, tone of voice).
- Responses may lack the spontaneity of spoken interviews: the conversation is structured in a more linear fashion than most personal conversations, where we do not wait for the other person to finish before replying, or do not completely finish sentences.
- You can never be sure whom you are talking to as no one's identity is certain on the net.

Kind of interview

The choice of the kind of interview will depend, like the choice of recording format, on what is appropriate to the subject of your research.

(i) Unstructured interviews

The 'informal conversational interview' (Patton 1990: 280) can take place in any situation where the interviewer and interviewee can comfortably communicate. If the person being interviewed does not even know that this is an interview, then you cannot use recording apparatus, except clandestinely, which raises ethical problems. It is therefore preferable for the interviewer to explain the purpose of the conversation, which allows taping. However, this may also introduce a temptation for the researcher to redirect the conversation by comments or questions, even if they do not try to control the response of the interviewee. Informal conversation is the interviewing technique most commonly used in field research, or to add depth to data obtained by participant observation. It is particularly useful in cases where the interviewee needs to feel completely comfortable before speaking about sensitive topics (which, once again, places a heavy ethical responsibility on the interviewer). For examples, see Burgess (1993: 101–22).

The strengths of this kind of interview are the highly individual responses that it generates, and the possibility of continuing the interview later, or even several times, allowing the information to build naturally.

The problems of informal conversation are:

- It is too unwieldy to be useful with groups.
- It needs good rapport to be established between the interviewer and interviewee, so it is likely to take more time than other forms of interview, both preparation time before the interview and moving slowly and carefully during the interview.
- It still requires great skill and care in making comments and asking questions, so that the interviewer avoids leading the responses, but takes advantage of any openings that occur.
- The information that it elicits is random, and so:
    - It may take either a very long session or (in order not to tire or bore the interviewee) more than one session before you cover all the desired areas.
    - You can never be sure that the data you collect from one interviewee will be in a form that makes comparison possible with other interviewees.

If your primary concern is with individual descriptive responses – for instance building upon observational data from field work – these problems may not matter, but if you wish to use your interviewees as a sample of a larger population it *will* matter, and you will choose a more structured interview.

(ii) Structured interviews

There are at least two forms of structured interview – the general interview guide approach (semi-structured) and the standardised open-ended interview approach (structured).

The standardised open-ended interview is usually done with an individual, as it takes the form of a survey questionnaire administered by the researcher (or an assistant). The questions are carefully worded and arranged to be delivered identically to all respondents: even alternative wordings or questions asking for clarification or elaboration are written into the schedule. In the second subsection of this section our focus was on written questions, but interviews can also use both open and closed questions, depending upon the circumstances.

Like questionnaires, standardised open-ended interviews can be conducted face-to-face, or by telephone, with similar advantages and disadvantages. For examples of a standardised open-ended interview, see Patton (1990: 363–8), or Docherty et al. (1987: 125–42).

The advantages of the standardised open-ended interview are:

- It is economical of time.
- It reduces interviewer impact within the situation, allowing more than one interviewer to be used with minimal effect on the reliability of data.
- The interview schedule can be shown in advance to managers, decision makers and ethics committees, to reassure them concerning the research, and so to maximise the chances of the researcher being permitted to conduct the research within institutional settings.
- It keeps data comparable, and so easier to analyse. This is particularly useful if interviews are to be repeated, for instance before, during and after a research programme.
- It allows complex questions (for instance, responses to 'gratifications' statements) that are difficult to cover adequately in an unstructured interview.

The disadvantages are:

- The interviewer cannot respond to any situation which emerges during the course of the interview, such as an interviewee raising a valuable issue that does not appear on the question schedule.
- Individual differences among interviewees cannot be taken into account, which may impoverish the data.

The general interview guide approach starts with a basic checklist of areas to be covered in the interview, sometimes, but not necessarily, in the form of questions. Acting as moderator, the interviewer guides the interview, but permits the various aspects of the subject to arise naturally, in any order, and can allow digressions if they seem likely to be productive. In structure, it falls somewhere between the standardised open-ended interview and the informal conversation, so it can be called 'semi-structured'. For an example of an interview guide, see Patton (1990: 360–2).

The advantages of this approach are:

- Preparing an interview guide forces the interviewer to clarify their own goals.
- The interviewer can respond to any situation which emerges during the course of the interview, such as an interviewee raising a valuable issue that does not appear on the question schedule.
- Like informal conversation, it can elicit very personal responses, without taking as much time as informal conversation.

The disadvantages are:

- It takes more time than the structured interview, and time during the interview needs to be carefully monitored so that the desired information is covered within any time limit.

- Like informal conversation, the data elicited from one respondent (or group) is not necessarily comparable with that from another respondent (or group).
- Like informal conversation, the data requires complex analytical and interpretive techniques.

To make the best use of this interviewing method, the interviewer should:

- avoid closed questions;
- avoid presuppositions (ask 'What is your opinion of this programme?', NOT 'How satisfied are you with this programme?', as this implies satisfaction);
- avoid 'either/or' questions (requiring yes/no, or good/bad as an answer);
- ask only one thing at a time;
- be clear and neutral, define terms or give examples (alternatives which do not prejudge);
- avoid 'why' questions, as these require the interviewee to make causal inferences about the world or their experience, and the answers are almost impossible to interpret (see Patton 1990: 313–16);
- ask followup questions, restate a question to clarify (and to invite more), invite rather than challenge ('That's interesting. How do you do that?');
- maintain control, keep to the checklist, but do so discreetly;
- be attentive and *listen*, so you can be flexible and respond to the situation as it changes;
- avoid making comments that appear to evaluate what the interviewee is saying (say 'that's interesting' rather than 'that's good').

This form of interview is appropriate for individuals, but also for groups, sometimes called 'focus groups'. Interviewing several people at once has advantages:

- It can increase the size of your sample, without increasing time and costs, so it is relatively economical.
- It invites participants to monitor each other, providing checks and balances that do not operate for individual interviews or for surveys.

The disadvantages are:

- The time is spread over several people, so no one person has much time to speak and the number of topics that can be covered is fewer than for individual interviews.
- Because it is not obvious from a tape recording of a group just who is speaking at any one time, it is necessary to take notes. This can be just a list of the initials of each speaker, including when two people speak at once. It is difficult for the researcher to take these notes and to facilitate the

interview (act as moderator) at the same time, so it may be necessary to bring in an assistant researcher as note taker. Because it reduces their participation in the group, and because they are not usually trained for this role, members of the group should be used as note takers only as a last resort.

- The internal monitoring can lead to the phenomenon of 'false consensus', that is a more uniform response than would otherwise be obtained.

Focus group interviews are different from individual interviews – not only logistically, but in underlying principle. The individual interview aims to obtain information from a person, away from others who might influence the interviewee's response. In former years, the focus group was simply an extension of this, used to save time and money by providing more interview subjects, selected by similar (random) sampling techniques to those used for selecting individuals. In more recent times, the focus group interview has been used precisely to find out how people respond in a group, that is how their feelings/opinions can be shaped by the experience of discussing the subject with others. It can even be seen as simulating the kind of group process usually studied in the field by ethnographic research. In this case, the group is likely to be selected purposively, and the group process (as in most ethnographic research) becomes part of the subject of your investigation. Focus group discussions can also be seen as empowering participants, for instance in feminist research (Madriz 2000).

Some points about running a focus group (see also Morrison 1998):

- Six to ten participants is usually accepted as the ideal size for a focus group, providing enough people for lively discussion, but not so many that the moderator has difficulty keeping the conversation on track.
- Select your sample appropriately to both your project and your intellectual framework. People who know each other will settle into debate easily, but will also bring their past history into the discussion; people who do not know each other will have fewer preconceptions, but will take longer to talk comfortably with other members of the group. A homogenous group (eg all teenagers) will produce evidence of agreement and conflict of opinion within that group: a varied group (of differing ages) will provide evidence of agreement and conflict of opinion between different groups.
- Prepare a checklist of topics or questions, including alternative questions or wording in case the conversation falters.
- In addition to the usual equipment checks, make sure there are enough microphones to record all members of the group. If you are using a text (for instance, an episode of a soap opera) as a discussion starter, check before the session that the replay equipment is working well and that you are familiar with its operation.
- Record in writing the sequence of speakers, note occasions when more than one person is speaking at a time, body language, gesture, comments

addressed to a specific member of the group, etc. When the budget allows, videotaping makes this clearer (but see discussion of video interviews above).

- Start by introducing yourself (and any members of the group who do not know each other), explain the purpose of the session, have a general chat to relieve any tension, remind of the necessity of the tape recorder and the role of the note taker, show them you have a checklist and explain its purpose (but do not read it out, as this may inhibit discussion).
- Start the discussion with a focus question and invite response. If you get no answer, address someone by name: keep the conversation going …
- Minimise your own input: do not volunteer your own opinions, do not try to adjudicate or to reach consensus.
- Monitor the discussion: keep track of what has not been covered from your checklist, interrupt politely but firmly if the discussion has gone too far from the point, keep track of time and of how much must be covered.
- Be flexible, despite monitoring: that is, be prepared to let things go if there is good (useful and interesting) debate happening.
- Listen carefully, so that you can respond to new ideas, encourage people who have something interesting to say, recognise when a silence is acceptable (a natural pause, rather than an awkward gap), throw in a question or comment to keep the discussion going.
- Follow up with encouraging comments or requests for further information. If you do not understand something someone has said, assume you are at fault and ask for explanation or additional information.
- Establish rapport, by providing encouraging remarks, using eye contact. Help the shy ones without being obtrusive, keep the loud ones tactfully in check.
- Verbalise where necessary (for instance if someone answers a question with a gesture), or take notes.

To sum up: stay (unobtrusively) in charge, and keep the talk moving.

4.4 Observation

Observation can be a research method in its own right (for instance in fieldwork), or it can be a supplement to other methods (particularly surveys and interviews). Observation in the context of research is more than just looking: it is purposeful looking, and recording the results. Gold (1958) proposes four categories of roles for the researcher in the field. Two of these (the 'complete participant' and the 'participant-as-observer', discussed in the fourth sub-section of section 7.2 in Chapter 7) involve the researcher taking part in the research situation while observing it. The other two involve simple observation, from outside the situation: the 'observer-as-participant' is acknowledged to be an observer, but the 'complete observer' is covert (undercover) (see Lindlof 1995: 146–9).

Webb et al. (1966: Chapter 5) use the term 'simple' observation to cover the researcher personally observing samples over time of exterior physical signs, expressive movement, physical location and language behaviour. Such observation has been called 'non-reactive' or 'unobtrusive' (Kellehear 1993; Webb et al. 1966), but it is never quite so innocent as this sounds. Just taking observation notes can be intrusive: Professor Higgins (in Shaw's *Pygmalion*, later turned into the musical *My Fair Lady*) was confident that taking notes of the dialect of Covent Garden flower sellers was acceptable science, but Eliza Doolittle saw it as an unacceptable intrusion into her privacy, and suspected him of being a police informer. Setting up 'contrived observation' (Webb et al. 1966: 142) with hidden cameras or tape recorders would now be considered, as Kellehear points out (1993: 4, his emphasis), to be '*socially* as well as *ethically* intrusive'.

If you are seeking objectivity, the advantages of observation are:

- It allows the behaviour under examination to continue in its natural setting, which is often precisely the point of the research.
- It minimises the impact of the researcher on the situation being observed.

But it still has problems:

- The researcher is necessarily implicated in the situation under observation, and (if she is taking notes) is a more fallible recording instrument than audio- or videotaping.
- Audio- or videotaping, or taking notes during the observation, can be intrusive: the subject may object, or may change behaviour as a result of being aware of being observed. Taking notes after the observation, even immediately after, may not adequately record what happened.
- Audio- and videotaping are difficult and time-consuming to analyse, but are relatively objective. Notes are easier to analyse, but are subjective, possibly skewed by the researcher's own experience or bias.
- Across time or location there may be unpredictable variations in the population being observed, creating biases that the observer may not even be aware of.

Unless you are seeking objectivity, you need to decide how to factor your own subjectivity into the process – that is, how to identify it, to understand it, and to express it in your report.

Methods of observation are specific to the research project; however, all forms of observation share a common goal – 'thick description'. This is a term borrowed by Clifford Geertz from Gilbert Ryle, to explain what ethnographers do:

> Ethnography is thick description. What the ethnographer is in fact faced with … is a multiplicity of complex conceptual structures, many of them superimposed

> upon or knotted into one another, which are at once strange, irregular, and inexplicit, and which he [sic] must contrive somehow first to grasp and then to render ... Doing ethnography is like trying to read (in the sense of 'construct a reading of') a manuscript – foreign, faded, full of ellipses, incoherencies, suspicious emendations, and tendentious commentaries, but written not in conventionalised graphs of sound but in transient examples of shaped behaviour. (Geertz 1973: 9–10)

This is clearly not a simple business of recording what you see, but a much more complex matter of recording all the nuances of the situation you are observing, including your own part in it. Simple observation is rarely encountered in media audience research: participant observation, discussed more fully in section 7.4, is much more common.

4.5 Conclusion

Audience data is commonly gathered by survey or observation. The methods of doing this may appear much the same for all intellectual frameworks; however the goals are so different that it would be a mistake to make that assumption. The positivist is likely to prefer quantitative methods that can produce results which can be analysed statistically and inferences which can lead to truth claims. The post-positivist may use either quantitative or qualitative methods and will not expect results or conclusions to be so rigorous. The critical theorist may also use either quantitative or qualitative methods or both and will seek to use the results to understand and improve the social world. Both the critical theorist and the constructivist expect their results to be contingent and do not make claims to objectivity and truth. The participatory action researcher's primary concern is to involve participants in the research, no matter what research methodology is applied.

In the next chapter we consider how these different intellectual frameworks analyse and interpret their data differently.

CHAPTER 5

Audience Research – Analysis and Interpretation

In this chapter we discuss analysis (systematising) before interpretation (relating to a broader framework), acknowledging that these phases are actually interdependent.

5.1 Analysis

In the analysis phase, it is sensible to separate quantitative data from qualitative data, however the distinction is not always clear-cut: terms such as 'highest' or 'typical' are quantitative, yet they are used frequently in qualitative research reports.

Quantitative analysis

For detailed advice on statistical methods, try textbooks such as Levin and Fox (1997) or Phillips (2000). What we offer here is an overview of the kinds of statistical concepts and principles that might be appropriate for quantitative audience data.

Quantitative data gathering starts with the simple counting of units or measuring of quantities. We will use a comparatively small example, a mythical sample of 256 viewers who regularly watch the television soap opera *Neighbours*. That raw number tells you very little. It does not tell you who these viewers are or what they are like: that would require **demographic** information about the sample and about the population from which it was taken. It does not tell you how popular *Neighbours* is: that would require comparative ratings, for instance for other programmes scheduled at the same time as *Neighbours*, or for other soap operas. It does not tell you why these viewers regularly watch or what they like or dislike about the programme: that would require interview or survey data about their responses. Let us assume that our question arose from the proposition in previous research that more women view soap operas than do men, and that the target audience for *Neighbours* is young people. Your search for the relevance and significance of the data begins with description, and then moves on to inference.

At the level of description, you need to consider:

- the relation of this data to other data: regular viewing of *Neighbours* is our constant; age and gender are our variables;
- the qualities of this data: as discussed below in more detail, this includes the configuration (the way values are distributed, for instance as a normal curve), the values of central point(s) (mean, median, mode), and variability (the extent to which individual scores deviate from the central value). This can then be presented in a table (Figure 5.1) or a graph (Figure 5.2).

The graph shows clearly that the distribution of the age ranges of this sample is in the form of a normal curve – with few cases at either extreme and most bunched up in the middle. However, we have already lost some information.

Age in years	Gender		Total cases
	Male	Female	
15 and under	3	10	13
16	13	27	40
17	23	60	83
18	41	41	82
19	20	10	30
20 and over	0	8	8
	100	156	256

Figure 5.1 Quantitative data displayed in a table

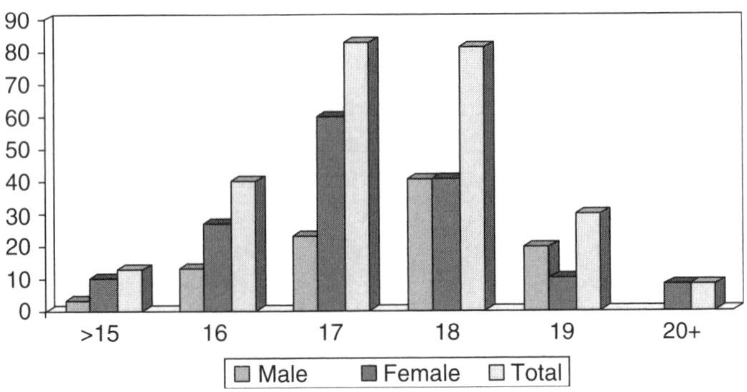

Figure 5.2 Quantitative data displayed in a graph

Grouping the extreme values as '15 and under' and '20 and over' implies that there were an insignificant number of cases in each of these categories: it simplifies our table, and allows random variations to cancel each other out. However, it also disguises aberrant cases, which can be acceptable (to avoid excessive skew) or unacceptable (if the information lost is significant to our enquiry). For instance, if our sample was drawn from college classes, and there were two mature students aged 40 (in this case, both women), we have avoided the excessive skew, but we have also lost the opportunity to take into account the phenomenon of mature-age women returning to study. As the graphs stand, the age distribution of male viewers is skewed slightly positively (towards the higher end of the age range), and that of female viewers is skewed slightly negatively (towards the lower end of the age range). This draws attention to the central point of the age distributions. For the whole sample the central point is 17, no matter which of the three forms of calculation we apply. The mean (or average) is 17.4, derived by dividing the sum total of all the cases (256) into the sum total of all their ages (4452). The median is also 17, derived by finding the half-way case, that is the point halfway between case numbers 128 and 129. The mode is again 17 – the most common value. For females alone, the mean is 17.2, the median is 17 and the mode is 17. For males alone, the mean is 17.6, the median is 18 and the mode is 18.

The mode, or the most common value, is the central measure least commonly used because it provides the least information. However, there are times when this value is precisely what you are seeking, and it is certainly useful in understanding a set of cases that has not been ordered, or that cannot be ordered because it is not numeric (such as finding the most common soap opera gratification in a questionnaire). It is also the easiest central value to locate, so it can be useful in making a quick estimate in a frequency distribution, in combination with the range, which is the highest and lowest values in the distribution. The median, or exact half-way point, is also sometimes just what you are seeking, and it can be useful when data is ordered but not numeric, or when numeric data does not follow a normal distribution. Most commonly, the median is used in conjunction with the mean, to give additional information. The appropriate measure of spread to link with the median is the inter-quartile range: this is the two values located at the end of the first and the third quarter after dividing the full range into four equal sections.

The mean is the most useful and exact central measure, when the numeric information exists to make it possible, and the distribution is in the form of a roughly normal curve. The appropriate measure to use with the mean is the standard deviation – a measure of spread that takes into account all values across the whole range. This is derived by a mathematical formula, which you can find in any standard statistical textbook.

But there are other ways of describing this data. We could not talk sensibly about the gender distribution in the same way as the age distribution, because gender is given as mutually exclusive non-numeric categories, so it has no mean/median/mode, and no dispersion. But it is still valuable information. In our sample there are more females than males, but it is difficult to immediately estimate the significance of gender while age is represented as individual raw scores. There are, for instance, exactly the same number of both male and female 18-year-olds in our sample. Common sense tells us that this figure is probably more important for males, because there are fewer males in the total group. We can express this importance statistically in at least two ways: as percentages, or as proportions. For instance, expressed in terms of percentages, the data in Figure 5.1 looks as shown in Figure 5.3.

We have now described the qualities of our data in relation to other relevant data and have found a difference in the spread of age across male and female members of our sample. The next stage is to examine the relationships more closely.

Although our tables and graphs relate two variables (age and gender) to a constant (regular viewing of *Neighbours*), they do not allow us to make assumptions about the type of relation we have discovered: we cannot, for instance, conclude that age or gender cause people to watch *Neighbours*. In any case, cause-and-effect relationships are not the only possible relationships among variables. Of the list of tactics provided by Miles and Huberman (1994: Chapter 10) for generating meaning from qualitative research, the following can also apply to quantitative data: patterns, clusters, contrasts/comparisons, partitioning variables, factoring, finding intervening variables, and building a logical chain. So, if we want to find out what sort of relation we have here, we need to apply the rules of logic to our statistical information. For instance, to establish a causal relationship we would need to:

- demonstrate association between the variables (that one changes in some predictable fashion as the other changes);
- demonstrate sequence (that one follows the other in time);
- control for other variables (to establish that the variable being studied is the only possible cause);

Age in years	Gender				Total #	Total %
	Male #	Male %	Female #	Female %		
15 and under	3	3	10	6.40	13	5.10
16	13	13	27	17.30	40	15.60
17	23	23	60	38.50	83	32.40
18	41	41	41	26.30	82	32.00
19	20	20	10	6.40	30	11.70
20 and over	0		8	5.10	8	3.10
	100	100	156	100	256	99.90

Figure 5.3 Quantitative data displayed as percentages in a table

- check that other possible kinds of explanation are not valid (that there is not some third variable that controls or influences both the variables we are considering, and that they are not linked in some sort of chain of causation).

Establishing causal relations is very difficult – some would say impossible in the social world, and certainly impossible in our example. In audience research we are more likely to be interested in finding patterns, making comparisons, or demonstrating that one variable appears with a certain frequency in association with another.

With interval data (numbers and frequencies, particularly when normally distributed) association is measured by tests of correlation. Perfect correlation (that a change in one variable allows an absolutely reliable prediction of a change in another variable) is impossible to find in the real world, but if it existed it would be expressed as a 'correlation co-efficient' of 1.0. The correlation can be positive (+1.0: the two variables change in exactly similar ways) or negative (−1.0: the changes move in opposite directions). In the real world, what we end up with is a measure of the probability that as one variable changes the other will also change in a predictable direction – a positive or negative correlation co-efficient of somewhere between 0.0 and 1.0. The most commonly used is the product-moment correlation, but there are other forms of correlation, each with its own strengths. The statistics textbooks can help you to decide which is more appropriate to your needs and what formula you will need to apply.

For nominal data (categories rather than numbers, like the gender data in our example), ordinal data (rank data rather than frequencies), and interval data that does not follow the normal curve, the textbooks can provide guidance on non-parametric tests, for instance chi-square tests. Still further procedures are required for comparing two different forms of data: in our example, for relating the dichotomous gender score to the normal curve age score. The data analysis process leads us to do one of the following:

- look more closely at the sample (our 256 viewers of *Neighbours*), to consider other variables, such as education or place of residence;
- compare this sample with others, to relate this data to other data, perhaps in a matrix showing the gender and age of regular viewers of *Coronation Street*.

Correlation calculations allow us to quantify whatever relation we turn up empirically. The value of these calculations is entirely dependent on the quality of the initial research design, which attempts to ensure that the variable(s) being currently measured, and only it/them, can be held responsible for the relationship(s) being found, by 'controlling for' other variables. Once all your data has been analysed, you need to decide to what extent the results you have found for your sample (those 256 regular viewers of *Neighbours*) can be assumed to tell you something about the population from which the sample was drawn (all regular viewers of *Neighbours*). Even if you used one of the forms of probability sampling (see the second sub-section of section 4.2 in Chapter 4), your sample is unlikely to be perfectly representative of that larger population. So you follow statistical procedures (again, from the textbooks) to measure '**standard error**', and hence with what level of confidence you can generalise to that larger population. This will allow you to judge the probability of a '**null hypothesis**', that is, that any difference in results between two samples within a population is due entirely to sampling error.

Statistical analysis can be applied to large amounts of data, and to many types of data. It allows the researcher to consider:

- the strength and direction of the associations between two or more dependent variables across two or more groups of subjects (**multivariate analysis**);
- the nature of the impact of the combination of two or more variables on some outcome (**multiple regression**);
- what associated variables (factors) can produce a result, or a range of possible results, including reducing many measured variables to a much smaller number of latent (not measured) underlying variables (factor analysis).

The statistics textbooks can help you decide when these more sophisticated procedures become relevant, and assist you to apply them.

Quantitative data analysis leads to:

- quantitative descriptions of the data, often in the form of tables or graphs;
- statistical inferences in the form of statements of probability about the data;
- statistical comparisons (both descriptive and inferential) of two or more sets of data;
- statements of the statistical significance of all aspects of the data and of the inferences drawn from the data;
- statistical measurements of the probable level of error, and hence the reliability and validity of all aspects of the data and of the inferences drawn from the data.

Quantitative data can be enlightening, and statistical methods can be useful in understanding such data: they are particularly useful in establishing that there is a question worth asking. But be careful not to place too much reliance on quantitative data alone:

- The results of quantitative analysis are always ultimately dependent on the quality of the initial data:
  - Their value can be eroded by inadequate definitions, insufficient controls on inter-coder reliability, or other mistakes or inadequacies in the data-gathering phase.

  - Even if your methodology was flawless, you are dealing here with human behaviour, which does not reduce easily to numbers.
- Tests of significance aim at establishing the level of probability, in a range from zero (impossible) to 1.0 (absolutely certain), and there are also statistical measures of reliability and validity (see the first sub-section of section 12.2 in Chapter 12). It is comparatively easy to achieve statistical significance with large samples, but that still does not necessarily mean that the results are useful in the real world: that depends on how 'significant' the original question was – something which cannot be measured statistically.
- No matter how convincing quantitative results are (no matter how high the levels of significance and how low the probability of error) they remain mathematical/statistical concepts. In order for researchers to make use of them, statistical statements have to be turned back into meaningful prose: this is just as difficult to do and as prone to error as the initial conversion of human behaviour into quantifiable categories. It is also no more inherently valid and/or reliable than the analysis of qualitative data.

Qualitative analysis

Miles and Huberman (1994: Chapter 10) provide a list of tactics for generating meaning from qualitative research: in addition to those listed above as also applicable to quantitative data, they mention noting themes, seeing **plausibility**, making metaphors, subsuming particulars into the general, and making conceptual/theoretical coherence. These authors (Miles and Huberman 1994: Chapters 5–9) also give good advice on devising displays both as an analytical tool and as a way to present data succinctly and visually. Audience researchers will find the advice provided by such general methods textbooks useful, but you still have to decide what forms of analysis are appropriate specifically to your audience data.

If you have collected documents (see the first sub-section of section 4.3 in Chapter 4), you can analyse these quantitatively (discovering what position was held by a majority of correspondents to the newspapers, or applying content analysis to the discursive content) or qualitatively (using methods such as those described for historical documents in the first subsection of section 8.1 in Chapter 8 or the semiotic analysis of texts in the third sub-section of section 10.1 in Chapter 10). If you have collected data by observation (see section 4.4 in Chapter 4), you will probably be analysing it qualitatively, using some of the methods described in the third sub-section of section 8.1. But most of your audience data is likely to be survey data, in the form of questionnaires (second sub-section of section 4.4) or interviews (third sub-section), requiring the qualitative analysis of texts (open questions in questionnaires), and talk (audiotaped interviews, which are converted into text by transcription). A video record will be much richer than any audio recording, and should also be analysed by a system which takes the visual into account – content analysis or semiotic analysis.

Some advice on audio transcription:

- Do it as soon after the session as possible, while it is still fresh in your mind.
- For the novice, allow at least five to eight hours for the transcription of every hour of recording.
- As you transcribe, incorporate the information from the notes taken during the session, for instance identification of voices.
- Transcribe all the actual conversation about the research topic as accurately as possible, including hesitations and incomplete phrases and sentences, but you need not transcribe irrelevant details, such as casual comments while tea is being served.
- Develop a standardised format. One convention has the interviewer's speech in italics, to stand out from that of the interviewee. Most transcribers use only initials to identify each speaker. Some incorporate the confirmatory noises of the interviewer ('Uhuh', 'Right'), or the non-verbal sounds of either speaker ('laughs'), in brackets within the text of the interviewee's response. You can develop your own format, but until you have experience, it is wise to look at what others have done, for instance Brunsdon (2000: 219).

Now you have written texts ready for analysis, that is, the systematisation of the information they contain (see Ryan and Bernard 2000; Silverman 2000). Your discursive audience responses are a different kind of text from those discussed in Part III: written answers to open-ended questions or transcribed interviews are most commonly analysed by a form of content analysis called 'code-and-retrieve'. For detailed advice on doing this, see Miles and Huberman (1994), or Strauss (1987: 27).

Our general recommendations in the code-and-retrieve process are:

- Keep a clean copy for your records and for submission with your report: work always on a duplicate.
- You are looking for the patterns in the evidence: mark these with coloured highlighter pens on hard copy, or use the search and highlighter functions of your computer software, or apply a computer package designed for such analysis.
- Be prepared to adjust your categories and revise how you allocate your evidence as you work through the text: if you notice omissions or inconsistencies these might suggest new coding categories, requiring you to go back over what you have done already.
- Transfer quotes from the text to headings on another sheet, or copy them from one computer file to another computer file.

You may start with coding categories developed by others (for instance, Herzog's uses and gratifications categories, see section 3.3 in Chapter 3), testing these against your data and adapting them as you find discrepancies and gaps. Or you can develop your own coding categories, finding them within your data by analytic induction (see the third sub-section of section 8.1 in Chapter 8), as described in Brown (1994: Appendix).

This system of analysis remains basically intuitive. More specialised forms of analysis have been developed, to reduce the influence of the coder on the analysis, either by systematising the procedures (conversation analysis, discourse analysis) or by providing the human coder with computer assistance. For a discussion of how these can be applied within a post-positivist approach, see Ryan and Bernard (2000).

One such post-positivist approach is 'sociolinguistics', a term which encompasses a variety of approaches to the study of relations between language and society, examining the rules and protocols which determine language use in a variety of social situations. It can be used when interpreting interview transcripts.

Conversation analysis

The main focus of **conversation analysis** is on the interpersonal interactions between speakers talking together – how they take turns, how they defer to or over-ride one another, how they adopt roles within the conversation, who chooses to respond or to be silent and when, etc. It is most commonly used on ethnographic field records, particularly audiotaped talk, but it can also be applied usefully to focus group discussions.

The strengths of conversation analysis are:

- It provides a more structured and systematic procedure than simple code-and-retrieve, reducing (but still not eliminating) the dependence on coder intuition.
- It provides a way to understand personal interactions (the positioning of each participant within the group process) as well as to analyse the words spoken.

Some basic advice about the method:

- The peripheral information (tone of voice, pauses, interjections, stumbling over words, mispronunciations, etc) will be just as important as the words actually spoken: take the time to get this into the transcript.
- Take note of how the talk can be broken down into sequences, like the sequences of a film.
- Watch for moments of resolution (such as laughter), and work back to explore how the talk reached that point.
- Identify anomalies and ambiguities, such as persistent silence, and try to account for these, for instance by rethinking your analytic categories.

For more detailed explanations and examples, see ten Have (1998), Miller (1997), Heritage (1997). For a critique of these systems, see Watson (1997).

Discourse analysis

The term 'discourse analysis' is used with a wide variety of meanings ranging from positivist to constructivist or post-structuralist conceptions of language. All the different uses of this term (see the Glossary at the end of this book) agree that discourse analysis focuses on the structure of written or spoken texts, attempting to understand how participants constitute a world in the course of their linguistic interaction. It is used for the analysis of talk, but also of visual and aural texts (newspaper reports, films, videos and radio programmes – see the second sub-section of section 10.2 in Chapter 10), and it can be applied to transcripts of both individual and group interviews.

The strengths of this method are that it provides a way:

- to understand the deeper structure of any text as well as its surface content;
- to consider interpersonal interaction between speakers;
- to position discourses within a larger communication (and, ultimately, social) context.

Standard principles for the different forms of this kind of analysis have been established over time (see Potter 1996: 137–9; van Dijk 1985), and examples of some of these variants are provided in Wetherell et al. (2001) and Potter (1997).

Computer-assisted analysis of qualitative data

A computer can handle large amounts of data quickly and systematically, and, because of the increased consistency of coding, teams can operate on the data without the usual problems of inter-coder reliability. Computer programs can also 'enhance the confidence with which generalizations are made' (Silverman 2000: 161), and so contribute to the strategy of constant comparison – Glaser and Strauss's 'grounded theory' (Glaser and Strauss 1967; also see the third sub-section of section 8.1 in Chapter 8). But you must understand exactly what you wish the computer to do, and use its resources appropriately: for instance, it is inappropriate to expect computers to assist with the close analysis of very small textual extracts.

The usual function of computer-assisted analysis is to reliably locate all usages of those code terms identified by the researcher. It is possible to simply use the 'search' facility of your word processor for this purpose, but there are also now computer packages (such as NUD*IST or NVivo) that will do this more efficiently, and with functions that your word processor cannot replicate. Data analysis packages are constantly being updated and new ones developed: you should explore these, as well as the advice given by authors such as Miles and Weitzman (in Miles and Huberman 1994: Appendix), Weitzman (2000) or Silverman (2000). It is to your advantage to spend time learning how to make the best use of the package you eventually choose.

In summary, qualitative data analysis leads to:

- qualitative descriptions of the data, either discursively, or in the form of data displays;
- logical inferences in the form of explanations of the data;
- discursive comparisons (both descriptive and inferential) of two or more sets of data;
- discursive explanations of whether these descriptions and inferences can be assumed to apply more broadly than to the cases being analysed, and the conceptual and logical grounds for such explanations.

The meaning of data, even after analysis, is not self-evident (Miller and Glassner 1997): it must be interpreted. However, analysis and interpretation are interdependent. For instance, if your chosen method of data analysis was discourse analysis, you have taken a step towards interpretation by acknowledging that audience responses are discourse, rather than a window into either the real world or the unconscious of the respondents: however, you still need a theory/theories through which that discursive meaning can be understood.

5.2 Interpretation

The interpretive framework pre-exists the research design and is basic to its development, so it is difficult to determine which is the chicken and which is the egg. Theories (that is, forms of explanation) arise out of and support frameworks (that is, views about the world), and all of these are constantly changing: for audience research the most commonly used may be primarily concerned with how we know (positivism, **behaviourism, structural-functionalism**, post-positivism) or primarily concerned with what we know about social categories such as class (various forms of Marxism), and gender (various forms of feminism, or other approaches to identity politics). We recommend that readers follow up our brief explanations through the writings of the people discussed, or through more general texts on social theory, such as Collinson (1987), Beilharz (1992), or Lechte (1994).

Positivism/post-positivism/empiricism/ behaviourism/structural-functionalism

Among the paradigms proposed by Lincoln and Guba (2000), the earliest to be applied to audience research was *positivism*. The positivist's search for verifiable truth leads her to ask questions about what the world is objectively like: in the case of television audiences, questions such as 'Who watches soap operas?'

'What effects do soap operas have upon their viewers?' 'How accurately do soap opera characters and narratives reflect the real world?' The positivist prefers empirical research on the model of the physical sciences, and assumes that the best research is that which most effaces the researcher. So positivists trust quantitative over qualitative methods, and in the results seek the highest possible level of generalisability, validity and reliability and the lowest possible level of error (see the first sub-section of section 12.2 in Chapter 12). You will have gathered that this is not the position favoured by the present writers: we have serious reservations about the early effects studies – the audience research most clearly associated with the positivist and empiricist tradition.

The related terms '***empirical***' and '***empiricist***' have been called 'among the most difficult words in the language' (Williams 1988: 115), their imprecision both resulting from and producing conflicting views among social theorists and commentators. There is general agreement that 'empirical' methods require observation of the real world, and, in one sense, 'empiricism' simply refers to the theoretical framework supporting such empirical methods. Empiricism has also, however, been associated with the demand for scientific objectivity, an issue about which heated and partisan debate continues, despite Smith and Deemer's confident assertion (2000: 878) that '**relativism** is nothing more or less than our condition in the world.'

Allen (1985: 31–4), for instance, describes the empiricist position like this:

- 'Facts' exist objectively and can be known by a researcher, who exists separately from and outside the world of facts.
- 'Knowledge is equated with regularity and absolute knowledge with absolute regularity' (Allen 1985: 32), from which covering laws can be induced.
- The researcher can set up a closed system, controlling extraneous data and so isolating only one variable to be measured at a time.
- 'Theory' can be understood either as untested speculation, or as statements of observed regularity.
- Absolute regularity in the social world is impossible to locate, which leads to increasing reliance on probability, and on increasingly sophisticated tests of significance to support claims of probability.

Critics of this position (including Allen) would respond that:

- The researcher is a part of the world being researched, so cannot produce completely objective knowledge.
- The piling up of facts as if they are self-explanatory means that explanation (what we have called 'analysis') remains at the level of data collection and the generalisations that follow logically from this (omitting what we call 'interpretation').
- The human sciences cannot accommodate closed systems as the physical world does, and even physical science is increasingly suspicious of claims to closed systems.

- Causes can only be explained in terms of regularities, of greater or lesser degrees of significance, but these can only be judged as not the result of chance: what eventually causes the regularity cannot be explained by the scientific method alone, so 'Empiricists confuse predictive power with knowledge' (Allen 1985: 43).

This debate over objectivity arises periodically within media research as it does in other research communities. Within both the social sciences and the humanities research traditions there are factions that reject any difference between 'empirical' methods and 'empiricism', avoiding empiricism by avoiding the empirical. We consider, on the contrary, that empirical methods are not only acceptable, but necessary: if we are to understand our world, we must examine it carefully and systematically, even if we deny the possibility of objective knowledge arising out of such an examination. Among many commentators who agree, Frow and Morris (2000: 332) insist that cultural studies must be built upon an empirical base.

Meanwhile, even researchers who reject positivism and empiricism need to understand these frameworks, if only to be able to recognise them in their reading. One approach which builds upon the empiricist tradition in the social sciences is *behaviourism*, commonly associated with B. F. Skinner (1904–90), who sought to understand human behaviour by observing how real people act and interact. He theorised a causal connection between a Stimulus (S) and a Response (R): S can be a media message, R can be an attitude or a form of behaviour. Behaviourism aims to establish predictive rules: that S will always generate R, given certain determining conditions. The behaviourist approach dominated psychology and sociology in the 1930s and 1940s, when 'behaviour modification' was an approved social goal.

In media and communication studies, the behaviourist influence was strongest in the 1950s and 1960s. Gitlin (1978: 207) attributes the introduction of behaviourism into media research to Katz and Lazarsfeld, who referred (1955: 18) to four kinds of media effects previously identified by Lazarsfeld (1948): 'immediate response, short-term effects, long-term effects and institutional change'.

Gitlin (1978: 207) is highly critical of this approach, suggesting that:

- It assumes commensurability of the modes of influence, that is, that personal and media influence are comparable in power.
- It assumes that power can be assessed in discrete incidents, denying the power of the structure within which people and media operate.
- It assumes that the consumption of media (and of the ideas and values assumed to lie within the media) is analogous to the buying of goods.
- It constructs attitude change as the dependent variable, but this requires a finite definition of 'attitude', and hence of 'attitude change', when these are notoriously imprecise.
- It defines opinion leaders as other members of the audience, ignoring the structural influences on opinion.

- It does not explain discrepancies between the data and the theory (the two-step flow of personal influence; Lazarsfeld et al. 1948) derived from the research.
- It does not sufficiently acknowledge the place of historical change: it assumes that conclusions derived from data on radio could be applied to other, later forms of media, such as television.
- It was allied with the media organisations that commissioned research within a marketing orientation, so it could not ask the important questions about the social context of media consumption.

Whatever the judgment of later researchers, Paul F. Lazarsfeld made a significant contribution to sociology in general and to communication studies in particular, refining survey methods and hypothesis testing. His discussion of the difference between administrative and **critical research**, and the value of integrating both within communications research, can be found in Lazarsfeld (1941): his influence is still felt, particularly in '**administrative research**', which is still frequently encountered within American communication studies (described in Halloran 1981). Lazarsfeld was the first director of the Office of Radio Research, set up at Princeton University with a grant from the Rockefeller Foundation in 1937, and moved in 1940 to Columbia University, New York. He later headed the Bureau of Applied Social Research. His own work (for instance, Lazarsfeld 1940; Lazarsfeld et al. 1948; Katz and Lazarsfeld 1955) was central to the effects tradition of audience research, but did not concern specifically soap opera. His work was based on the structural-functionalism of Emile Durkheim and Talcott Parsons, and like them he sought to apply 'scientific methods' to the study of societies as social systems.

Structural-functionalism is a powerful 'tendency of thought', with strong links to positivism, and is associated particularly with Talcott Parsons (1902–79). Parsons set out to link positivism with **idealism**, but used scientific models (at first physics, later biology) in developing his 'general theory of action'. This proposed four systems of human activity (cultural, social, personality and behavioural), all related to the physical-organic environment which supported them. In later years he modified this substantively, but retained the emphasis on linking the structure of society (how the elements of social systems combined) with its functions (the use-value of human activity) (Parsons 1977). Functionalism sees media effects as either positive (functional) or negative (dysfunctional). Uses and gratifications research is sometimes categorised as functional research (Allen 1985: 220–1), asking questions about the positive functions of the media in society.

These positions derive ultimately from a positivist faith in the growth of objective and verifiable knowledge through the scientific method. The **post-positivist** also seeks objective knowledge, while admitting (as positivism does not) that this is probably not achievable in the human sciences. Post-positivists have, therefore, used similar methods of audience research to positivists, though they interpret the results and measure their success by rather different criteria (see the second sub-section of section 12.2 in Chapter 12).

We next consider some theories of how the world works, specifically theories of class and of gender: some strands within these intellectual frameworks support positivist research methodology, some support post-positivist or non-positivist methodology.

Theorising class and ideology (various forms of Marxism)

Marxists are fundamentally concerned with economic questions – who owns and controls the means of production – but they are also interested in how this is related to the circulation of ideas. Marx himself revised his theories during his lifetime and what is now called Marxism has been developed further by his followers. Each strand of Marxism has its own assumptions about what constitutes good research, and therefore preferences about methods and methodologies: see, for instance Vaillancourt (1986), though the picture has also changed since that book was written.

Marx

Karl Marx (1818–83) was an historian, philosopher and economist. As an historian, he was concerned with the relation between technological developments and the social structure: he divided historical time according to the dominant social and economic system of the period – the Asiatic, the ancient, the feudal, and eventually the capitalist systems.

As an economist, his major premise is that labour (rather than property) creates wealth, and that in a capitalist system those who labour (the proletariat/working class) are not properly recompensed by those who own the means of production (the bourgeoisie/capitalists). The resulting power struggle is inevitable, and he predicted that the working class would seize power, leading eventually to a classless society.

As a philosopher, he proposed that the ideas that would benefit the ruling class circulated freely (as the dominant ideology), and that this gave rise to 'false consciousness' – the acceptance of bourgeois ideology (roughly the values, attitudes and interests of the property-owning class) by the working class because they did not recognise its class basis. In his early writings he constructed a model of the world in which the (economic) base totally determined the (ideological) superstructure: he later revised this model, to propose that economics determine 'in the last instance' rather than always and absolutely.

The Marxist dismisses earlier social theories as idealist, and proposes instead 'historical **materialism**' (the science of social formations) and 'dialectical materialism' (the theory of scientific practice). From this perspective, research about the social world (including media research) should be capable of producing generalisations, possibly even predictions, but in practice not all

Marxists are positivists. Some use both quantitative and qualitative methods, and in recent years there have been many examples of ethnographic audience studies from a Marxist perspective. In audience research, Marxists might ask questions about which classes are being addressed by particular media forms (such as newspapers or radio) or genres (such as soap opera or television news), or how audience opinion has been shaped by the owners of media production houses, or how audiences are sold as 'eyeballs to advertisers' in a commodity exchange.

Gramsci

Marx's theory was developed before the modern state, and did not adequately foresee either the technological/information revolution of the twentieth century or the social changes that accompanied those developments. As an explanation of the repeated failure of proletarian revolutions from the time of the Paris Commune (1870), Antonio Gramsci (1891–1937), in the *Prison Notebooks* (1971, written 1927–37), proposed the concept of '**hegemony**' (the capacity of the state to achieve the co-operation of its citizens, by a mix of force and consent).

The state, he proposes, engineers consensus through a bureaucracy which administers state decisions, and an educational system that reinforces the wisdom of compliance. Because the consensus seems to be popular or democratic, opposition is interpreted as anti-social as well as unreasonable. However, a minority always rejects state hegemony, either because they recognise and wish to break through its ideological effect, or because they see their own self-interest as not being served and so they break the law. For Gramsci, socialism remains preferable to state hegemony, even when the state is democratic: democracy requires that people act only as individuals in their own interests, while socialism requires that people think of the good of the whole social formation.

The concept of hegemony has entered the general vocabulary of media research. It helps to shape questions about how media reporting influences public opinion, or how audiences come to accept unquestioningly the 'truth' offered to them in newspapers and electronic media, or how the public's perceptions of the society they live in (for instance, its level of violence) are constructed by the media rather than by their personal experience.

Althusser

'Ideology' is another term originating within Marxist theory, but taking on a life of its own within the broader study of culture (including the media). Louis Althusser (1918–90), whose writings became influential in English from the early 1970s (his book *Pour Marx* was published in French in 1965, and an English translation by Ben Brewster – *For Marx* – appeared in 1969), challenged the concept of ideology as 'false consciousness', and redefined it as those ideas which are taken-for-granted – and therefore invisible – in any social formation. This means that a person may recognise that what someone else believes is mere ideology, but that person may not recognise their own beliefs as ideology, because the truth of their own beliefs appears self-evident and unquestionable.

Althusser maintained that, while economy was ultimately determinant, it was not always dominant within society: he insisted that ideology maintained hegemony, winning (by overdetermination) the consent of the governed to the rule of the state. In a key essay (Althusser 1971) he proposed an explanation of the relationship between the Repressive State Apparatuses (police, prisons, the military, government agencies) and the Ideological State Apparatuses (education, the family, the legal system, the media). In the 1970s and early 1980s, his ideas were central to cultural debates, including within media studies, where they influenced research about both audiences and texts.

Within audience research Althusserian concepts interacted with post-structuralism and psychoanalysis in the theorisation of pleasure, but there were also more direct Althusserian influences. His concept of a 'symptomatic reading', demonstrated in his own *Reading Capital* (Althusser and Balibar 1968), has been central to the development of **textual analysis**: Ben Brewster defines 'symptomatic reading' as analysing 'the textual mechanism which produces the sightings and oversights rather than merely recording it' (Glossary; Althusser 1971: 318). For audience research, Althusserian concepts of reading as production (of knowledge) suggest that media consumption is more than just another example of capitalist exploitation of the masses: if the 'watching time' of audiences is conceptualised as productive labour, audiences can create necessary value (their own meanings) as well as surplus value (meaning for the advertisers) (Jhally and Livant 1987; critiqued by Allor 1988: 221).

The application of the term 'ideology' within media studies (and, indeed, within cultural studies more generally) has been irrevocably altered by Althusser, though the period of his personal eminence was cut short by illness.

Terms such as 'class', 'ideology' and 'hegemony' remain central to Marxist theory and practice, but also circulate more widely outside Marxism. Similarly, many intellectuals owe a (not always acknowledged) debt to Marxism, for helping to shape their conceptual framework.

Some have been influenced by other schools of thought, influenced in their turn by Marxism. The 'Frankfurt School' is the popular name for the Institute for Social Research, founded in Frankfurt in 1923, as the meeting place for Marxist intellectuals in several fields. With some of its members Jewish, the Institute felt compelled to leave Germany in 1933 when Hitler came to power, spent some time in Switzerland then in the USA, and returned to Frankfurt in 1949, leaving several members in America. The Frankfurt School is primarily associated with the notion of 'critical theory', and consequently with critical research, in opposition to the 'administrative research' associated with

Lazarsfeld. This is also the origin of the 'critical' research paradigm listed among Lincoln and Guba's five paradigms (see the fourth sub-section of section 1.1 in Chapter 1).

For media studies, the key member of the Frankfurt School was probably Theodor Adorno, who, though he rejected classical Marxism, agreed with others of the Frankfurt School that the mass media acted as agents of state hegemony in disseminating the dominant ideology. He articulated this position in *The Dialectic of Enlightenment* (Adorno and Horkheimer, English translation 1979), equating the mass media with 'low culture' (commercialised art appealing to the lowest common denominator) and suggesting that this preserves state hegemony, by providing undemanding fare that challenges neither the intellect nor the aesthetic sense of the public. This view, labelled 'mass culture critique' by Herbert Gans (1974) and others, has implications both for textual analysis (demonstrating how mindless popular cultural texts are and how they disseminate the dominant ideology) and for audience research (demonstrating how gullible the mass audience is). Adorno later revised this position, becoming somewhat less pessimistic (Adorno 1991).

The Marxist inclinations of the Birmingham Centre for Contemporary Cultural Studies were evident in the choice of class, age, gender and race as its key areas of study, but its greatest contribution was in the establishment of cultural studies as an interdisciplinary field of research and teaching. The Media Group was an influential part of the Centre, particularly after 1968 when Stuart Hall (see section 3.5 in Chapter 3) became its director. In the early 1970s, the Group critiqued the journal *Screen* for its insistence on psychoanalytic readings of texts: the Group preferred to take into account real readers as well as textually positioned subjects. It was Hall's Marxist position which led him to postulate the theory of encoding/decoding, in which meaning-production takes place in a context of the viewer's ideology and past experience, allowing multiple viewing positions. The *Nationwide* project (see section 3.5 in Chapter 3) was an effort to test this theory in practice.

Meanwhile, the Glasgow Media Group was formed in 1974 within Glasgow University, and began its long study of television news (see the first sub-section of section 9.1 in Chapter 9), demonstrating television's ideological bias against trade unions in the reporting of labour conflict, and so its hegemonic role in upholding the status quo.

The Frankfurt School, the Birmingham Media Group and the Glasgow Media Group all provide examples of the application of Marxist concepts, even though not every person associated with these groups would explicitly acknowledge their debt to Marx, and some would even position themselves against classical Marxist theory. But there is a sense in which all discussions of class derive ultimately from Marx – including everything from the ethnographic studies of the Birmingham School to Pierre Bourdieu's class-based theory of taste (Bourdieu 1980). We have reached a point, then, where Marxist concepts permeate the study of the media and culture, including those which deny such 'grand narratives' as classical Marxism.

Theorising gender (various forms of feminism and identity politics)

Initially questions of gender in relation to audiences were raised by feminists. All the questions that we have listed as possible to ask about audiences can be asked specifically about the female audience: 'Very simply, to do feminist research is to put the social construction of gender at the center of one's enquiry' (Lather 1991: 71). However, different sorts of feminists concentrate their attention on different aspects of this process, as 'feminism' is not a simple term, despite being used so widely and so pejoratively. One of the clearest expositions of the discourse around feminist terminology is by E. Ann Kaplan. Using categories developed by Julia Kristeva, she divides the field of early second-wave feminism philosophically into two (Kaplan 1992: 252):

- essentialist: believing it is possible and even necessary to define 'woman' and 'female' as essentially different from 'man' and 'male';
- anti-essentialist: believing that language constructs concepts such as 'woman' and 'man' or 'male' and 'female' just as much as it does 'feminine' and 'masculine'.

She then develops political categories, concerning the action preferred to further the cause of women (Kaplan 1992: 251):

- 'Bourgeois feminism' struggles for equality and equity, still within the capitalist system.
- 'Pre-Althusserian Marxist feminism' relates culture to economic power and the oppression of other groups such as gays, blacks, and the working class.
- 'Radical feminism' sees women as autonomous but different, and requiring separate social structures such as health and education facilities.
- 'Post-structuralist feminism' accepts that language constructs social categories such as 'men' and 'women'.

These are useful categories, bearing in mind Kaplan's own caveats: that later usages of the term built upon earlier models rather than replacing them, and that new definitions and usages arise as feminism 'mutates'. As a fifth category, she draws attention to the way post-modernism interacted with feminism in new ways (Kaplan 1992: 252), and we would also point out the developments since Kaplan's chapter was written, sometimes called 'post-feminism'. This makes six categories, each with its own take on the appropriate questions and methods for a feminist researcher, as shown in (i)–(vi) on pages 104–5.

For specifically media research, the best general text on feminist research is still van Zoonen (1994). We also suggest that each of the six categories of feminism has its own approach – both to the media in general, and also to the ways in which media, and media audiences in particular, should be studied. The first two are compatible with positivist approaches (though sometimes they use post-positivist methods), the last four really require non-positivist approaches (see the fourth sub-section of section 1.1 in Chapter 1).

(i) The search for equality and equity led bourgeois feminists to campaign for work opportunities (and so to conduct institutional research on gender imbalance within media industries), and for improvements in the way women were represented in the media (and so to conduct textual research, usually by quantitative content analysis, measuring media representation against either the roles of women in the real world or an ideal of what these roles might be, leading to the concept of 'positive' and 'negative' media images of women: see, for instance, Gallagher 2000). Audience research from this perspective usually assumed that female audiences were passive victims of a repressive patriarchal system.

(ii) Early (pre-Althusserian) Marxist feminists were concerned with women as consumers of media within a capitalist economic system, which led them sometimes to quantitative content analysis of texts, but at other times to study real women in the audience by surveys and interviews (broadly, ethnography). But Marxist feminists were also increasingly prepared to link ethnographic methods with psychoanalytic concepts: Kaplan's example (1992: 257–9) of this model is Lillian S. Robinson (1976/1986).

(iii) Radical feminists focus on, and celebrate, gender difference, rejecting the male symbolic order, and encouraging women to seek individual solutions to their individual problems. Their research is more qualitative and descriptive: Kaplan (1992: 259–61) quotes Carol Lopate's research linking texts to audiences, which we have already discussed in section 3.5 in Chapter 3.

(iv) These first three categories arose in the period commonly known as 'women's liberation'. The term 'feminism' came into the ascendant when post-structuralist feminists shifted the argument from rights to language, and became immersed in the theoretical matrix of the late 1970s and 1980s, which included French psychoanalysis (particularly Lacan; see the second sub-section of section 11.2 in Chapter 11), Althusserian Marxism (see the second sub-section of the present section), and theories of symbolic systems (such as semiotics, see the third sub-section of section 10.1 in Chapter 10). The interest of post-structuralist feminists in the construction of subject positions through language led to media research that considered how the interaction of texts and readers through media institutions such as television can be inflected through concepts of 'desire, identification, fantasy, and subjectivity' (Penley 1992: 499). Of the studies discussed by Kaplan in this category (1992: 264–5), we have already considered Modleski and Brunsdon (section 3.5 in Chapter 3).

(v) Post-modernism (see the third sub-section of section 11.2 in Chapter 11) can, at its extreme, deny linguistic categories such as 'gender' altogether and be increasingly cynical of the possibility of recognising either textual or social meaning. But feminism has linked to post-modernism in its less extreme variants, as

Kaplan herself does in her discussion of the post-modern aspects of MTV (Kaplan 1992: 269–75).
(vi) In recent years, the category of the 'post-feminist' has been proposed, though there does not yet appear to be an agreed definition of this. It certainly seems related to a generation gap – a mismatch of perceptions between younger and older women. New technologies, and particularly the growth of the internet, are playing an important role, and the relation of women (including feminists) to these developments is still very open (van Zoonen 2001).

One reason for choosing soap opera as our focus for Part I was the range of feminist research in this area, best discussed by Brunsdon (2000). Such studies arose out of both the uses and gratifications tradition, and the cultural studies tradition, with individual researchers inflecting feminism differently.

Feminist research has been conducted both through ethnographic studies of audiences, and through symptomatic readings of texts to understand the reading positions available to women. Feminist ethnography has developed, and is still developing, strategies of research, a number of which are discussed by Lotz (2000):

- Selecting as subjects those audiences of which the researcher is or was a part forces the researcher to reevaluate her own speaking position, and to either avoid or acknowledge her 'colonising gaze'.
- Studying audiences with more social power than herself can help a researcher to avoid being patronising, as some studies of soap opera audiences (even some of those which set out with a feminist agenda) have been.
- Adopting a reflexive methodology includes being required to 'account for the subject position of their voices', admitting the researcher's own privileged position while still trying to avoid becoming 'overly self-focused and indulgent'.
- 'Interrogating silence as well as speech' includes consciously trying to extend the right of speech to more participants.
- 'Attention to the affective components of research' includes acknowledging the emotional aspects of the research, for both researcher and research subjects.
- The subjects of the research can be empowered by having their words quoted at length, having the entire interview available for the consideration of a reader, obtaining the subjects' approval of a draft before publication, or even allowing the subjects to participate in the writing process.

Some of these strategies are employed in the work of Walkerdine (1986), Seiter et al. (1989), and Hermes (2000). Lotz (2000: 463) warns that 'There will likely be some bad work produced this way, but that should not usher in critiques of the whole-scale failure of innovation.'

There are, however, still female researchers who seem to be adopting some form of the post-feminist position. Speaking of her own women students, Brunsdon says:

> Feminism, to the young women in the seminar room, seemed to mean moralism, miserabilism, and the posing of false unities between women – and their reading of founding feminist texts rather confirmed this. These attitudes coexisted with assumptions that they would work for a living, that they might not necessarily get married, and that their sexuality was their own business. (Brunsdon 2000: 13)

Such women may well not ask the sort of question that earlier feminists were interested in and may decide to stick with more traditional research approaches.

Meanwhile, there has been an increasing concern with questions of gender which are not restricted to women, but include a range of forms of identity. Gauntlett (2002) deals with questions of gender and identity in relation to the media, relating the theoretical contributions of Anthony Giddens, Michel Foucault, and Judith Butler to the way concepts of gender are played out in popular culture.

5.3 Conclusion

You will have absorbed elements of all these frameworks of interpretation as you read, and before you are able to recognise your own speaking position. Every time you use the term 'class', you are drawing on the Marxist tradition. Every time you refer to 'patriarchy' you are drawing on the feminist tradition. Every time you speak of 'truth', you are admitting the influence of positivism, and if you deny the possibility of locating or recognising the 'truth' you are positioning yourself within post-positivism or another of the non-positivist traditions. It is these influences which lead you to select a research topic. Those questions which ask about the economic basis of audience behaviour and preferences must ultimately position themselves within or against Marxism. Those questions which address issues of the role of gender within audience behaviour and preferences must ultimately position themselves within or against feminism or other forms of gender politics. Linking the substance of your research to its methodology requires you to consider *how* we know about the phenomena we wish to explore, and so to position ourselves within or in opposition to positivism, behaviourism, structural-functionalism, post-positivism, or other forms of non-positivism.

The more you understand these influences, the more effective your research will be and the more clearly you will be able to communicate your conclusions to others (see section 12.3 in Chapter 12).

PART II

RESEARCH ON INSTITUTIONS

Humans live in society, which runs by principles – unstated (moral and social) rules, as well as publicly specified (legal) rules. We express our principles through the institutions we create, and the institutions then implement and reify the principles. We become members of a community by learning the rules and habitually obeying them, and we expect the rest of the community to obey them too: the institutions hold the community together. Most of the time, institutions were formed before we were born, so they seem to exist independently of us: we, in turn, transmit them to the next generation, which also assumes they are permanent and continuing. But institutions also change over time: perhaps they lose touch with what produced them in the first place, so people lose respect for them and insist on radical change, or perhaps they just slowly mutate as new people and new ideas percolate through them.

Language is an over-riding institutional context, within which all other institutions in any society operate:

> our internal perception of the world around us is greatly influenced by the verbal categories which we use to describe it ... We use language to cut up the visual continuum into meaningful objects and into persons filling distinguishable roles. But we also use language to tie the components together again, to put things and persons into relationships to one another. (Leach 1976: 33)

In Western society, some institutional contexts are codified, like law or religion: some are more amorphous, like the media. Most exist informally within a broader social context: family within kinship system, courtroom within legal system, supermarket within commerce. Most also have physical contexts, which can suggest boundaries and limits: the Houses of Parliament in which the institutions of government function, the cinemas in which films are screened.

The term 'institution' applies to both a set of rule-governed practices (abstract concepts, such as 'language', 'law' or others mentioned above), and also the formal organisations which administer the practices within social and physical contexts (universities, courts, government departments, etc). Most also contain or relate to smaller organisations still: so a university is made up of Schools which contain Departments which in turn contain courses, while a court relates to various legal services and law firms as well as to the prison system. Institutional research, then, can be directed to understanding either an organisation from any of these levels, or the wider institution which encompasses potentially many organisations.

Building on our definition of culture (section 1.2 in Chapter 1), Part II concerns research on the expression of culture through media institutions. Such research concerns relations between governments and institutions, as well as how institutions work internally – how they worked in the past (historical studies), how they work in the present (descriptive studies and reports), and how they might work in the future (policy and policy-oriented studies).

This 'work' can be defined in different ways. We might study how the functions of various parts of the institution interrelate (for instance the owner, management and staff of a radio station), how the institution deals or interacts with clients or customers (the radio station with its audience or with advertisers), how the products of the institution are produced (a radio programme from idea to broadcast), how the technology is managed and what effects that has on the products of the institution (how a change from broadcasting to narrowcasting might affect news production), how change is managed within the institution (the decision-making process), how power is distributed (between the radio station and the network, the owner and the management, the management and the staff), the place of the institution within a broader industrial or social context (government ownership and content regulation, news bias, the construction of audiences).

In many ways, institutional research mirrors audience research. If the media institution is seen as powerful, then the audience is assumed to be vulnerable: if the audience is seen as powerful, then there seems less need to be fearful of the power of the institution. It is therefore important to understand how the media wield influence within society – the old question of the relationship between the sender and receiver of messages, or the producer and consumer of texts.

We do not have a heuristic model to cover institutional research like that offered for audiences. Within sociology, there have been several strands of organisation theory (see Jary and Jary 1995: 467–9). Silverman (1970), for instance, divides research on organisations among systems theory (open/closed systems, conflict/consensus), structural-functionalism (see the first sub-section of section 5.2 in Chapter 5), organisational psychology (theories of personality of the people involved), socio-technical systems (interaction of technology and social systems), action analysis (how meaning is attached to behaviour), and patterns of interaction (individualism versus group action, rule-compliance, conflict management). There are examples of most of these in institutional research on the media, but much media research focuses less on the organisation (the individual television station or network) than on the broader institution ('television' as a category), and its relations with other institutions (such as governments). It may also narrow down to a **case study** (a particular television programme in production at a particular time).

In the absence of a model, we have divided the field of institutional media research into three strands, each of which has its own take on the ontological and epistemological divisions among researchers (see 1.4). Historical studies are primarily concerned to understand the past, though they often see that as providing important lessons for the present. Contemporary studies often apply sociological methods, to describe how institutions work in the present, though they may often have to take into consideration how they got that way, and where they are now heading. Oliver Boyd-Barrett (1995: 186) describes this approach as being concerned broadly with 'political economy', which:

> in media research has a broadly 'critical' signification, often associated with macro-questions of media ownership and control, interlocking directorships and

> other factors that bring together media industries with other media and with other industries, and with political economic and social elites. It commonly looks at processes of consolidation, diversification, commercialization, internationalization, the working of the profit motive in the hunt for audiences and/or for advertising, and its consequences for media practices and media content.

The methods of sociology may also be applied to policy studies, which are primarily concerned with the future, though they must start with examining the present and may also take the past into account. James Halloran (1981: 36) makes a useful distinction between 'policy-oriented research' and 'policy research':

> The latter is frequently of the variety that seeks to bring about the efficient execution of policy and thereby make the existing system more efficient. On the whole it is not concerned with asking questions about the validity of the system, challenging predominant values, or suggesting alternative policies or modes of action. Policy-oriented research, on the other hand, ideally addresses itself to the major issues of our time. It is concerned with (among other things) questioning the values and claims of the system, applying independent criteria, suggesting alternatives with regard to both means and ends, exploring the possibility of new forms and structures, and so on.

This allies policy research with an administrative approach, and policy-oriented research with a critical approach.

In institutional research on the media, then, the boundary between the social sciences and humanities is being constantly breached – from both directions, and both can benefit from a clearer understanding of the methods commonly used by the other. In fact, the historian's traditional methods (discussed in Chapter 7) produce what the sociologist would call 'thick description' (see section 4.5 in Chapter 4).

So, no matter which institutional context the research comes from (social science/humanities; media studies/communication studies/cultural studies), similar questions will be asked:

- Studies of the past: What was the institution like and how did it come to be that way?
- Studies of the present: What is the institution like and how did it come to be that way?
- Studies of the future: How can knowledge of the past and present of the institution help us to determine what the institution might or should become?

Chapter 6

Researching Media Institutions

Our chosen focus for this discussion of institutional research is censorship, defined broadly. Couvares (1996: 9–10) reminds that the term:

> ... has been used to refer to related but quite different practices: governmental prior restraint on expression; criminal prosecution and punishment for obscenity; administrative regulation of expressive content by either independent parties or producers themselves; the intentions, activities, and effects of individuals and groups who exert pressure on producers to alter their products or on distributors to cease marketing them; conscious and unconscious editorial evasions and silences practiced by writers, directors, and other personnel involved in the production of cultural commodities.

Most of the research we will discuss concerns the first of these – the actions of the government: however, many of the other aspects of censorship become tangled up with the official censorship procedures. Government censorship is an 'institution' in both senses of the term: the process of censoring is a rule-governed practice which occurs systematically within a social context (making it an abstract 'institution'), but that process is carried out by a group of real people operating within a named organisation which is concrete in the sense of having premises and personnel and terms of reference. Censorship involves the whole media community – owners, producers, and consumers of media, and also the government agencies that oversee the institutional processes. Media censorship began as soon as technological developments enabled mass circulation of media, so it crosses all media, beginning with early popular print publications – the 'yellow press' and the 'penny dreadful'. However, we will be concentrating on only two – film (where the principles of media censorship have been fought over since 1896) and the internet (which is the current battleground). This allows us to address historical studies (of the past), sociological studies and government reports (contemporary, in the present) and also policy studies (directed to predicting or changing the future).

Because censorship is a controversial topic, on which debate continues and feelings still run high, the wide range of publications on censorship include some that support and defend it, some that oppose and deprecate it, and some that report on it without admitting to a position. Few report on action research, so common in audience research. Many are polemical, designed to argue for one side of the debate or another: in some cases these draw on other people's 'research' to bolster their argument, not always checking first on the rigour of that research.

In Part I, publications such as Lopate (1977) and Modleski (1982) were considered as research, though they are largely speculative and intuitive: in the same spirit, we will consider any publication that treats the subject of censorship seriously (that is, by supporting claims with evidence drawn from systematic study, rather than merely making polemical assertions) as a contribution to the research on the subject, appropriate to be evaluated as research, regardless of the writer's motivations. Our selection from this broad field is arbitrary – a convenience sample of what is easily available to us. Within this sample, it is not easy to separate the research out into categories: at first glance, they all seem to use similar methodology and to present the reports in similar formats, but we will attempt to tease out some of the differences in order to evaluate the reports.

6.1 Historical studies

Change over time can be studied by historical or sociological methods, or a combination of both: in many ways these methodologies overlap, though researchers do not always recognise this. The sociologist is more likely to be concerned with changes in the very recent past, though she may also look further back to put the present into context. The historian is more likely to be concerned with long-term change, though she may well bring this story up to the recent past. In addition, as academic boundaries (for instance between history and historical anthropology) become increasingly porous even these distinctions cannot always be sustained.

Historical audiences for film were for many years difficult to locate, but recently there has been a burgeoning of research, producing both specialist journal articles such as Harper and Porter (1999) and collections such as Maltby and Stokes (1998) and Stokes and Maltby (1999). Research on the history of media institutions, however, has always been prolific – in film there have been countless histories of the people and the practices within studios, distribution and exhibition companies, and government agencies. In fact, the historical audience has often been sought through the institutional history, by examining institutional practices such as market pre-testing, fan magazines, or hierarchical systems of film distribution.

Christine Geraghty's study (2000) of the cinema as social space in the 1940s and 1950s is one such study of audience through institutional practice. She draws on evidence from two British film magazines, *Picturegoer* and *Films and Filming* – not their coverage of the films, but any mentions she could find in articles or the letters columns concerning the experience of going to the pictures. She then backs up this archival research with interviews (oral history sources) and with references to cinema-going in sociological studies of the period, including mass entertainment statistics (Geraghty 2000: 2). From this she infers both the importance of cinema-going as a social activity, and its routine and everyday nature. She also acknowledges that the soaring popularity of television coincides with changes in the role of the cinema over the period: a general decline in attendance, a decline particularly in the family audience, an increase in the proportion of young people attending cinema, and the growing sensationalism of the films themselves.

This is an excellent example of a particular kind of sociological/historical research. The report is basically descriptive, with explanations couched in terms of associations rather than of (much harder to defend) cause-and-effect. This is typical of data gathering concerning the past: when the researcher cannot directly examine the subject of research (through experiment, observation or survey), indirect methods must be used. In surveying recent research on British cinema audiences of the 1920s and 1930s, Street (2000: 119–68) discusses the use of social science surveys, cinema owners' surveys of audience preferences, and the huge amount of data generated by the Mass Observation project (which is only now beginning to be mined for meta-analysis, for instance by Harper and Porter 1996). In the USA, similar social science surveys, such as those of Alice Miller Mitchell in Chicago and of Helen and Robert Lynd in Muncie, Indiana, are used by Stokes (in Stokes and Maltby 1999) to reconsider the female spectator of the 1920s and 1930s.

Like the audience surveys, some of the earliest written studies specifically of film censorship were not intended to be historical: they presented issues that were live in the present of their writing, and they became historical data only with the passage of time. Publications such as Quigley (1937), Moley (1945), Hays (1955) or Harley (1940) can now be mined by scholars, in the same way that contemporary debates about censorship of the internet will become historical evidence for future historians – even when such publications are polemical tracts.

The history of film censorship is addressed directly but superficially in some early general film histories (for instance Hampton 1931/1970). By the 1960s it was possible to look back with a little more distance on the history of censorship, so new research appeared, describing how official censorship bodies had come into existence, and considering the major developments in the bureaucracies and their decisions. Writers such as Randall (1968) for USA, Phelps (1975) for Britain, or Bertrand (1978) for Australia, often drew on the international comparisons provided by Schumach (1964) and Hunnings (1967). Robertson (1985, 1989) and Matthews (1994) brought the British story up to date, and Watson and Shuker (1998) surveyed all forms of censorship in New Zealand.

In all regions, once the survey histories had laid down a framework, more specialised research became possible, such as Jacobs (1991) on the censorship of the 'fallen woman' film. Among the specialised reports are those which take a 'slice' approach to the subject – perhaps a more limited period (Kerekes and Slater 2000, Maltby 1996), or key individual decisions (Aldgate 2000), or the effects of censorship on a specific studio (Kramer 1999). Edited collections of articles on such specialised research began to appear: for USA, see Couvares (1996) or Bernstein (1999). All of these works are engaged in the process of adding detail to the historical accounts of the development of the institutions of censorship, while also producing new understandings based upon both more extensive data and altered frameworks of interpretation.

Where the survey works are mainly narrative and descriptive, the specialised works can provide more focused argument. Lewis (2000) is concerned with the interplay of economic and ideological motivations, in the period following the introduction of the 1968 MPAA film-rating system. He draws on evidence from the early history of censorship and from the period of the House Un-American Activities Committee hearings and the blacklist, from ratings decisions and legal battles over the First Amendment. He presents it as an explanatory narrative, or rather several narratives that eventually link as explanation, but claims that 'it is structured less like an academic history than a novel' (Lewis 2000: 9), with heroes and villains, and a climactic pay-off.

The application of the anthropologist's 'case study' methodology to history produces historical anthropology (see, for instance, Sider and Smith 1997). In USA, there was in the 1980s a sudden surge of research on film censorship, when the opening of the case files of the Hays Office (the national film censorship organisation, administered for many years by Will H. Hays) allowed detailed study of individual films by a 'case study' approach. For instance, Maltby (1986) examines the negotiations about the production of *Baby Face*, as an example of the links between the ideology of film (particularly the representation of female sexuality) and the politics of the depression era in America.

All of these works are film history, but, as Street (2000: 2) reminds us, 'film is a part of history and history is a part of film': so increasingly social historians use film (and the films that have been censored) as evidence for social history more broadly. Several works (for instance Pernick 1996 for USA; Bertrand 1998 for Australia) discuss the connections between the eugenics movement, the 'social problem' films (concerning birth control, venereal disease, and prostitution) and film censorship in the early twentieth century. The interests of social history and film history intersect most obviously in those works concerned with the political function of film and the censorship that sometimes follows. This group includes the political aspects of sex (Ghosh 1999; Haralovich 1990) and race (Doherty 1999) as well as the more traditional political issues of government and resistance (Higginbotham 1988).

For the media researcher all these histories (film history, social history, and political history) contribute useful information on the development of censorship as an institution. In recognising their differing perspectives the media researcher becomes aware of their frameworks of interpretation – their social, political and epistemological assumptions – and can judge them as examples of historical research.

Subject-matter is not the only way to categorise these varied works: we might also consider their different modes of presentation. For instance, Hays (1955) tells his own story in the biographical first person, with a total lack of methodological self-consciousness. Vieira (1999) presents his argument visually, in a glossy coffee-table presentation, with glorious black-and-white illustrations from the films, and minimal text. Robertson presents short entries on 'a random selection of films especially noteworthy from a censorship angle' (Robertson 1989: 5), organised chronologically (so the changes in the censor's procedures and criteria for judgment become apparent), with an alphabetical index to lead a reader to any specific case, and a concluding summary. Street (2000) uses her own template for the analysis of individual historical documents (discussed in the first sub-section of section 8.1 in Chapter 8), leading to an interpretation of the meaning and value of each.

There are also different approaches to the acknowledgement of sources. Because censorship is such a controversial topic, and can be presented in a titillating or sensational fashion, books about it circulate within the general market. Publishers often assume that academic citation systems interrupt and irritate non-academic readers, so some general books (Matthews 1994; Trevelyan 1973) have an informal writing style, that simply claims truth: they either provide limited citation and bibliography, or abandon both entirely, producing an effect more like polemic. Some academic books (such as Hunnings 1967, or Schaefer 1999) provide full citation and reference lists, but others (such as Doherty 1999) list the references for specific claims under a page number in a special 'notes' section at the end of the book.

Because the methodology of historical research is usually disguised, it is not easy to list the strengths and weaknesses of various approaches. The major strength of historical narrative is its capacity to bring the past to life for a reader: the major weaknesses are the risk of evidence being presented as if it is finite and absolute (rather than tentative and contingent) and of allowing readers to assume that sequence implies causation (that what happened before something else also caused it). The major strength of historical explanation or argument is that it can provide evidence more clearly and deal more easily with doubt and contingency: the major weaknesses are that it is often drier and less engaging than narrative, and historians can be tempted to select evidence that fits a theory rather than insisting that the theory arise out of the evidence.

Whether historians like it or not, readers always do assess and evaluate what they read – a task that is easier for those who have some knowledge of the debates about history and historiography discussed in the first sub-section of section 8.2 in Chapter 8. Some of the above works (notably Street) couch their case studies within an historiographical context, explicitly exploring issues of authority and plausibility.

As you read, you might judge the authority of the text by:

- the specialised knowledge of the writer. John Trevelyan (1973) was a censor from 1951 to June 1971, and Secretary of the British Board of Film

Censors for the last 13 of these years. He could be presumed to know more than the lay person about the internal workings of the Board. Kerekes and Slater (2000) were collectors of horror films, caught up personally in the 'video nasties' controversy which they describe. It is up to a reader to decide whether such a privileged position makes the writer more convincing (because she is in a better position to know) or less convincing (because she is likely to have a personal agenda);

- the specialised knowledge of the other people who contribute information, for instance interviewees. Kerekes and Slater quote extensively from correspondence with other collectors engaged in the black market and with the managers of video businesses affected by the Video Recordings Act 1985. Where they can, they name the person and give some background to allow a reader to evaluate this person's special expertise: but they also expect readers to accept some unnamed sources, with the explanation that these informants would be placed at risk (of harassment or of legal action) by being named;
- the qualifications and/or reputation of the writer. A reputation develops slowly: it is unlikely to help in the judgment of a first book or article. Qualifications, however, can confer authority at any time. Information about qualifications is often found on the dust jacket, for instance, James M. Skinner's (1993) academic qualifications are listed (Professor of History and Film at Brandon University, Manitoba for 26 years), as well as his qualifications in film scholarship (Director of the Brandon Film Festival for 22 years and contributor to various film publications), and his censorship qualifications (Vice Chairman of the Manitoba Film Classification Board). On the other hand, a doctorate does not make one an authority on everything (see the discussion of Rimm's research in section 6.3 of this chapter);
- the access that the writer had to relevant sources, often acknowledged at the start of the book. Through Stephen Murphy, then Secretary to the British Board of Film Censors, Guy Phelps was given unprecedented access to the Board's files and to its viewing theatre. So his book (Phelps 1975) acquires authority, though such a privileged position may also place the writer under obligations which constrain his or her writing about the institution which conferred the privilege;
- the citation procedures used. The journalistic style, with its absence of citation, may not be a sign of inadequate research, but it does demand that the reader take the writer on trust.

The plausibility of the text might be judged by:

- whether evidence is offered for claims. A reader has every right to be sceptical about assertions such as this:

> Not surprisingly the film trade despaired. The only reason why they had created a censorship board was to neutralise the 'faddists' on local councils, and

> now every crank on the country's 688 local authorities was threatening to take up the cudgels against them. (Matthews 1994: 25)

Not only is this an excessive claim to make ('the *only* reason', '*every* crank'), but the lack of both citation and evidence places the whole weight of the claim on the author's authority;

- whether the evidence offered seems authentic. The procedures described in the first sub-section of section 8.1 in Chapter 8 can be used to authenticate evidence, but most of the time readers are left to make their own judgment, which is why citation (which shifts the weight of the claim from the writer to the source) becomes so important;
- whether the claim is internally consistent, that is whether the logical processes applied to the evidence make sense. The evidence offered should be strong enough to support the contention, and/or exceptions should be judiciously considered, which is not done in the claims of Matthews (above) about all 688 local authorities;
- whether the claim is externally consistent. It should agree with what other people have said, or the areas of disagreement should be judiciously considered. Kerekes and Slater are angry: their tone is often strident or sarcastic, making a reader wary despite the overwhelming evidence they offer.

It must be admitted that every historian has lapses – moments when a citation is omitted or bungled, evidence is not provided, or the evidence that *is* provided is inadequate to support the claim being made. Occasional lapses might be forgiven (though reviewers are seldom so generous), but ignoring academic apparatus places the report into a different category from academic research and writing – into popular history (Matthews 1994) or polemic (Kerekes and Slater 2000). We do not wish to argue against passion and conviction in historical research and writing: however, in academic writing we would like to see the passion supported by argument, rather than the argument weakened by passion.

As usual, for all of the research discussed above, the researcher/writer's methodology and style – as well as the reader's response – will depend upon their intellectual framework. A positivist will avoid passion in the belief that it must utterly undermine the research; a post-positivist will set the passion aside for the duration of the research; a constructivist will read the passion as one of the ways in which meaning has been constructed; a critical theorist will use the passion as a springboard for the research which will be directed towards changing those aspects of the world that fuelled the passion; and a participatory action researcher will have started with the passion and drawn in others who have similar feelings. Whatever your framework, remember that in the field of historical writing it is very easy to cross stylistic boundaries, so it is important for researchers to be aware of, and for readers to notice, such category shifts.

Popular history usually ignores theory altogether, providing a preferred explanation as if it were self-evident (a 'voice-of-God' pronouncement).

The academic historian cannot afford to ignore theory, though the meaning of the term is notoriously shifty. Within classical social science, theory is extrinsic to data: it is what a researcher applies (deductively) to data or derives (inductively) from data. Historians who consider history to be a science (for instance classical Marxist historians) think of theory this way too: as something they apply to or derive from the evidence. Academic historians differ from popular historians in presenting the conclusion as conjecture, still tentative and contingent, subject to change if new information comes to light.

The linguistic turn discussed in Chapter 8 has complicated this simplistic picture. If not only value, but meaning itself is constructed, then theory cannot be separated from evidence, but is always intrinsic to it and inherent within it. The linguistic turn has certainly changed how the history of film censorship has been written about: the more recent reports discussed above are very different in tone and in presentation style from earlier examples. But these differences are subtle and complex, not easily identified in individual research reports. None of the examples discussed above is a full-blown post-modern history, as defined by Jenkins (1997) and discussed in the first sub-section of section 8.2 in Chapter 8. However, Street (2000), at least, acknowledges recent moves in this debate, and tries to accommodate the linguistic turn in her discussion.

6.2 Contemporary studies and reports

Research on organisations has been a central focus of sociology from its beginnings, including studies of how organisations are structured, how they operate and how individuals operate within them. However, a survey of research reports in the major sociological journals indicated that until the 1970s such research was primarily quantitative (Faulkner 1982: 70–3). By 1998, the ground had shifted sufficiently for the first volume in a series on 'the foundations and current direction of organisational theory and behaviour', sponsored by the *Administrative Science Quarterly* and republishing key articles from that journal, to be entitled *Qualitative Studies of Organizations* (van Maanen 1998).

Research in media sociology similarly began with a heavy emphasis on quantitative methods: some of the earliest research on media institutions came from within the 'administrative research' paradigm, established by Paul Lazarsfeld (see the first sub-section of section 5.2 in Chapter 5). This paradigm developed the two-step flow theory of communication, that is, that messages reach receivers indirectly, through the mediation of opinion leaders. It is closely allied to the effects tradition in audience research, and led to the conclusion that media institutions were not as powerful as many people feared (Katz and Lazarsfeld 1955).

The administrative tradition, with its preference for quantitative methods, was already beginning to falter by the time it was challenged by Todd Gitlin

(1978). He declared that the 'dominant paradigm' had been asking the wrong questions: it had been concentrating on the attitudes and behaviour of individual audience members rather than thinking of the larger issues. Some of these questions are addressed by policy research and policy-oriented research, but to some extent the gap still remains: sociological research often seems to focus on organisations, without recognising the larger institutional context.

For instance, if behaviourism (see the first sub-section of section 5.2) aims to establish predictive rules (that stimulus S will always generate response R, given certain determining conditions), then administrators within institutions (for instance schedulers within television stations) can make decisions based upon what can be predicted of audience response. Audience research concentrates on determining what the response of audiences will be: institutional research concentrates on the way the administrators use or might use this information. Katz and Lazarsfeld (1955: 18) described four kinds of media effect: 'immediate response, short-term effects, long-term effects and institutional change'. The first three lead to effects studies on audiences (see Part I): the last can lead to positivist research on institutions themselves. In the case of Lazarsfeld's 'administrative research' paradigm, however, the central focus remained on the audience rather than on the institution:

> The administrative theorist is not concerned with the corporate structure of ownership and control at all, or with the corporate criteria for media content that follow from it: he or she begins with the existing order and considers the effects of a certain use of it. (Gitlin 1978: 225)

There is a similar gap in the Cultural Indicators (CI) programme, which comprises three theoretical threads: institutional process analysis (studying how institutions operate to control media representations), message system analysis (studying the content of representation), and cultivation analysis (studying audience perceptions of the media and how this influences behaviour – see section 3.2 in Chapter 3). Wober (1998) points out, however, that in practice the emphasis has been on the last two of these, with very little institutional research done explicitly under the CI banner.

The gap extends even into the present century: Sonia Livingstone (2000) argues that convergence has irreversibly linked audience and text in media research, but does not pursue the link of each of these with institutional research.

Nevertheless, sociological research on media institutions did continue, much of it still quantitative. Quantitative research on censorship is not common, and when it occurs it is likely to be centred on audience perceptions (that is, to link audience research with research on the institution of censorship), for instance (Hoffner et al. 1999). These researchers interviewed by telephone a random sample of 253 residents in a small, Midwestern metropolitan area concerning their support for censorship of television violence. They found the 'third-person effect' (the belief that others are more affected by televised violence than oneself) (Hoffner et al. 1999: 726), with variations according to how violent the interviewees perceived the real world to be. This is a basically quantitative study, from a positivist perspective, and can be evaluated as we did similar studies in Part I.

However, since the mid-1970s quantitative research has been losing ground in favour of qualitative methods, particularly ethnographic field work, involving participant observation and the use of documentary evidence. This kind of research produced exposés of production practices such as Lillian Ross's story (1950) of the making of *The Red Badge of Courage* or Michael Macliammoir's reminiscences (1952) on the making of Orson Welles' *Othello*. There have been comparable, but more academic, studies on television programmes, which have contributed a great deal to our understanding, not only of the production process, but also of the resulting texts and how audiences have received them (for instance, Tulloch and Moran 1986). Tulloch (2000: 7) proposes that:

> ... the ethnographies of television production that were beginning to appear in the early 1980s were much closer to being 'true' ethnographies than the 'active audience' analyses of the same period. Researchers of the former did spend considerable lengths of time within the various cultures of the TV industry, whereas audience researchers (particularly in Britain) tended to rely on qualitative interviews and brief observation (my own work in the mid-1980s on the Australian soap opera *A Country Practice* was symptomatic of this, in that, while I spent several months with the production team, I relied for my audience analysis on nine focus group interviews).

Production ethnographies share the strengths and weaknesses listed for other kinds of ethnographic research, already discussed in section 3.5 in Chapter 3.

We know of no comparable ethnographic studies of the workings of censorship authorities or of pro- or anti-censorship lobby groups: censorship is just too sensitive a subject to allow outsiders that kind of access. The nearest is the memoirs written by censors after they have left the job – the personal reminiscences (akin to oral history interviews or *testimonio*) of people like Hays (1955).

Over the years, the variety of methods available for institutional research has increased and researchers have become more willing to try new ideas. In 1982, Faulkner presented what he called the 'Triad method' as an innovation: it is now taken for granted that approaching a problem from several different directions can enrich research (remembering that using a 'triad' of research approaches is not the same as **triangulation** to establish validity: see the second sub-section of section 12.2 in Chapter 12).

How, then, have these methodological developments affected the research on censorship – research on current practices and future policy? Such research reflects and responds to public debate. At the beginning of the twentieth century, opposition to the censorship of film was considered extremely radical, even anti-social, and was seldom expressed openly. In those early years, controversy about the censorship of film centred on its implementation, and most of the debate about that occurred in the newspapers. The 'permissive sixties', however, produced a vocal anti-censorship lobby. As with more recent debates about internet censorship, opposition to film censorship has been based both on civil libertarian grounds (as an interference with the rights of the citizen) and on practical grounds (both doubting the quality of the research which claimed to establish a link between anti-social behaviour and the media, and questioning the effectiveness of censorship in achieving its stated aims of reducing social problems). Once the principles sustaining film censorship were a matter for debate, a new kind of publication (for instance, Hunnings 1967; Schumach 1964; or Stevas 1956) began to appear – not necessarily opposing the principles behind censorship, but certainly critically examining its social and legal foundations. Then came several works summarising key court cases, such as Carmen (1966), Devol (1976) and de Grazia and Newman (1982).

There is history in all of these, but it is incidental to the argument about the present. Most are library-based, constructing their philosophical and social arguments about the value of censorship around the data and interpretations of others. Their primary data is opinion – expressed informally in the press, or more formally in legal judgments. They also depend upon sociological research into the effects of media representations on behaviour in the real world (all those studies of the effect of violence or sex on film and television audiences: see, for instance, Brody 1977).

This is also the kind of data gathered by the various Government-appointed committees and commissions, which hear evidence from experts (teachers, psychologists, medical experts, police, social scientists) and from the general public (churches, women's lobby groups, parents' organisations). They weigh this evidence and prepare a report on present practice and recommendations for future action: these are available for India (*Report* 1969), the USA (*Report* 1970), Great Britain (*Report* 1980), Canada (*Report* 1992) and Australia (*Report* 1993). Like those early works describing the censorship system, as time passes these reports become valuable as historical evidence.

The major strength of these reports are:

- the wide range of opinion represented by those who made submissions;
- the care and attention to detail taken in synthesising these opinions, to produce policy;
- their capacity to represent an historical moment in a particular country in the debate about censorship.

The weaknesses are:

- that the opinions they represent are those of a vocal minority, but are often discussed as if they represent, or even constitute, the whole of public opinion;
- that it is very easy for opinion to be presented, by both those who made submissions and those who wrote the report, uncritically as fact.

No enquiry, however thorough, satisfied the lobbyists for long, and in Britain a key report resulted from an unofficial enquiry chaired by Conservative politician Lord Longford (Longford 1972). Former censor John Trevelyan described this as 'a curious document which in its 500 pages ranged from prejudiced subjective judgments unsupported by evidence to an objective and scholarly appendix by an expert psychologist ...' (Trevelyan 1973: 145). As research the Longford Report appears to have been fundamentally flawed, but it (and the response to it by Trevelyan and others) is now very useful historical evidence of attitudes to censorship at that time.

Like the historical research discussed in section 6.1 in this chapter, these government reports assume that their methods are beyond criticism. This places the responsibility on the readers to constantly evaluate what they are reading, taking into account how many people made submissions and how wide a range of interests were represented in these, how responsive the writers of the report were to the submissions and to what extent they seem to have pre-judged the issue. Knowledgeable readers (like Trevelyan, above) can identify both those issues that have been overlooked, and those occasions when the report's authors have slipped away from 'best practice' in research methods. It is also necessary to remember that even the best of these reports is never objective: they represent and express opinion rather than fact, and are quickly out-of-date. This is not a problem for the constructivist researcher, who can continue to use the reports indefinitely, as expressions of a particular construction of the world at a particular moment in time.

6.3 Policy studies and policy-oriented studies

We have argued elsewhere (Bertrand 1995) that debates about censorship have resurfaced each time a new communications technology has become available: so we now wish to shift the discussion from film censorship to censorship of online services such as the internet, where public debate is currently highly visible, much of it on the internet itself (Dworaczek 2001).

For instance, in July 1995 the US edition of *Time* magazine reported on a research study conducted by Marty Rimm (Rimm 1995), a student at Carnegie-Mellon University, which claimed that 'trading in sexually explicit imagery ... is now "one of the largest (if not the largest) recreational applications of users computer networks" ' (Elmer-De Witt 1995). The publication of the article drew a rapid response from critics, including Mike Godwin, the legal advocate of the Electronic Frontiers Foundation (US) (Godwin 1995a, 1995b), and Donna Hoffmann and Thomas Novak (Hoffmann and Novak 1995a, 1995b), two academics working in a school of marketing. Hoffmann and Novak argued that *Time* had 'given the Rimm study a credibility it does not deserve' and that this in turn had fuelled 'the growing debate over first amendment rights and restrictions on the internet' (Hoffmann and Novak 1995a). Rimm was an undergraduate student of electrical engineering when he conducted his research, a training which (as Hoffmann and Novak point out) presumably did not include the methodologies of social research which he claimed to have used. However, the possibility of 'disinterested' research on censorship is remote: Godwin was arguing from a libertarian social perspective and within a legal framework, while Hoffmann and Novak wrote their detailed critique of Rimm's work from within a positivist research paradigm within a management framework.

The kinds of public concern demonstrated in this case have prompted governments all around the world to consider taking control of online sources by the introduction of some form of censorship. So old debates about the value of censorship have resurfaced, complicated by the technical difficulties of controlling the content of something that can so easily cross national boundaries. We are still very close to these debates, so it is difficult to provide the kind of overview that we have offered earlier in this chapter. Instead, we are opting here to discuss selected examples in more detail, acknowledging that it will be some time before it is possible to see how these fit into the larger picture.

For the remainder of this chapter, we are also limiting our discussion to Australia, which presents a good example of the difficulties (both political and technical) of developing and implementing content restrictions of online services, even when centralised censorship of film and television already exists. We agree with Dwyer and Stockbridge (1999: 227), who argue that debates about censorship of the internet are 'in part characterized by liberalizing and self-regulatory tendencies and that regulation inevitably has a strong commercial and market orientation'.

We have already referred to the public enquiries set up by governments concerning film censorship, and the reports that these commission. In a similar spirit, in July 1995 the then Minister for Communication and the Arts in the Australian Parliament directed the Australian Broadcasting Authority (ABA) to investigate 'the content of on-line information and entertainment broadcasting services, including any broadcasting services provided on the internet'. This required policy research, to determine the appropriateness of any measures which might be introduced to encourage or require online service providers and users to meet community needs, through means such as self-regulatory codes of practice, educational programs, complaints handling procedures, devices for blocking or filtering certain material and offence provisions.

Their report (ABA 1996) is not primarily concerned to justify censorship as an institution, but rather to investigate the desirability and practicality of extending the current censorship system into a new media environment: the ABA was being asked to obtain information which would make possible the prediction of future technological developments, and to inform policy decisions. The underlying assumption of the study (ABA 1996: 88) was that the online environment (predominantly the internet) had created new types of services and expanded technological possibilities which challenged traditional classification paradigms and enforcement, and so required appropriate regulatory mechanisms (including, if feasible, technological mechanisms) to address 'community concerns' (ABA 1996: 9). This concern with new 'threats' posed by online services and with attempts to provide a technological response are common threads in much of the material which follows.

The ABA established 'an extensive consultation process', released an issues paper for public discussion and response, established a web site, and undertook 'the monitoring of national and international developments' (ABA 1996: 14). The 'extensive consultation process' included meetings with 'some sixty different representatives of on-line service providers, content providers and users, businesses, government departments, academics, educational and community organizations and individuals' (ABA 1996: 14). This study, then, is similar to the various national reports on film censorship listed in section 6.2 in this chapter, and can be evaluated in similar ways, however it is at the same time clearly different in several respects from these. It did not undertake the study of historical documents, nor use observation, formal surveys or questionnaires, although Chapter 4 (ABA 1996: 70ff) draws on attitudinal studies of audiences (using methods such as surveys and focus groups) conducted previously by the ABA and the Office of Film and Literature Classification (OFLC).

Following an introductory chapter which constructs a narrative about the origins and methods of the research, the report presents a series of chapters based on issues, in each of which background information is provided, options are canvassed and the results of consultations and submissions are presented, leading to recommendations to the Minister. The overall thrust of the recommendations was supportive of 'a self regulatory framework based in industry codes of practice and labelling schemes and a large-scale community education scheme' (Dwyer and Stockbridge 1999).

This is very clearly 'policy research', aimed at providing recommendations to the commissioning body, the government. Much of the research we have examined to this point has sought to establish certain 'facts' and then to provide frameworks for their interpretation. However, policy research deals with the future, which cannot be 'known' but only speculated about, so this research report is dominated by statements of value rather than fact, statements which cannot be 'proven' and so are always contestable and the subject of ongoing political debate. Participants in such debates often seek to bolster their arguments with statements which claim to be factual, or to refer to the 'facts' of the historical past and to argue that situations in the past are analogous with the present, or can provide guidance for the future. Ultimately the claims made by this report are value claims: for instance, 'to be effective, these objectives should be achieved as much as possible through industry self regulation, rather than by more prescriptive, interventionist methods' (ABA 1996: 32). Statements of this type are presented as if they are self-evidently true: they are, however, a priori claims which ultimately cannot be 'proven' but will be accepted or rejected by readers (including government) on the basis of their accordance with previously held values and attitudes.

The research process in this case involved the canvassing of many opinions (often contradictory), through meetings and submissions. In interpreting such contradictory data the researchers were required to mediate between different views expressed, a process of applying explicit or implicit frameworks of interpretation. The result is a measured and judicious document, disguising its own interpretive framework, and with similar strengths and weaknesses to the other government reports discussed earlier.

Lobby groups also contribute to the public debate, both by presenting their views to official enquiries, and commissioning their own research and publishing the results. *Regulating Youth Access to Pornography* (Flood and Hamilton 2003b) is a report produced by such a lobby group, the Australia Institute (AI), in March 2003. Confusingly its public release was accompanied by a discussion paper (Flood and Hamilton 2003a) by the same authors, dated February 2003. The larger report refers, for evidence of some of its claims, to the discussion paper, so it is necessary to read the two documents together, as an attempt to intervene in the process of policy formulation in Australia.

The preface to *Regulating Youth Access to Pornography* includes a statement that the paper:

> was motivated by a concern that young people are being exposed to a wide range of pornographic material, some of it of a violent and extreme kind, and that this exposure may be having long-lasting detrimental effects on some young people and on society at large. In particular, the internet has in recent years seen a proliferation of pornographic content of a disturbing kind. This material is easily accessible to children. (Flood and Hamilton 2003b: iv)

There is no indication in either document that they have been produced in response to public debate or concern, or that the research being reported was commissioned by any individual or group, however the thrust of the reports is to argue for significant changes in the direction of public policy concerning the regulation of access to aspects of the world wide web. As research, both documents are seriously flawed, and would not be worthy of comment except that their release was accompanied by a flurry of attention in the popular media and at least one carefully argued response, from another lobby group – Electronic Frontiers Australia (EFA 2003).

Regulating Youth Access to Pornography asserts that 'children in Australia have extensive exposure to pornography,' and (even though there is, in fact, no system of content regulation of the internet) argues that 'the existing system of regulation of sexual content on the internet' has failed and needs to be replaced. The report recommends the following changes:

- the development and implementation of a nationwide school-based program of media and health 'literacy';
- the development of a system of mandatory ISP-based content filters;
- the implementation of age verification technologies;
- the requirement for pornographic websites to have 'plain brown wrappers';
- instant help functions available for children exposed to offensive material. (Flood and Hamilton 2003b: vii)

The first and second of these recommendations receive the most detailed discussion in the report: the latter three, all of which face major practical barriers (detailed in the EFA response), are largely undeveloped. This illustrates a common limitation of much critique of internet policy: the people with the greatest expertise and interest in internet policy are often technical people, who write about technical issues and do not usually produce systematic, published research on internet policy (Sam Hinton, personal communication, May 2003). The authors of *Regulating Youth Access to Pornography* were clearly not technical people. They report on a study conducted on behalf of the AI by the polling company Newspoll which was commissioned to survey 16 and 17 year olds 'to determine the extent of their exposure to X-rated videos and Internet pornography' (Flood and Hamilton 2003: v). Some results of this survey are presented both in verbal summary and in tabular form. For example it is reported that 84 per cent of the boys polled believed that watching of X-rated videos 'is widespread among boys of their age'. This statistic is confusing: it does not mean that 84 per cent of those polled actually do watch X-rated videos (which would indeed indicate that such watching is 'widespread'), but that 84 per cent of those polled *believed* that such watching was widespread among their peers (which makes the *belief* 'widespread', but does not provide any evidence at all concerning the actual behaviour). It also depends upon self-reporting, which is notoriously unreliable, especially in relation to sexual behaviour for which particular groups may see advantage in 'boasting'. The statistics are, in fact, presented confusingly throughout the two documents, requiring careful reading to distinguish between self-reported behaviour and self reported attitudes.

There seems to be little understanding of methodological issues, and no discussion about this in the report: there is no explanation of the method of sample selection, of the size of the sample, of their geographic makeup or spread, and there is no copy of the survey or interview schedule. The EFA response suggests that in a news release the AI indicated that the survey sample consisted of two hundred 16–17 year olds surveyed by telephone, however the telephone survey is only mentioned in passing in the discussion paper, with no mention of the sample size. From reading both documents, it becomes apparent that this Newspoll survey is the only research conducted, and the sole evidence for claims of 'the extensive exposure to pornography' of young people in Australia. For example:

> Just under three-quarters (73 percent) of boys and 11 percent of girls report that they have watched an X-rated video. Eighty-four percent of boys and 60 percent of girls say they have been exposed accidentally to sex sites ... (Flood and Hamilton 2003b: x)

A significant feature of the report is the reliance on assertion unsupported by evidence. For example on page 2 of *Regulating Youth Access to Pornography*

(Flood and Hamilton 2003b) the comment is made:

> While definitive conclusions must await further research, it is our view that the research literature's documentation of significant associations between adult use of certain types of pornography and sexual aggression provide grounds for real concern.

This comment is followed by a footnote that indicates that 'the research literature is reviewed in Flood and Hamilton (2003),' that is, in the discussion paper. However, we could find no literature review or bibliography in Flood and Hamilton (2003a).

On page vi of *Regulating Youth Access to Pornography*, the following statement is made: 'web sites showing pornography, some of it of the most extreme kind, are easily accessed by children.' This statement is repeated verbatim on page 7. There is a logical flaw here: the fact that it is possible to access a particular web site does not necessarily mean that it is in fact being accessed, and no evidence is presented of such access by children. Their sample consisted of adolescents, and no evidence is presented that these respondents were asked about the nature of the pornography they had seen, including whether it may have been 'of the most extreme kind'.

A key claim of *Regulating Youth Access to Pornography* is that 'the existing system of Internet regulation is failing to limit the exposure of children to pornography on the internet' (Flood and Hamilton 2003b: x). However no evidence is supplied, other than the Newspoll survey, to support this claim. The major thrust of the report is the recommendation of a mandatory system of Internet Service Provider (ISP) based filters to screen out offensive material. Content filters on the web have been proposed for a number of years (Kruger 1998) and generally rejected as impractical by those who have researched them (this is the main thrust of the EFA argument).

To sum up the weaknesses of this report:

- It does not sufficiently explain its methodology.
- It presents evidence inconsistently, making it difficult for a reader to judge the strength of the argument.
- It is technologically naive, not sufficiently aware of the debates that have already ruled out as impractical some of the policy proposed.
- It is logically flawed, allowing terminology to shift confusingly and drawing conclusions that are not sustained by the evidence.

Heath Gibson's (2000) critique of the prevailing internet content regulation regime in Australia is a better example of policy research. It should be read in the context of the development of the internet at a time when neo-liberal economic and social policies are dominant. Most governments have tended toward minimal regulation of the internet, and therefore often do not have a formal internet policy, preferring to engage in ad hoc policy formulation, including attempts to regulate content through censorship. Consequently critiques of internet policy may be critiques of government regulatory proposals, or of neo-liberalism and of laissez-faire economic policies (such as Schiller 1999).

Following an executive summary, Gibson's report is in three main sections: introduction and background; issues raised by the Online Services Act (OSA); and summary and concluding comments. Like the Australia Institute report, this document is an intervention by a privately funded 'think tank' into debates on media policy formulation, and indicates one direction in which policy formulation has gone in each of the UK, the USA and Australia in recent years.

The first section of the report establishes the historical background to the development of the legislation being critiqued, proposing that 'public policy in relation to the Internet should be driven by informed research on the relevant issues' (Gibson 2000: 2). Gibson argues that much of the impetus for the introduction of the OSA was an attempt to regulate the type of content that the Australia Institute report is concerned about: pornography on the internet. He presents the main arguments usually advanced in favour of tighter regulation: protecting children from content likely to be offensive, limiting the spread of child pornography online, and ensuring that internet content conforms to community standards.

However, he questions the need for tighter regulation in relation to each of these. He comments that protecting children is likely to lead to all internet content being reduced to the level of children, particularly as frameworks already exist which make the distribution of child pornography illegal. He argues that the diversity and global nature of the internet pose a challenge to community standards, which in themselves are difficult to determine in a diverse culture (such as Australia, the US or the UK). Although he does not explicitly say so, the implication is that it is not worth the effort to try to determine and then enforce community standards.

Following a brief history of the OSA, Gibson raises a number of issues to do with its implementation. Again underlying each of these are several related elements: a concern for consistency – which might be seen as related to efficiency in that an inconsistent regime creates inefficiencies; a concern over the likely economic impacts of the regime on the emerging internet content industry; and underlying liberal assumptions, especially to do with the desire to minimally restrict the freedom of autonomous individuals.

Gibson's concern for consistency is evident in the argument that although the OSA sees the internet and television narrowcasting (pay-per-view TV) as commensurate media, it imposes standards on the internet which are stricter than those for other media forms. For example, he argues that much of the regulation of internet use should properly be undertaken by parents, and that in adopting the narrowcasting model the OSA imposes an 'unduly restrictive' regime (Gibson 2000: 7). In a second argument Gibson supports greater openness and transparency of censorship decisions than is provided for by the OSA, partly on the grounds of fairness (decision making is less open in relation to the internet than other media), but more significantly from an underlying, liberal, assumption that autonomous individuals require access to information in order to make informed decisions. He also suggests that a more transparent regime would provide guidance to Internet Service Providers (ISPs) about the basis for making decisions about what content is unacceptable. Finally he argues that a number of provisions of the OSA are likely to prove economically onerous to ISPs and content providers, and so are likely to be anti-competitive, causing some flight overseas of content providers, and increasing concentration of ownership in the industry as smaller companies close down or are absorbed by larger companies.

This report presents a clear and well-argued case, which does not have the logical problems of *Regulating Youth Access to Pornography*. However, it could have been strengthened by making clearer the author's position within the current critical climate: as it stands, only a knowledgeable reader could identify the author's underlying liberal assumptions.

The reader, concerned to evaluate such research reports, can apply (as we have done in our discussion) standards of **authenticity** and plausibility like those proposed in section 6.1. In cases where the research builds upon other research (like Flood and Hamilton 2003b builds upon the Newspoll survey) it is necessary to evaluate at both levels. However, because all policy research is directed towards the future, using a priori arguments, presented as if they are self-evidently true, such reports will (as we have already noted) be accepted or rejected by readers on the basis of their accordance with previously held values and attitudes, that is, on how well the report matches the reader's own intellectual framework. While the main thrust of the arguments advanced by the Australia Institute comes out of a moral concern to protect vulnerable sections of the population, but without empirical evidence that this population is vulnerable, the main thrust of Gibson's report is based on a liberal assumption of the benefits of minimal regulation based largely on arguments of economic benefit and efficiency. Both of these are most likely to fit comfortably within a post-positivist framework.

6.4 Conclusion

Research on institutions is less often action-oriented than research on audiences, particularly in the case of censorship, our chosen focus for this part of the book. If the research is primarily concerned with the past and present of an institution, it may be either empirical or rhetorical, but policy research is directed towards the future, and so is inevitably rhetorical, even if it supports the argument with empirical information from the present or the past. All of these, however, may also be distributed across the frameworks already identified – positivism, post-positivism, constructivism, critical theory or action research. Your evaluation of any individual research report will draw upon both your application of critical judgment to the processes of the research and the form of the report, and your awareness of how well your own research framework matches that of the researchers/writers.

CHAPTER 7

Gathering Data on Institutions

Some of the research methods employed to study institutions have already been mentioned in Part I (on audiences), but all of these are inflected differently when the object of study changes from audience to institution. Remember to have an ethics policy in place before you start to gather data (see section 1.5 in Chapter 1).

7.1 Records and documents

These are the written and/or printed and/or web-based evidence left by and about institutions and the people who work in them. **Documentation** is a form of **material culture** (see section 7.2 in this chapter), so it has two aspects:

- a material aspect: it exists as books, pieces of paper, electronic recordings;
- a discursive aspect: the messages/texts it contains can be interpreted.

Sociologists have traditionally been wary of documents: Webb et al. (1966) was a brave foray into forms of data rarely used at the time, when sociologists preferred to place more reliance on observation and oral data. By the 1980s, ethnographers were routinely acknowledging the value of documentation (Burgess 1993: 123–42; Hammersley and Atkinson 1983: 127–43) and more recent writers (Atkinson and Coffey 1997: 47; Hodder 2000: 704) note that this trend has strengthened among sociologists generally.

Historians, on the other hand, have always used documents, and have developed sophisticated methods for dealing with these. The distinction made by some historians between primary and secondary documents is difficult to sustain when the dividing line constantly shifts: the same document can be a **primary source** for one kind of enquiry and a **secondary source** for another. For instance, Beman (1931) was written as a debaters' handbook, providing a bibliography and quotes from contemporary sources supporting arguments both for and against censorship: it can be read as a secondary source, restating and summarising other people's opinions, or as a primary source of the state of public opinion on censorship in 1931. So, if you find us using the term 'primary evidence', remember that we intend it as a relational term, not an absolute.

At first sight, using documents appears to be a cheap and easy alternative to action research. However, locating documents, gaining access, and learning to interpret them is never simple and may involve hidden costs, such as access fees, travel or photocopying.

The advantages of using documents produced within the institution being studied are:

- It 'documents' a particular moment, thus allowing a researcher to follow changes in policy and practice.
- It is written in the institution's professional language, which may well be part of what the researcher is studying.
- It is relatively permanent, so can be consulted repeatedly.

The disadvantages of such use are:

- Documentation may be difficult to track down, if the recordkeeping processes within the institution have been flawed, or if documentation has been culled over time:

> For example, during an interview with the art director Maurice Carter I was promised access to surviving documents from the Art Directors' Guild. These would have been invaluable to me, but it turned out that they had been consigned to the garbage the week before by Mr Carter's wife. (Harper 1994: 6)

- If it is incomplete (which is more likely as you move back in time), skews may be occurring which the researcher may not even know about.

You may choose to use documents written from outside the institution you are studying – by journalists, competitors, commentators or critics of the institution. This, too, is relatively permanent so can be revisited, and in addition it opens up for debate the context within which the institution operates.

Forms of documentation relevant to institutional research

Documents generated within private or non-government institutions

Some of these (such as annual reports, audited financial statements) are on the public record, and should be found in public libraries, or freely available from the institution itself. Others (such as policy documents or day-to-day financial records) may be considered private and sensitive, and may not be easily accessible without the co-operation of the institution.

Some private and non-government institutions jealously guard their current documentation, but may have lodged early records with libraries or archives: there may, however, be restrictions on use, such as a protection period or a requirement to obtain the institution's permission before publication.

Documents generated by government bodies

In a democratic society, government bodies are expected to open their activities to public scrutiny, except where this might produce a risk to the security of the state. However, there are also usually provisions allowing the Government to make its policy decisions in private. This conflict of interest is commonly resolved by a requirement that all government documentation be lodged with the national archive, but that public access be restricted.

This means that public documents (such as parliamentary records and debates, or departmental reports) are available quickly, often published and distributed through public libraries, with subject indices, which save a researcher valuable time. The more private documents (such as cabinet minutes, or correspondence between ministers) are lodged in archives. Access provisions vary: in Australia, material lodged with the federal government archive is not available till 30 years have passed, and even then public access to the more 'sensitive' material (such as cabinet minutes) may still be refused. Each layer of government may have its own archive: national, regional and local.

Newspapers, journals and books

We are not referring here to your 'reading around a subject', but rather to the contribution that newspapers, journals and books can make as research data in their own right.

It is unwise to take shortcuts through published collections of extracts. Foerstel (1998) provides a brief overview of the history of media censorship in the USA; but most of his book is thumbnail sketches of key legal cases, and extracts from interviews with participants. An academic researcher might find useful pointers in such collections, but should not depend upon them: this data has been taken out of its context, selected and organised by an editor, so a serious researcher needs to go back to the original.

Regional and local newspapers can be very useful. They may be held in the large central (national and state) libraries, or in a local library or in the collection of a local historical society. Chris Watson (personal email 9 November 2001) found a full run of the Nelson local newspapers at the Isel Park Museum in Stoke, New Zealand, and comments:

> They enabled me to check stories around the making of 'Nellie of Nelson' and reviews of the sex hygiene films of the twenties (like 'Damaged Goods'). I discovered that segregated audiences were mandated before the famous 'Ulysses' case.

Private documents

Diaries and personal correspondence are often hard to locate, and may have restrictions placed on their use. They may be found in the specialist manuscript collection of a public library, in a private collection (perhaps one devoted to a specific person), in the collection of the local historical society, or just picked up serendipitously in a book sale.

They are idiosyncratic, but often invaluable:

> ... 1950s film director Wendy Toye has these marvellous little drawings which she puts in her papers – she calls them 'comic cuts'. They are a kind of aide-memoire and give you very clear access to her intentions and desires – comparing them with the finished film helps you to understand what kinds of constraints the director is under. (Sue Harper, personal email 22 October 2001)

They can also be personally revealing. Harper reminds that:

> ... private materials ... often give you access to the very raw feelings of the person who wrote them, and you feel like an intruder. The diaries of Muriel Box in the BFI library are like this, and film scholars have to learn to be very sensitive in how they interpret and use such material.

Locating documentation

Start with the reference lists provided within books on your subject. For censorship, even an older example such as Jacobs (1991: 188–91) can alert you to historical sources: if your research project is more current, you may need a more recent book. You could also check entries in the various national dictionaries of biography or volumes of *Who's Who*, or published guides to archives such as Helferty and Refauss (1993), Reynard (2000) or Foster (2001). Follow all these up in library catalogues (see Chapter 2), which will take you to public sources, but also sometimes to finding aids to archival holdings, such as Kelson (1996), which lists the catalogues of the censorship authorities in occupied Germany. Large public libraries may also have specialist book collections (perhaps a rare book section, such as the Lilly Library within the library of Indiana University, Bloomington), or manuscript or archival collections (such as the Turnbull Collection held at the New Zealand National Library). The catalogues of most public libraries are available on the web (for instance, the National Library of New Zealand: www.natlib.govt.nz).

If the books on your subject use unpublished material, they should give complete citations, including the archival information which will alert you to the collections that might be useful – public (national, regional or local government collections) or private (collections for commercial organisations or individuals). For instance, Jacobs (1991: 187) lists the location of the personal papers of Will Hays, as well as the papers of the Catholic Legion of Decency, the Motion Picture Producers and Directors Association, and the major studios (MGM, Paramount, RKO, United Artists and Warner Bros).

When seeking archival sources, always begin with the web. URLs change and sites come and go, so if you can't find any of those listed here try surfing the net for their new URLs or for alternative sites. There are web sites for most major television programmes and new films, and some of these (for instance www.summerbayweb.com/menu.htm or www.homeandaway.org on the soap opera *Home and Away*) contain information about the programme's past, thus forming a living archive. Most of the time, however, you will be looking for a physical repository. Some university departments of media studies have links on their web sites to other useful sites, including sites for research resources: for instance, the Department of Film, Television and Media Studies at the University of Auckland at www.arts.auckland.ac.nz/ftvm. Some media journals are similarly useful, for instance *Screening the Past* (www.latrobe. edu.au/screeningthepast). There are also the various international archiving federations: start with the Association of Moving Image Archivists (AMIA at www.amianet.org) or the International Federation of Film Archives (FIAF at www.fiafnet.org).

Using archives

(i) Most archives require that you establish your credentials as a bona fide researcher before you use the collection. Even if they do not require you to apply for a 'reader's pass', you should write first, giving information on who you are, what you are doing, and what will happen to the results. Ask about opening hours, charges, limitations on access, whether finding aids are open to researchers, what equipment you may bring in with you (laptop? portable scanner? digital camera?), what photocopying is available.

(ii) Preparing for the visit:

- Read up as much as you can, both about what you are researching and about the institution you are visiting.
- List (for yourself, not for the archive) what you hope to get from the visit: both what sorts of information you are after and what forms of documentation you wish to consult.
- Many archives insist that, for the preservation of fragile documentation, readers must not use pens or biros: some provide pencils and

means of sharpening them, others expect you to provide your own. You may also be asked to leave your jacket outside, or to wear white gloves for handling delicate materials. Access to fragile documentation may be restricted to more senior researchers, and photocopying or scanning may be entirely forbidden which means you must allow time for taking extensive notes.

- Avoid disappointment by acknowledging before you start that you may well find much less than you hoped. However, your effort is never really wasted: finding out that there is nothing there is actually useful information.
- Avoid panic by acknowledging before you start that you may need more than one visit. Sometimes the first visit only allows access to finding aids and you may then have to follow procedures for ordering materials to be available on a second visit. These procedures may include:
    - obtaining written permission from the copyright holder (whether an individual or a department). For government documentation, this may involve an exclusion period. For unpublished scripts and/or media productions, clearance may be refused if the copyright holder believes that some commercial value still exists in the item.
    - obtaining clearance on politically sensitive documentation. National Archives of Australia (NAA) checks each file before it is released, and may mask cabinet papers or anything judged sensitive, but leave the rest of the file available to the researcher. Any documentation that has not already been cleared has to be processed before it will be made available, and this may take some time.
    - obtaining clearance on culturally sensitive materials. Russell Campbell (personal email 6 November 2001) points out that the New Zealand Film Archive 'prides itself on being a bicultural institution and one must understand that in Maori culture being granted access to information is a privilege that must be earned'. Similarly, ScreenSound Australia and the Institute of Aboriginal and Torres Strait Islander Studies (both in Canberra) are careful about access to records of indigenous communities.

In the case of audio-visual archives, you may find that, in order to protect the original archival copy from wear-and-tear, researchers are only allowed to see a viewing copy: if this does not already exist, you may have to wait until one is made. This may take a long time, particularly if the archive is more concerned to protect the original from deterioration than to provide access copies for researchers.

(iii) Getting the most out of the archive:

- Archive staff know their collection(s) better than you ever will. Take their advice about the best routes into the material or what finding aids to use.

- You know better than they do what you want. As you become familiar with the archive, you will have ideas of how to use it to your advantage, even if these are not the ways previous users have found most helpful. In such cases, be politely insistent.
- Keep scrupulous records: of everything that seemed relevant at the time (whether or not it eventually turned out to be helpful), and everything you requested (whether or not you actually got to see it). If you record the disappointments (and the date and reasons for disappointment, such as 'file missing'), you are less likely to find yourself wasting time on a later visit going back over old ground.
- Every archive has its own procedures, depending on:
  - the nature of its collection: film and television programmes are relatively well-catalogued (eg ScreenSound has MAVIS – a cataloguing system that is easy to use and accessible on the web), but written documentation may turn out to be less easily traced;
  - the provenance of the collection: private papers are the most idiosyncratic in their principles of collection and ordering, government documents are more systematic;
  - when the system was put into place: what was acceptable practice in the 19th century is very different from what is expected in the 21st century.
- Learn the procedures, so that you can:
  - interpret the organisation and numbering within the filing system, and so make the best use of the finding aids;
  - understand how clearance may be obtained, so you can obtain copyright permissions efficiently.

The starting point is the overall name of the collection, usually the government department where it originated. For instance, if you were working in the Public Record Office in Kew on film in the 1950s, you would look up the finding aids for the BT (Board of Trade).

Within the NAA the files are organised first by the Ministry or Department where the documents originated. In the early 20th century, when a letter arrived in a department it was entered first in the correspondence registry – a large volume with columns for date, a few words about the subject matter, and the number of the file into which the document was placed. A separate registry listed the files in sequential order, with a summary of the contents. So, a file called A27/1417 would be the 1417th file created for that Department within A series in 1927. To trace documentation relevant to your enquiry, you might search (manually, if there are no computer databases available for 1927) the file registry and ask for files on subjects which might contain the correspondence you are looking for. Or you might check the correspondence registry for letters referring to your subject (for instance complaints about a film), and ask for the file that they were placed into.

However, files cannot always be found, and if this happens don't assume it is the fault of the archive.

- It could have been destroyed, accidentally or deliberately: for instance, all files of the Australian Commonwealth Censors were destroyed up to 1929, simply to save office space.
- It could have been misfiled, in the source institution before it reached the archive, or after someone has used the file in the archive. Most archives do not have the time or resources to search for a missing file but most are willing to do what they can incidental to other searches, and get back to you if the file turns up at a later date.
- It might be a quirk of the system. In the 20th century, some departments of the Australian government had a 'top-numbering' system. The number in the correspondence registry indicated the file where the document was first placed: this file had more and more documents added, each one entered at the same file number, until the events being documented drew to a natural conclusion. If new material appeared later on the same subject, and someone remembered that earlier occasion, they might have incorporated the first file into a new file, under a new number: the old file will simply disappear unless the new number is noted beside the final entry for the old file.

(iv) Building on what you find in the archive:

If the information you want is not where you expect it to be, don't give up! In the examples given above (censorship records destroyed, top-numbered files no longer traceable), it was possible to find substitute (if partial) documentation:

- Good bureaucrats keep both the correspondence they receive and the replies they send. This means that if the document you want is not in the archive holding the papers of the sender it may be in the archive holding the papers of the receiver. For instance, the Australian Commonwealth Censor corresponded irregularly with the authorities in charge of censorship in the states and some of that correspondence was found in state archives.
- People who work for institutions often keep their own records, so documentation missing from the institutional archive may turn up in personal archives. So, Stanley Hawes' papers were able to shed light on the history of the Commonwealth Film Unit, and Professor Alan Stout's papers were able to contribute to a study of the Australian National Film Board. It is not always obvious where such collections of personal papers may be found: the Hawes papers are in ScreenSound Australia while the Stout papers are in the National Library of Australia.

7.2 Non-written forms of material culture

In defending historians against charges of 'a fetishism of documents', Marwick (1993) defines historical evidence very broadly, under thirteen headings which include non-written sources such as 'media of communication and artefacts of popular culture', and 'archaeology, industrial archaeology, history-on-the ground and physical artefacts'. For a sociologist, observation of non-written forms of material culture is recognised as a useful 'unobtrusive' or 'non-reactive' research method (Webb et al. 1966/1981).

Like documentation, all material culture has two aspects:

- a material aspect: artefacts have a physical existence, while behaviours and processes leave physical traces;
- a discursive aspect: artefacts, and the traces left behind by behaviours and processes, can be interpreted.

Webb et al. (1966: 2) list examples such as the rate of wear on floor tiles in a museum indicating the popularity of exhibits, or the rate of library withdrawals being a measure of the impact of the introduction of television to a community. Hodder (2000: 705) provides further examples:

> Shortcuts across lawns indicate preferred traffic patterns, foreign-language signs indicate the degree of integration of a neighbourhood, the number of cigarettes in an ashtray betrays a nervous tension, and the amount of paperwork in an 'in' tray is a measure of workload or of work efficiency and priority.

The audiovisual media may be used in this process by the visual sociologist (Dabbs 1982; Harper 2000), who studies current social processes either by recording them in photography, video and film, or by analysing already existing data: store windows, family photographs, current television or radio programmes.

A cultural studies researcher (Frow and Morris 2000) may be interested in similar forms of media, with the addition of newspapers and of sound (radio or popular music): their interest is in material elements of a culture, which may be studied as they now are or as they were in the past.

The media historian is interested in the materials produced within media institutions (such as radio and television broadcasts, film and video and television productions, newspapers and journals), or in the physical contexts for media (for instance cinema buildings). These might be studied either as evidence of the history of media institutions, or as evidence of how the media contribute more generally to social or cultural history.

The goals of these researchers are different, but their preferred data and the means of obtaining it are often similar. Again, the reference lists in books and articles on your subject can provide a starting place for tracing collections of material culture, or ideas for gathering your own records.

As with documentation, the first source is libraries and audiovisual archives: the process of locating and using these was included in the discussion of documentation archives (see the first sub-section of section 7.1 in this chapter). Audiovisual archives provide materials for many different kinds of research:

- A study of the operations of an institution, such as a radio or television station, or a film production company, may require the study of its products (radio or television programmes, or films).

- A study of funding or regulatory bodies (such as censorship boards, or government funding agencies) may require research into the audiovisual productions about which such institutions are making decisions.
- Audiovisual archives may also hold scripts, lodged with the product. These can be useful in tracing changes that occurred during the production process.

The technology used for making and presenting programmes (cameras, projectors, sound recording apparatus) may also be relevant, and may take a researcher to museums and specialist collections (public and private).

7.3 Oral sources

'Oral tradition' includes stories, riddles, songs, proverbs, legends – everything passed down by word of mouth from one generation to the next. From the middle of the twentieth century, attempts have been made to codify practices of collection and interpretation (for instance Vansina 1965). Oral traditions may also be written down – in fact there is a whole branch of history constructed around the content and process of this tradition, not only in pre-literate cultures, but also in those areas of literate societies which do not produce many written records (children, under-classes, transient populations: see for instance Factor 1988).

Then there are those oral sources constructed for this particular research project. The usual forms of (structured and unstructured) interviewing common in sociological research (see the third sub-section of section 4.3 in Chapter 4), and the 'life history' interview familiar in ethnography can also be applied within institutional contexts (Heritage 1997; Tierney 2000). Ethnographers at first collected 'life histories' in order to 'illuminate cultural, historical, and social facts rather than individual lives or aspects of personality' (Tedlock 2000: 459), but over the years they have become interested also in the particular stories of individuals, regardless of how representative these might be. A specialised form is the *testimonio*, which starts out as an interview, but ends as a personal statement by the interviewee (Beverley 2000; Randall 1985; Tierney 2000). These sociological methods are coming ever closer to the historian's 'personal testimony' (sometimes called oral history) interviews, such that the terms seem to be interchangeable.

In institutional research, personal testimony has the advantages that it:

- adds a human dimension to the written records discussed in the first sub-section of section 7.1 in this chapter: what appears on the written record as a simple decision may in fact have been fiercely debated;
- allows people at all levels within an institution to have a voice, not just those decision makers whose names appear on the written record;
- allows people to speak for themselves, and to reflect at leisure and with hindsight on their actions and decisions.

The disadvantages are:

- Eyewitness testimony is often assumed to be indisputable. However, the value of oral sources depends on the reliability of memory, which varies with age and with mental alertness, and memory is in any case always selective and likely to have reshaped events.
- The research may be skewed by the selection of the people to be interviewed, and this can occur, perhaps without the researcher being aware of it, because of the availability of people to give testimony, which is often serendipitous – those who have survived, and who are still living close enough to be interviewed.
- It is easy to forget that interview transcripts should be read as texts, interpreted rather than taken at face value as expressions of 'the truth'.

Selecting research subjects

Because every interview subject is unique, it is never intended to 'prove' a hypothesis through oral history interviews. But there *is* usually an intention to understand broader phenomena by exploring individual experience(s), and in this sense the people interviewed are being considered as a sample of a larger population. Clearly probability sampling is inappropriate in such circumstances, but the various kinds of non-probability sampling (see the second subsection of section 4.2 in Chapter 4) should be carefully considered, to determine which is more relevant in your case.

Most oral history interviewees are selected purposively, usually because (on the basis of earlier experience or on the recommendation of others) the subject is judged to have a valuable story to tell. The most likely method of selection is convenience sampling, or a form of snowballing, finding new interview subjects by asking each interviewee to suggest who else might have similar or comparable or related experience. For institutional research, this allows you to tap into the intellectual or commercial or industrial or administrative networks, which may be part of the institution that you are studying.

Chris Watson (personal email 14 November 2001) describes how he found informants for his research on early films in the country areas of New Zealand:

> I tracked down surviving players in small towns by checking the credits against the telephone directory. It helps if it is a rare name. I got the son of the man whose taxis were credited in one of the 'Community Comedies'. And he had a wealth of family anecdotes about the production. In Nelson I found the villain from another of the comedies was still alive (at 90+) and still drinking whiskey and smoking (he said he had 'given up' women).

This process could be called convenience sampling, though at the time it probably just felt like common sense.

The comments on sample size in the first sub-section of section 4.2 in Chapter 4 still apply. The results of oral history are never intended to be predictive, and are only presumed to be transferable within very broad parameters, so there are no rules on the size of the sample: in some cases, a large sample will be wise, and in others a single case is sufficient and illuminating.

Interviewing

Like all interviewing, oral history interviewing is purposive conversation. It is usually conducted with an individual, though group interviews are possible. It is usually somewhere between a totally unstructured interview and a general interview guide approach. The basic advice about interviewing (given in the third sub-section of section 4.3 in Chapter 4) still applies, with some refinements specific to this type of interview.

- Preparation is essential:
  - Read all you can about both the context of the interview (the general historical period or subject) and about the individual being interviewed. For instance, if the interviewee was a censor you should know in advance of the interview what were the dates of her appointment to the Censorship Board, positions and responsibilities held over the course of the appointment, date of leaving.
  - Prepare a background paper from available information. If you are taking a life history, then the best background is a family tree; if you are interviewing about only a part of the person's life (say their association with an institution you are researching), the best background will list dates of the phases the institution has gone through (for instance, the dates of appointment for all chief censors over the history of the Censorship Board).
  - Prepare a list of questions. If this interview is one of a series, it is helpful to have a basic question checklist, which you can adapt to the specific person being interviewed.
- Select an appropriate recording medium and follow the technical advice given in the third sub-section of section 4.3.
- When you first contact your subject(s), explain the project and the interview process, describe the type of consent required and the use to which the interview will be put. If time allows, arrange for a brief pre-interview, to meet your subject and to check background. Do not be too thorough in this pre-interview, or you will find that the real interview has lost its spark: subjects are inclined to remember what they said the first time and either to provide an abbreviated version on the record or simply not mention things at all as they think they have already said them.
- It is usually preferable to interview the subject in their own environment (home or place of work), where they feel at ease. If this is not possible,

suggest a neutral place, but with sufficient privacy: cafes are noisy, and university campuses are intimidating to people who have not had experience of them before. No matter what the location, check out its suitability beforehand.

- When you arrive for the first recording session, check that all equipment is working well. Be prepared to control extraneous noise: to close doors or windows, take phones off the hook, stop noisy clocks.
- Begin with one or two simple questions, previously agreed to, to allow everyone time to settle down into the interview situation. That might be the general question(s) 'Where and when were you born?' or it might be more specific to the research project, such as 'Where were you working before you became a censor?'
- The primary purpose of the background notes and the question list is to make sure you are fully prepared. Once the interview actually starts, you may not need to consult them again at all. Throughout the interview, your role is to encourage the interviewee to tell their own story, perhaps asking the subject to clarify something, but never offering your own opinion.
- Time may need to be carefully monitored: keep your eye on the clock, and have a clear idea of what areas you wish to cover, so you can intervene to direct the conversation.
- Conversations have their own rhythm, even if you have no time limit. Recognise when it is time to stop, and be prepared to continue at a later date if you consider there is more to be covered. Having a second session allows you time to think about what has been said already and to adapt your questions to incorporate the new knowledge.
- In general, it is unwise to interrupt the subject in mid-flight, but once a natural pause occurs do not be afraid to ask for further clarification of something, or to return to an aspect that you feel has been insufficiently addressed.
- Do not try to take notes during the conversation: however, do have a notebook and pencil at hand, and, when the subject uses an unfamiliar name or place or term, jot down how it sounds to you. After the recording is finished for the day, but before you leave, clarify these names and terms with the interviewee, to minimise the checking you would otherwise have to do at the transcription stage.
- When the subject uses gesture or body language, clarify it for the tape by a verbal comment. For instance:

  Interviewee: The room was about the size of this one …
  Interviewer: About 6 metres square? …
  Interviewee: With a window there and there (pointing)
  Interviewer: In the centre of the south wall and the west wall?

- Always end the session by thanking the interviewee, and always send a written acknowledgment and thanks a few days after your final meeting.

Normally, a single interviewer would speak to a single interviewee, but there are occasions when the same principles might be applied to a group conversation.

For instance, a researcher wishing to speak to past and present members about the history of an association might speak to individuals (to obtain information uncontaminated by the memories of others), or to past members in a group and present members in another group (to allow interaction within each group but not between the two groups), or to a group consisting of both past and present members (so allowing interaction between the groups). Ideally, given enough time and resources, a researcher might try all of the above, probably in the order listed.

Much of what has already been said about focus groups then applies. You will need a note taker, and you should also:

- limit the size of any group to maximise opportunity for discussion;
- take care with the recording apparatus, to ensure all participants are audible on the tape;
- listen carefully, monitor discussion and be prepared to intervene if it gets off track or too heated;
- ensure that everyone has an opportunity to speak;
- verbalise gestures for the sake of the tape.

7.4 Observation and participant observation

Observation is not simply looking – it is looking purposefully (see section 4.4 in Chapter 4). Observation provides a key form of data for sociologists and ethnographers: the method was first developed within a positivist framework, but is now applied much more widely than this (see Angrosino and Perez 2000). Marwick (1993) reminds us that 'observed behaviour, surviving customs, technical processes, etc.' are also valuable sources for historians.

Traditional ethnography has generated a number of positions for the researcher as observer in relation to the subjects of the research (Gold 1958; see also section 4.4 in Chapter 4 of this book). The debate about whether the ethnographic researcher could or should be 'inside' or 'outside' continues (for instance, Miller and Glassner 1997): positivists still seek objectivity, while non-positivists assert that 'the colonial concept of the subject (the object of the observer's gaze) is no longer appropriate' (Denzin and Lincoln 2000: 634).

Though there are ways of observing institutions unobtrusively from the outside, this is difficult in the case of the media: in institutional media research, the most common kind of observation is 'participant observation'. This means that the researcher is directly involved in the social practices of the institution being studied. Though this method is difficult and time-consuming, it also has great advantages:

- Social interaction is best observed in the social setting in which the behaviour would normally occur, rather than in the controlled environment of an experiment or survey.
- Rich and varied data can be obtained, making possible 'thick description' (Geertz 1973; see section 4.4).
- It is possible to gain access to participants' own understandings of the situation, in their own words.

Because participant observation involves working 'in the field' – that is, inside the social situation under study – it is sometimes equated with '**field research**'. This can be misleading, as 'participant observation' rarely occurs in isolation: it may be backed up with document analysis, interviews with other participants, and possibly questionnaires and surveys, in which case, it may well be described as a 'case study' (see Stake 2000). For a more detailed description of field research, try Burgess (1993), or Bailey (1996): we will discuss participant observation as just one technique available to a field researcher.

One area of media research which often involves participant observation is studies of the production process, in which the researcher was attached to the production team of a film or television or radio program. However, our focus for this part of the book is on censorship, so our example will concern film censorship. You might, for instance, be researching the effectiveness of the censorship classification system in excluding the attendance of under-age children from restricted classification films. Among several ways of tackling this, you might start by simply observing the patrons lining up at the ticket booth, and watching how they interact with the ticket seller. You would need the management's permission to hang around in the foyer, or you may find yourself ejected as a nuisance! However, such informal observation might well help you decide whether there is a real question at issue here: perhaps attempts to deceive are so rare that researching them would be pointless.

If you decide that the issue is sufficiently alive to warrant further exploration, you might wish to study it from inside the institution which is required to enforce the regulations – the cinema. When you explain your project to the management, you may even find they are really interested in the research: they may wish to know how frequently patrons try to bend the rules, or how willing staff members are to allow patrons leeway. The management may be sufficiently interested to pay you to do the research, or at least to provide you with access and facilities. This would take you from simple observation to participant observation: you might be allowed to observe the ticket sellers at work (either directly or by video- or audiotaping them), or you might even be given a temporary position as a casual employee in the ticket box. You might also decide to interview other ticket sellers (about their practices), or the cinema management (about their policy, and how they implement it). You might distribute a questionnaire to patrons, or arrange focus group interviews with groups of parents and with groups of children or teenagers. Participant observation then becomes just one tool in a complex of research strategies.

Of Gold's four categories of roles for the researcher in the field (Gold 1958), the two that we are concerned with here are the complete participant, and the participant-as-observer. Covert research, as a complete participant, is no longer acceptable within most ethical frameworks (see section 1.5 in Chapter 1), and is unlikely to be approved by your supervisors.

You are more likely to be a participant observer, engaged in overt research:

- There may still be problems of initial access to the institution, but once these are overcome the researcher is free to move around inside it, without subterfuge, and so with more likelihood of obtaining access to a wider range of information (requesting an interview with the manager, for instance).
- There is little chance of the researcher becoming so caught up in the situation as to lose sight of the original intention or to compromise the research process. Early ethnographers particularly feared the possibility of 'going native', but immersing oneself in the culture being studied is now more likely to be considered favourably (Tedlock 2000: 457).
- There are still ethical problems. The researcher may have difficulty avoiding taking sides in any conflict situation arising within the group being studied, and there is still the question of the rights of the people being observed, and of the institution itself (in this case the cinema management) over the final report and publication.

In practice, the role of the researcher may shift among the various categories of observation, and it certainly changes over time, as professional and personal relationships develop between the researcher and people in the institution being studied.

As well as the issue of whether the research should be overt or covert, there are other problems of participant observation. From a positivist or post-positivist position, the problems are:

- If the researcher is already (before the research begins) an integral part of the situation under observation (already employed at the cinema, for instance), objectivity is difficult.
- If the researcher enters the situation for the sake of the research, he or she may not be familiar enough with the situation to understand fully what is going on.
- The presence of a researcher within a situation may subtly alter the situation, compromising the data gathered.
- Audio- or videotaping, or taking notes during the observation, can be intrusive: the people being observed may object, or may change their behaviour as a result of being aware of being observed. Taking notes after the observation, even immediately after, may not adequately record what happened, and may be skewed by the researcher's own experience or bias.

- Audio- and videotaping are difficult and time-consuming to analyse, but are relatively objective. Notes are easier to analyse, but are subjective, possibly skewed by the researcher's own experience or bias.

From a non-positivist position, objectivity and bias are not of the same concern, but serious problems remain:

- Like other oral testimony, the information obtained during interviews with participants is not objective truth, but the expression of a point of view, which complicates analysis and interpretation.
- There are always issues of the comparative status of the researcher and the people within the situation under study. Even if the researcher and the research subjects are of similar gender, marital status, age, religion and social status, the researcher is still always in the position of asking for information and the subject of providing it.

Finally, it is possible that the relationship between the researcher and the host institution (or individuals within it) may sour. This can lead to problems in finalising the research or in presenting the report, or even – in extreme cases – physical danger to the researcher (for examples see Punch 1994: 85).

These problems do not invalidate the method: they just require caution in gathering data, and even greater care during analysis and interpretation. This is one method that cannot be broken up into sequential stages: everything seems to be happening at once, but, despite this, you will need to think about each one separately, as we do here (continuing to use our example of a study of under-age children's access to restricted-classification films):

- Choose your question or area of interest. As well as the general principles outlined in Chapter 2, for participant observation you need to take into account how easy it will be to obtain access to the social situation you wish to study.
- Start keeping a diary. The first entry should be your basic question, a set of goals derived from this question, and your reasoning in reaching these. This will help you when the exigencies of the research start to squeeze, and you find it necessary to amend some of your original plans. Your diary will help you to constantly monitor what you are doing, locate what is fundamental and what is peripheral, what can be adjusted without doing violence to your original intention and what will require a complete rethink of your priorities and goals. You will continue to use it throughout the research, recording both what happens (and your reflections on this) and what you feel and think (and how these feelings and ideas change). The more often you record in your diary, the more useful it may turn out to be. Examples of a rather more attenuated approach to keeping a diary are provided in Silverman (2000: Chapter 2).

- Obtain access to the situation. In the narrow sense, this happens as you enter any field of research, but 'access' more broadly defined is also something which is constantly negotiated and renegotiated as your research proceeds. You will find that some people understand the institution better than others, and may control the flow of information and the circulation of instructions within it. These are called 'gate keepers' (cf. the use of this term in relation to news, in Chapter 9), and you will have to come to a (formal or informal) understanding with them before you can fully negotiate your way around the situation (Punch 1994: 86–7). In our example, the cinema manager, the head ticket seller, and the union representative may all be serving as gate keepers.
- Establish your definitions:
  - of the institution, its activities, personnel, the period which your research will cover, the special issues which your research will concentrate upon;
  - of your own place within the institution, your relation to the activities and personnel, how long you will be there and how this relates to the period under study, any special interest you have in the issues under study;
  - of the terms to be applied during your research.
- Consider the ethical issues: When and how will research subjects be informed of the observation? Will you use an informed consent form? What rights will research subjects have over the form of the final report?
- Decide on your approach to the observation:
  - Will your recording be continuous or intermittent?
  - Will you record everything or be selective? If selective, on what principles of selection?
- Decide on your method of recording – video, audio, notes, checklists? Checklists will probably be useful in this case, either to supplement video or audio recording, or to replace it if it is not available, as they can be marked quickly and with minimal interference with your regular work. Miles and Huberman (1994: Chapter 4) give good advice on different forms of recording, such as contact summary sheets, category cards, etc.
- Prepare:
  - Familiarise yourself with the setting, make drawings or take photographs.
  - Familiarise yourself with what is expected of a person in the role you will be taking within this setting (this includes language, dress, ways of behaving, ways of relating to others in the situation).
  - Practise taking notes in other situations, and (if possible) perform a 'trial' observation in the field.
  - Test your approach. For instance, develop shorthand codes for note taking, and a checklist which will provide all the categories which you will later need for analysis. Test the scales and ratings that you intend to use for the analysis.
  - Test any equipment.

At the same time expect that anything that can go wrong will go wrong, so be prepared also to be flexible, to adjust your expectations and your behaviour as you go along.

- Observe and record, by the method(s) chosen.

  Formal observation, in systematic fieldnotes, will cover those areas of the observation that you already anticipate will be relevant to your analysis. Some useful headings for such notes are:
  - setting (spaces, appearance, activities, sounds);
  - actors (appearance, behaviour, speech: in this case the dress and demeanour of young patrons, and what they say to each other and to you which may indicate their age);
  - context (time(s), occasion(s) ...)

  Because these notes are systematic, they are easily comparable, allowing you to more carefully monitor changes in the situation.

  Your diary notes are different – less systematic, less easily comparable across time. However, these are likely to throw up the unexpected, and perhaps allow you to adjust later observation to take this into account.

  In any observation situation, there is an optimum time, after which your attention begins to wander and your recall to blur: work this out by trial and error. Every researcher and situation is different, but most people find that about three hours is as much as they can profitably do before weariness begins to affect concentration. The more detail you need to remember for recording after the session, the shorter the period of the session needs to be.

- Reflect on your experience. At the end of every observation session, record (probably in your diary) what you felt about it:
  - general observations ('I was too rushed between 10 a.m. and 10.15 a.m. to complete the forms adequately, so I completed them in green after the rush had passed');
  - reflective memos ('A is the most generally popular X-rated movie at the moment but it is B which seems to be drawing more younger viewers');
  - focusing questions ('Do parents prefer to take children to animated films? Do they think these will be "safer"? Do I place undue weight on makeup in determining age?');
  - theoretical development (Parents' definitions of 'childhood'? What studies have been done on peer pressure?).

- Leave the field.
  - Time the exit: If the research proceeds to its logical end (you reach your planned goal, or decide that you are no longer learning anything new), this is not a problem. But there are circumstances which call for you to leave early: certainly leave if you are at physical or psychological risk, or if the people in the situation you are researching make it clear that you are no longer welcome there.
  - Ensure you have fulfilled all obligations to people in the field. Ideally, you wish not to compromise the chances of other researchers entering this situation, or of you yourself returning to it.

- Give plenty of warning, and extricate yourself with as little disruption as possible both to you and to the people remaining.

Analysis and interpretation will inevitably happen as you gather data: you will be reflecting upon the data and devising categories for analysis, and this will then be incorporated into further data gathering. Miles and Huberman (1994) discuss this process usefully: they also provide models of data displays that can present your information visually.

7.5 Conclusion

The most common sources of data on institutions are documents or observation. Though historians are more familiar with documents and social scientists with observation there is no reason why each could not use either. Researchers from a media studies or cultural studies background are used to using both in the same project.

In all cases the keys to selecting your methodology will be the question you are seeking to answer and the intellectual framework within which you are working. In the next chapter we consider how the different intellectual frameworks analyse and interpret their data on institutions differently.

CHAPTER 8

Institutional Research – Analysis and Interpretation

In this chapter we discuss analysis (systematising) before interpretation (relating to a broader framework), acknowledging that these phases are actually interdependent.

8.1 Analysis

Your institutional research may produce some survey data, in which case the advice on statistics given in the first sub-section of section 5.1 in Chapter 5 may be useful, and there may be reason to use textual analysis on media productions, in which case the advice given in Chapter 10 (on content analysis, semiotic analysis and discourse analysis) may be useful. Startt and Sloan (1989: 57–62) provide a useful general discussion of 'quantification in history', but most institutional research produces qualitative data, so that is where we will concentrate for the rest of this chapter.

Material culture: documents and artefacts

There have been attempts to develop a theory of material culture (Hodder 2000: 706–9), but we consider it is more useful to apply already-developed analytic processes to artefacts. So, semiotics can provide a way to read an artefact as a sign within a context of signification (see the third sub-section of section 10.1 in Chapter 10). Written documents are also discourses, which can be subjected to content analysis, semiotic analysis or discourse analysis (see the second sub-section of section 10.2). Cognitive psychology can provide a way to understand the social processes in play when a person uses material culture (see, for instance, Berger et al. 1986). Analysing financial documents may require a knowledge of accountancy procedures: try Battistuta and Duncan (1998) for an introduction to the sort of skills you may need.

In all cases, documents must not be read as transparent records of the activities, finances and organisation of an institution. Rather they are representations of how the institution (and the people who work within it) wishes to present itself to the reader of the document: they use stylistic conventions (such as the layout templates required for financial statements) and formal language (often only completely accessible to the trained person).

The analysis of documents is at the heart of much debate about what 'history' is and does. However, with some exceptions (for instance Jenkins 1997, discussed below), there is general agreement about some methodological principles:

- The nearer your evidence is to the original person or event, the more valuable it is likely to be. At the same time, the status of a source is relative to the question being asked: a television programme such as *The Civil War* (USA 1991, dir. Ken Burns) must be considered a secondary source (one of many possible interpretations) on the history of the American Civil War, but at the same time a primary source (direct evidence) for how television programmes conceptualise that history.
- All evidence should be subjected to rigorous examination, both to establish its authenticity (by 'external criticism'), and to evaluate its credibility (by 'internal criticism'). The terms 'authenticity' and 'credibility' are used rather differently by post-positivists in the evaluation of the end product of the research (see the third sub-section of section 12.2 in Chapter 12).

External criticism

This requires the following three elements.

Identification

Sometimes it is immediately obvious what a document is, but more often the source and function may not be immediately obvious – names and dates have been omitted or are indecipherable, or the writer has deliberately disguised herself under a pseudonym or by changing her writing style. You identify the document and its writer by comparison with other similar documents, testing signatures and writing styles, checking that dates match what you already know, tracing references to this document in other documents.

Sequencing

In institutional research, you commonly have large numbers of documents of different kinds and different dates. Sometimes the sequence of these is obvious, as with annual reports. However, it is also important to retain the order in which you find documents, even if this appears totally random. You can better understand a drawer full of pieces of paper if you first list them in the order they appear in the drawer, then reorganise this list sequentially (perhaps chronologically). By comparing the two lists, you might find relations between adjacent pieces of paper that are not chronological, but thematic.

Intertextuality
Each document exists in relation to other documents. These relations may be:

- thematic (concerning the same or similar issues within the organisation);
- chronological (preceding or following other documents);
- generic (of the same or similar format);
- organisational (emanating from the same or a similar person(s) or section(s) within the organisation);
- functional (having the same or similar purpose);
- hierarchical (dependent upon one another).

You may find conflicting versions of events in different sources: Sue Harper (personal email 22 August 2001) describes such contradictory information about films of the 1950s in the records of the British Treasury, the Board of Trade, and the National Film Finance Council, all in the Public Record Office at Kew. When this happens, you need to decide whether you will try to work out a 'correct' version (the positivist or post-positivist position), or concentrate on understanding how and why such a contradiction can arise (the non-positivist position).

Internal criticism

This involves looking more and more closely at the document itself, considering the following two elements.

Authorship
Some writers acknowledge authorship: other documents appear without individual attribution. You need to consider whether a consistent authorial 'voice' (whether or not identified by the first person 'I' or 'we') represents the whole institution or individuals or sections within it. If there is no consistent authorial voice, then it may be possible to organise documents according to the separate 'voices' represented within them. Next, you ask questions about trustworthiness: Was the writer in a position to know what is being claimed? What sources might the writer have drawn upon to produce the document? Did the writer have any personal stake in what is being discussed?

Remember that even if you decide the signature is a forgery, and the document is not what it claims to be, it can still be a useful source, so long as it is read within a new context.

Readership
Each document is addressed to a reader (Seymour Chatman's 'implied reader', see the second sub-section of section 10.2 in Chapter 10). The language can be clearly aimed at the general public or at others within the culture which

produced the document, or it may be specific to the circumstances or to the time when it was written. You can examine the document rhetorically, establishing that it is aimed at recording, persuading, justifying, etc. You might subject it to content analysis or semiotic analysis or discourse analysis, if these are appropriate – making a shift towards interpretation.

Street (2000) offers a rather different model for document analysis: she proposes considering every document under the headings of 'type', 'authorship', 'agency', 'context', 'impact', 'archival scheme' and 'interpretive significance' and provides examples of such use. For further discussion of the analysis of historical documents, and practical examples, see Atkinson and Coffey (1997: 55–60) and Startt and Sloan (1989: Chapter 6).

In practice, most researchers do not follow the rather rigid protocols laid out above. When you enter a new field of enquiry you start out being very careful, until you begin to have a feel for the evidence: you come to recognise institutional structures in operation, recurring formats within the documentation, the signature and writing style of the key players. Gradually, you come to have confidence in your own capacity to 'read' the materials: you acknowledge the possibility of fraud, forgery, or deliberate deception, but you do not expect to find it. You will occasionally be brought up short by a conviction that something is not quite what it claims to be: however, you are unlikely to be able to 'prove' this. Very rarely, uncovering the deception becomes the centre of the enquiry: Medick (1997) describes how he was at first taken in by the 'so-called Laichingen Hunger Chronicle', which circulated in printed form for many years as a document authenticated by rigorous historiographical procedures, and the processes by which he eventually came to demonstrate that this was actually a forgery.

Historians are aware of the incompleteness and fallibility of historical evidence. Good historians will, therefore, always phrase their document analysis tentatively, using those irritating but necessary qualifiers – 'probably', 'possibly', 'perhaps'. They will also always include the evidence that does not support the present tentative conclusions.

All historians, whatever their interpretive framework, use some version of the above process of analysis of documents. Where they disagree, sometimes quite substantially, is on the status of the results. For the positivist or post-positivist, what they find by document analysis is the facts of history, the building blocks with which to construct interpretations. Researchers within other intellectual frameworks, particularly since the linguistic turn in interpretation discussed in the first sub-section of section 8.2 below, seek rather to increase understanding, find new ways to look at the evidence, create different (perhaps even conflicting) constructions.

Oral sources

The oral traditions you collect (songs, stories, etc) are primary sources for a study of oral tradition, for instance for a history of story-telling within a particular community. In a non-literate culture (or a non-literate section of a literate culture – young children, for instance), you may also wish to use them as evidence for the social structures represented within them (for instance, playground rhymes as evidence of family structures and relationships).

If you come across, for instance, a story circulating within an institution, about a particular person or event, you are likely to find interesting variations of this as it is told by different people. There is a whole research tradition based on this oral process, drawing upon Vladimir Propp's (1975) analysis of the Russian folktale. In considering variations in the oral tradition:

- A positivist or post-positivist might compare variants of the story against each other and against other sources, in an effort to find the 'truth' (and to assign to conclusions a particular degree of trustworthiness).
- A constructivist might examine the variants as evidence of the process of communication within the institution, teasing out who told whom, with no expectation of finding 'truth'.
- A post-structuralist might examine the story as discourse, looking for internal evidence of how it constructs a particular position for the author and the 'reader'.

Oral history interviews must be treated with just as much care as oral tradition. Sue Harper (personal email 22 October 2001) reminds:

> ... with oral testimony one needs to develop a sensitivity to 'paralinguistics' – the silences, the coughs, the yawns – which say a lot. And the tone and timbre of the voice ... There is often a secret text which lurks beneath the seemingly straight-forward word ...

The transcripts of oral history interviews must, therefore, be analysed like any other text (see the second sub-section of section 5.1 in Chapter 5).

Fieldwork data

Fieldwork produces complex data, and requires that the processing of the data occur simultaneously with its gathering, so that the research adapts to what is discovered along the way. Your fieldwork on institutions may well produce interviews, observation records (written, audiotaped or videotaped), field notes (including reflections on the process as well as on the information gathered), and documents – and each of these will require a different kind of analysis. Analysis of interview transcripts is discussed in the second sub-section of section 5.1 in Chapter 5, document analysis is discussed in the first sub-section of section 8.1 above (also Catterell and Jones 1994), and the analysis of videotapes and audiotapes in the second sub-section of section 5.1 in Chapter 5 and in Chapter 10.

Fieldwork notes have already been filtered through your own consciousness, so you need to think of them as representations, affected by your own ideological position(s) and the exigencies of the situation. To analyse your notes, you reduce the quantity of data, and find the patterns within it, which can lead to explanations: Lindlof (1995: 219–43) gives detailed advice about this process. You can try using computer-assisted data analysis, but be careful: the danger still exists of the self-fulfilling prophecy if you search for code words of your choice in a text that you, yourself, have generated.

The kind of 'thick description' that results from sociological fieldwork (or historical research) does not lend itself comfortably to empiricist views of scientific research: it is not easily replicable, validity and reliability are almost impossible to establish, and it is never predictive (see the second and third sub-sections of section 12.2 in Chapter 12). However, attempts have been made to fit these kinds of research into explanatory frameworks that can claim scientific value. Two of the social scientific methods used for doing this are analytic induction and grounded theory.

Analytic induction

Burgess (1984: 179, after Robinson 1951: 813) identifies the main steps in analytic induction as 'defining the phenomenon'; offering a hypothetical explanation; studying one case; reformulating the hypothesis or redefining the phenomenon if that case does not fit; repeating this process 'until a universal relationship is established'. It is a method that has limited application within audience research, which commonly produces large amounts of data (more suitable to deductive analysis), or is based on single cases or small numbers of cases, insufficient to sustain analytic induction. However, this method *can* be useful with research on institutions, when an optimum number of cases has been examined – for instance, if all the journalists in a large television newsroom have been interviewed.

Grounded theory

A specific application of analytic induction is 'grounded theory', a term devised by Glaser and Strauss (1967). The first stage is to compare incidences to establish initial categories and to decide what theoretical properties these possess. Then these categories are refined by further comparisons, gradually reducing the range until the theory is well-grounded. Though Glaser and Strauss initially denied the possibility of establishing prescriptive rules for qualitative research, Strauss later set out 'guidelines and rules of thumb' (Strauss 1987: 8), based on the principles of induction, **deduction** and verification that underlie qualitative research that aims for validity.

Grounded theory has been widely applied in the social sciences, sustaining a rich literature. In recent years, Anselm Strauss has worked with Juliet Corbin

(Strauss and Corbin 1990, 1998), while Barney Glaser has worked alone, both continuing his own interest in grounded theory (Glaser 1994), and challenging the interpretations of Strauss and Corbin (Glaser 1992).

There has also been considerable criticism of the method, but for beginning researchers the main argument against grounded theory is that once you start using it (or, for that matter, any form of analytic induction), you are beginning to interpret as well as to analyse, and the interpretive framework applied by the founders of grounded theory was positivism. It is precisely the tentative efforts of Strauss and Corbin to shift towards a post-positivist position that underlie their disagreements with Glaser. But there are also efforts to realign grounded theory completely, to fit it within a constructivist framework. This requires ethnographers to 'change our conception of [social life] from a real world to be discovered, tracked, and categorized to a world *made real* in the minds and through the words and actions of its members' (Charmaz 2000: 523, her emphasis).

8.2 Interpretation

Neither the sociologist's 'data', nor the historian's 'evidence' ever 'speaks for itself'. The interpretive frames commonly applied in institutional research are those of history and historiography for evidence from the past, those concerned with the politics and sociology of organisations for data from the present.

History and historiography

You are an historian if you do what historians do – regardless of your academic location (or lack of one), and what historians do is to research and write about history. 'History' has been variously defined as the events of the past, independent of the writing about them, and as the writing about the past, independent of the events being written about. 'Historiography' is the practice of the writing of 'history': it is what historians *do*, rather than what they *produce*. Historiography and the philosophy of history both have long and complex histories themselves: the traditional version is provided in general texts such as Nash (1969), and a more adventurous approach is offered by White (1973, 1987).

Following Nash, there have been, broadly speaking, in past centuries two powerful schools of historical thought. The idealist view approaches the past through broad speculations, seeking the pattern(s) of history, developing theories which are then tested against experience, or reaching generalisations by inductive processes. Induction starts with a single case, compares it with another case and another and so on till it builds towards a probability statement about the world. This is the older of the two early historiographical approaches, and in comparatively recent times it is represented by Benedetto Croce (1866–1952).

The scientific view of history develops an understanding of past events by the systematic study of the 'evidence' they leave behind. Generalisations are reached about this data by deduction, which is the process of applying the rules of logic to data in order to make statements about the world from which the data was extracted. Scientific history is a comparatively recent concept, starting with the German historian Leopold von Ranke (1795–1886), and developed in the 19th century by historians who established the facts by 'source-criticism', then connected these into general explanations, even to predictive theories. In this they were encouraged by Comte's arguments (see the fourth sub-section of section 1.1 in Chapter 1) that all knowledge is fundamentally similar, passing through three stages (theological, metaphysical, scientific). Marx (see the second sub-section of section 5.2 in Chapter 5) proposed such a scientific theory of history, with a predictive capacity, and from a very different political perspective Elton (1967) claimed that the objective facts of the past are knowable and can be interpreted. This is an empiricist/positivist view of the world – one which aims to observe the world and apply logic to the data so gathered.

Empiricism has become associated with '**historicism**', a term that at first referred simply to the interpretation of human experience through the concept of historical change, but became contentious from the middle decades of the 20th century, with the writings of Karl Popper (1902–1994). Popper defined historicism as 'an approach to the social sciences which assumes that *historical prediction* is their principal aim, and which assumes that this aim is attainable by discovering the "rhythms" or the "patterns", the "laws" or the "trends" that underlie the evolution of history' (Popper 1957: 3). He proposed that such claims both misrepresented science, which was never as determinist as this suggested, and misunderstood the operations of the social world, which always contained unique and unpredictable elements. More recently still, the term 'historicism' has been applied to the study of the past for the benefit of the present: it therefore may imply either criticism (from those who insist that the past must be understood 'in its own terms' and 'for its own sake') or praise (from those who claim that the only function of history is to assist us to learn from the past).

Though individual historians are inclined to speak as if these arguments have already been settled (in favour of their own particular brand of history), the debate continues. Till relatively recently, historical methodology was generally understood to consist of a choice between the relativism of Carr (1961) and the objectivity of Elton (1967). In the latter half of the 20th century, most of that general understanding of what history is, and how historians can or should operate, was fundamentally challenged by an intellectual climate that included post-structuralism and post-modernism, sometimes called the 'linguistic turn' (Iggers 1993: 34). Jenkins (1997), for instance, challenges the simplistic reading of Carr and Elton, and at the same time rejects these writers as effective representatives of the dominant schools of historiography: he proposes that Richard Rorty and Hayden White provide more useful models for contemporary historians.

Most historians would still agree with Marcus and Fischer that:

> The only way to an accurate view and confident knowledge of the world is through a sophisticated epistemology that takes full account of intractable contradiction, paradox, irony, and uncertainty in the explanation of human activities. (1986: 14–15)

The problem is how to achieve this ideal. Post-positivist historians accept that individual 'facts' (like names and dates) can be known, but may call this mere 'chronicle': for them, true 'history' seeks to understand the facts in context, to appreciate the 'how' and 'why' as well as the 'what' and 'when'. Constructivist historians insist that all knowledge is position-dependent, constructed, and fundamentally ideological.

The core of the problem is still to identify the relationship between historical facts (however defined) and historical interpretations (the generalisations, explanations or narratives that historians construct from the evidence). Many historians now place the emphasis on the interpretation rather than on the evidence, and therefore on the way history is written (on forms of historical explanation and on ways of presenting historical information) rather than on the events themselves.

Because history concerns change over time, it is not surprising that chronological narrative is still the most common form of historical writing. Startt and Sloan (1989: 156) propose the common-sense view, that:

> The historical narrative, a mixture of explanation based on evidence and intuitive reasoning, is one of the oldest forms of investigation that have characterized the study of humankind.

Denzin and Lincoln (2000: 375) propose the constructivist view, simply assuming that all history is story and that 'every historical method implies a different way of telling these stories'. From a structuralist position, White (1973: ix) describes 'the historical work' as 'a verbal structure in the form of a narrative prose discourse'.

Although narrative remains fundamental to history, its function in establishing causation is still problematic. In the past, it has often been implied that merely putting data into periods, or describing it in a chronological narrative makes a claim of causation. This is still how inexperienced readers may interpret your narrative – that if one event followed another it was presumably caused by the earlier event – even if you are carefully avoiding making such causal claims.

The first stirrings of new ways of thinking about history can be detected from early last century. The Annales School was associated with the French journal *Annales d'histoire économique et sociale*, founded in 1929. This group wanted to reconcile the interests and methods of historians and social scientists, by replacing the traditional view of history as chronology, particularly in relation to national and political themes, with a view of history as thematic, with emphasis on economic and social themes. This took them to the analysis of demographic and geographic data, often by methods familiar to the social scientists, but with the sensibility of the historian.

The work of Harold Innis in Canada (for instance Innis 1950) is concerned, in a way similar to the Annales School, with relating history to economics and to geography, through themes such as the production of staple commodities, or the way rivers function as communication routes. In the narrower field of film history, Barbara Klinger (1997) has proposed a 'cinematic *histoire totale*', analogous to the total history proposed by the Annales historians.

Hans-Georg Gadamer (1973) proposed an historical hermeneutics which recognises the dialogue between past and present: he requires that historians operate at the horizon of the present, and address the horizon of the past, as they cannot avoid either of these (see the third sub-section of section 9.1 in Chapter 9 for further exploration of the concept of 'horizon'). By doing this well, the historian recaptures the tradition as far as possible in its own terms, outside culture and context, just as ethnographers do, when they try to socialise within an exotic culture. Other hermeneuticists (for instance Paul Ricoeur) have also involved history as one site of interpretation (see the first sub-section of section 11.2 in Chapter 11).

Michel de Certeau (1988, first published in French 1975) builds upon Michelet's understanding of history as a discourse with the dead, positioning itself at the boundary of past and present and constantly shifting between these two and the future: events are real to de Certeau, but their representation is what makes them history, and this representation can never pin down their essence. He exemplifies for history the post-structuralist, perhaps even post-modernist, epistemological break, even though he continues to refer to history as a science.

Like literary deconstruction, this view of history places as much importance on what is not said – on the gaps and holes in the evidence of the past or in the discourses that surround it – as it does in what appears clearly on the record. And, at the same time, the writing of history becomes inseparable from the history itself: 'Thus historians can write only by combining within their practice the "other" that moves and misleads them and the real that they can represent only through fiction. They are historiographers' (de Certeau 1988: 14).

The post-modernist challenge (discussed again in the third sub-section of section 11.2) is dispersed across the disciplines, and individuals often cross disciplinary boundaries. In the 21st century a new map of the field seems necessary: however, different people draw this map in different ways.

Jenkins (1997), for instance, proposes post-modernity as our current condition in the world, not something that we have any choice about: he presents 'post-modernism', on the other hand, as a philosophical position that we can decide to accept, either in whole or in part. He nominates two contrasted forms of traditional history: upper case 'History' and lower case 'history', and condemns both. He describes upper case History as teleological (goal-directed, assuming progress) and openly ideological (whether of the right or the left), and suggests that it has collapsed with the failure of **modernism**. He proposes that lower case history claims to be inclusive (liberal/**humanist**, pluralist) and to seek understanding of the past 'in its own terms' and 'for its own sake', and has taken over the academy, effectively claiming to be the only legitimate form of history. His argument is that everyone has recognised the effect of the post-modern critique on upper case History, but that lower case history has also suffered (not always acknowledged) collateral damage. The selections he offers as readings then illustrate five positions in three sections: 'On History in the upper case: for and against post-modern histories', 'On history in the lower case: for and against the collapse of the lower case'; and 'Nuanced or ambiguous others'.

Jenkins positions himself clearly on the side of post-modernism, but his extracts cover both sides of this debate, his explanations are clear, and his categories helpful in finding a way through an intellectual minefield in which the positions are complex and constantly shifting. He is less successful in suggesting examples of what a truly post-modern history might look like: for Jenkins, even Hayden White is only tentatively accepted as post-modernist. Among those he mentions as possibly truly post-modernist, only Dening has demonstrated an interest in media history. Dening provides a fascinating interpretation of the *Bounty* mutiny in semiotic terms, treating behaviour as 'language'. He maintains that 'any question worth asking about the past is ultimately about the present' (Dening 1992: 366) and that 'the present is the creative product of our readings of the system in our signs and the occasions of their expression' (Dening 1992: 223). He closes the book with an exploration of the various filmic representations of the mutiny as examples of 'cultural literacy', and steadfastly resists evaluating them against any final 'truth'.

Though many historians (for instance, Evans 1997) would admit that these debates are changing the way historians think, some (like Iggers 1993, or those christened 'nuanced or ambiguous' by Jenkins) are cautious about committing themselves to a position. Meanwhile, 'traditional' history continues to be written, and its methodology to be defended (in addition to the selections in Jenkins 1997, see Kozicki 1993, or Marwick 1993).

In particular, some Marxist historians have insisted that the post-modern emperor has no clothes. They object to the relativism of post-modernism – its tendency to shift from the proposition that discourse constructs society to the claim that reality cannot exist outside discourse. If (as post-modernism insists) there is no external referent for knowledge, and all 'grand narratives' are repudiated, then there is no place for the emancipatory politics espoused by Marxists, no point in struggling against the capitalist system. This political pessimism leads the post-modernist to accept that capitalism has triumphed, and either become a helpless observer or collude with rampant consumerism. Marxists (for instance Wood and Foster 1997) determinedly resist this position.

A contemporary historical researcher needs to have some ideas concerning the following questions:

- Ontology: What is 'history' (the events? the writing about them? or both?) What is written history (speculation? science? discourse? ideology?) Is the concept of historical 'fact' or 'event' meaningful? If so, what constitutes a 'fact' or an 'event' of history and do these exist independently of being recorded? If not, what is left of 'history'?
- Epistemology: What constitutes 'historical evidence' and how can this be evaluated? Can historians know 'what really happened'? What is the relation of the historian to the history being written (is objectivity possible or desirable)? What is the function of narrative in writing about history? Do we write history for the sake of understanding the past 'in its own terms' or for the sake of the present?
- Methodology: What forms of data gathering, analysis and interpretation of the data, and writing of the report are appropriate to the ontological and epistemological position taken by the researcher?

The politics and sociology of organisations

Academics interested in institutions have not always recognised the similarities between historical method and the methods employed within sociology and cultural studies. All these researchers have been at one time or another influenced in the formation and application of interpretive frameworks by philosophers and theorists such as Marx, Foucault, or Habermas. Ethnographers (following pioneer anthropologists such as Margaret Mead) started out seeking objective 'truth'. But few remain truly positivist: the research approaches of most are now at least post-positivist, if not constructivist. Geertz (1973: 5), for instance, adopts the semiotic concept of culture:

> Believing, with Max Weber, that man is an animal suspended in webs of significance he himself has spun, I take culture to be those webs, and the analysis of it to be therefore not an experimental science in search of a law but an interpretive one in search of meaning.

This leads to his influential statement of world-view, and (consequently) method:

> An interworked system of construable signs ... culture is not a power, something to which social events, behaviours, institutions, or processes can be causally attributed; it is a context, something within which they can be intelligibly – that is, thickly – described. (Geertz 1973: 14)

From this perspective, theory must exist, to make sense of culture, but it is not separate from and above the culture or its description: analysis is 'sorting out the structures of signification ... and determining their social ground and import' (Geertz 1973: 9).

There are a number of post-positivist social science approaches that similarly view institutions as expressions of culture. Social **phenomenology**, following Husserl (see the first sub-section of section 11.2 in Chapter 11), is 'the starting point' for Berger and Luckmann's understanding of 'the social construction of reality' (Berger and Luckmann 1979: 34). The study of the constructed nature of everyday life and of intersubjectivity is the basis for social constructivism, ethnomethodology and symbolic interactionism (Berger and Luckmann 1979; Gubrium and Holstein 2000), each of which shares a methodological requirement to see social situations from the point of view of their actors (Lindlof 1995: 30).

Talcott Parsons (see the first sub-section of section 5.2 in Chapter 5) linked the structure of society (how the elements of social systems combined) with its functions (the use-value of human activity). His pupil, Harold Garfinkel, set out to study how people construct meaning out of the social world they inhabit, and so became one of the earliest practitioners of ethnomethodology, which seeks to probe the actual features and processes of intersubjectivity in real life contexts. Garfinkel's project was to understand how the character of everyday life comes to be taken for granted – how ordinary people construct sensible, orderly ways of doing things – through the accounts that participants construct of their realities (Lindlof 1995: 35). Ethnomethodology has been used both to study behaviour within media institutions and to do audience research. Its methodology is to examine 'the local construction of meaning' through interactional practices (Lindlof 1995: 35), including studying behaviour within media institutions such as newsrooms (see Tuchman 1978).

Symbolic interactionism is based on the work of George Herbert Mead, who argued that the self developed through processes of social interaction in which each individual constantly monitored the attitudes of others to the self through the use of significant symbols such as gestures (Lindlof 1995: 43). For George Blumer meaning arises from social interaction (Denzin 1992: xiv), and so methodologically he encourages an immersion in the life of groups under study through participant observation. Symbolic interactionism has shown an interest in organisational communication: the development of myths, rituals and multiple perceived realities within institutional contexts (Lindlof 1995: 44).

All these approaches retain some influence of positivism: Norman Denzin, for example, argues that many 'interactionists cling to a pragmatism which produces a crippling commitment to an interpretive sociology too often caught in the trappings of positivist and post-positivist terms' (Denzin 1992: 20). However, most also accept either a post-positivist doubt of the capacity of researchers to find definitive truth or a constructivist assumption that meanings in the social world are relative to the positioning of the researcher. Gubrium and Holstein (2000: 488), for instance, suggest that all these approaches are now turning into studies of interpretive practice: 'the constellation of procedures, conditions and resources through which reality is apprehended, understood, organised, and conveyed in everyday life', and that all such studies are concerned with 'how people methodically construct their experiences and their worlds and in the configurations of meanings and institutional life that inform and shape their reality-constituting activity'.

Some practitioners within these traditions admit that their own position, as well as that of the subjects of their research (the people working in the institutions under study), arises out of a broader world-view, a framework of understanding.

One of the clearest of these is the Marxist framework, introduced in Chapter 5. Marx's theories (see the second sub-section of section 5.2) combined history, economics and politics: his theory of how societies operate was based on his understanding of 'historical materialism', which he defined as the science of social formations. He saw human history as a series of shifts in the organic relation between how people lived (culture), and how goods were produced within a society (economics). Marx wanted a theory of history that would enable generalisation, and even sometimes prediction, but that would also make sense of the current world and so provide a basis for political practice. As a result, Marxism must be considered not only in the arguments around history and historiography, but also in the debates about social science and policy studies.

The comments in the second sub-section of section 5.2 about the necessary connection between Marxism and discussions of class apply just as much in institutional research as in audience studies (and they will again in textual research). In the case of institutional research, Marxists ask questions such as: Who owns the means of production (newspapers or radio or television stations)? Who controls and regulates the way owners conduct their businesses? In whose interests does this whole system operate? It is these questions that concern political economy research, much of which comes out of a critical theory perspective.

Critical theorists see the social world as divided into a number of realms or spheres, with the state serving the interests of a relatively small portion of the population: the owners of capital. The realm of culture is separate from the state, but the culture industries, contrary to their potentially revolutionary role, still serve the interests of capital. The critical theorist hopes, by studying, theorising and critiquing this subservient relationship, to provide a vision of an alternative role for culture, to encourage social change, and bring about less oppressive social structures.

The Frankfurt School (see the second sub-section of section 5.2) produced their critique within this framework, although they were revising some aspects of Marx's work. Other strands of critical theory have also been produced by Marxists such as Raymond Williams and Walter Benjamin, and the work of Gramsci and of Althusser (discussed in the same sub-section) has been of great significance and influence. Critical theory is not unified and monolithic, but its practitioners share certain values:

> Critical theory can be distinguished from what Max Horkheimer called 'traditional theory' – that is, rational social theory that privileged deductive scientific

> method, and served to reproduce social structures. Critical theory, by contrast, sought to retain the philosophical and the metaphysical in social theory, to oppose positivist methodologies, and to take an active part in striving to transform society for the better. (Hinton forthcoming)

The media are appropriate subjects of study for critical theorists because of their role as sites of cultural production, frequently owned by either the state itself or major corporations (increasingly transnational in structure and scope), and always in the service of capital. The approach which is particularly concerned with questions of ownership and control of the media is often known as 'critical political economy' (McChesney 1993, 1997, 1999; McChesney et al. 1998; Philo and Miller 2000). Critical political economy is a reaction to the rationalism of neo-classical economics and the positivism of scientific economics, and in many respects is a return to the political economy theories of Adam Smith and J. S. Mill as well as Marx. Because of their concerns with questions of ownership and control of the media, including the internet, critical political economists have been particularly involved in lobbying governments in the development of media and telecommunications policy, most recently in relation to 'privatisation' policies (Hinton forthcoming).

It follows that critical theorists have frequently seen themselves as oppositional or resistive to media institutions and texts, and particularly to popular culture. Adorno for example, as we have argued, favoured 'high culture'. This critical stance has remained strong within media and cultural studies (Bennett 1998), frequently assuming that power is located centrally: in the state itself and in the 'ruling classes', and more locally in institutions, including the boardrooms of media corporations. The media are seen as a site of ideological production and maintenance (or reproduction), because of their central economic role in modern economies and because of their reach and presumed influence in people's lives.

We can characterise both critical theory and critical political economy as being concerned, at least to some degree, with the exercise of power in modern societies. In this framework it is assumed that everything is based ultimately on economics, and that power is concentrated in limited sites in society and is generally applied in a 'top down' manner. However since the late 1960s an alternative explanation of power has gained considerable currency, particularly in cultural studies and in cultural policy studies. This is based on adaptations and interpretations of the work of Michel Foucault (1926–1984).

Foucault is variously regarded by his interpreters and critics as a philosopher, a social theorist, a cultural historian, an historian of political thought, an ethicist and a political commentator. His work spanned a number of years at a time when critical analysis was shifting and when **structuralism** and post-structuralism were engaging with Marxism and psycho-analysis.

In 1982 Foucault presented his work in this way:

> My objective for more than twenty-five years has been to sketch out a history of the different ways in our culture that humans develop knowledge about

> themselves: economics, biology, psychiatry, medicine, and penology. The main point is not to accept this knowledge at face value but to analyze these so-called sciences as very specific 'truth games' related to specific techniques that human beings use to understand themselves. (reprinted in Foucault 2000: 224)

Foucault did not directly discuss the media, but his work is relevant to media studies in a number of ways, of which two are relevant at this point in our discussion: on the relations between power and discourse, and on 'governmentality' which has been particularly influential in the development of cultural policy studies. His insights have also been applied within cultural studies, social science and ethnography (Miller 1997), and he has been a critic of historiography, his work being influential on Jenkins (1991) for example.

Foucault's work concerns how power is located within institutions such as the hospital and the prison: for him, power is not top down or only located in the state, but is diffused and dispersed throughout society and is intimately linked to knowledge. Much of his work consists of case studies, partly as examples of how to resist the dominant assumptions of critical theory, and partly as a substantial historical argument about how we came to think as we do in the present.

His early work participated in debates within structuralism and semiotics discussed in the third sub-section of section 10.1 in Chapter 10. His work on the 'death of the author' is a well-known example from this early period (Foucault 1986). Contrary to liberal humanist notions of human beings as in control of their lives, he considered at this point in his work that humans are 'determined' by language: he considered 'how historically and culturally located systems of power/knowledge construct subjects and their worlds' (Gubrium and Holstein 2000: 493). Later in his work he moved away from this structuralist position.

Unlike semioticians, who are concerned with language as an abstract system of rules (what de Saussure called *langue*), Foucault is concerned with language in action (what de Saussure called *parole*), which he called 'discourse'. In this application of the term, discourses 'shape our understanding of ourselves, and our capacity to distinguish the valuable from the valueless, the true from the false, and the right from the wrong' (Danaher et al. 2000: 31). Discourses are organised series of statements about the natural or social world which have, over a period of time, become formalised into 'rules' which govern the behaviour of members of a social or cultural field. These discourses also operate through architecture, habit, practices and ethics, and permit or constrain behaviour (including what it is permitted to think and say) and thereby shape the individual sense of self. A discourse is able to define an event or phenomenon as significant. Constellations of discourses are 'discursive formations', or domains of knowledge. One of Foucault's main contributions was to historically examine the ways subjects (roughly speaking, individuals) are shaped by particular discourses which are culturally variable over time. In *The Archaeology of Knowledge* (1972) Foucault sought to understand how discourses, such as medicine, the law, psychoanalysis and economics, derive their power from their ability, through discursive formations, to pronounce 'the truth' – through practices of confession and therapy for example.

Within the media, the more obvious sites of the 'quest for truth' would include news, current affairs programming and documentary, however we can also see various forms of popular factual entertainment as sites for ethical discussion and debate. For Foucault, because 'the self' is produced by discourse it is fluid and malleable. In the media, this view of the self as a 'project' to be worked on and improved is evident in popular television forms including *Big Brother*, *Survivor* and *Oprah*; in personal autobiographical web sites in which confessional and therapeutic discourses are evident; in soap opera, and in popular magazines (see Gauntlett 2002 for a discussion of popular magazines and personal improvement handbooks).

The issue of power is also central in another area in which Foucault is relevant to media study: 'governmentality' (Foucault 1979, 2002), or the 'microphysics' of the practices of government (Bennett 1998; Gordon 1991). He did not accept the view that power was centralised in particular social classes within society, nor in 'liberal democratic societies' was it centralised in the state: he saw power as a complex set of fluid and unstable relations between different groups. In a sustained examination of liberalism he sought to understand the relations between institutions and discourses and practices (sometimes at the most 'intimate' level).

Foucault traces an historical transition in the seventeenth and eighteenth centuries from a form of political thought based on the pursuit of interests by the prince as sole ruler to one oriented towards the sciences of the state and to a concern with territory, population and economy, within a context of a shift in liberal political thought to a concern with problems of governing and social administration. He discusses governmentality within the framework of the history of liberalism, as a series of political problems and strategies, which he sees as a style of thinking concerned with questions of how to manage government processes (Foucault 2000). The emerging rationality of government management of the state and populations produces particular types of knowledge, including 'policy' (a set of 'techniques' for securing stability and prosperity for the state and its population).

In any state which has eschewed terror it is necessary to regulate populations and their behaviour, but unlike Gramsci who sees hegemony as a mechanism for securing the 'consent' of subordinate classes, for Foucault 'governmentality' is as much about what we do to ourselves as what might be done to us (Danaher et al. 2000: 83).

Using a Foucauldian approach to questions of cultural policy, Tony Bennett argues that culture is increasingly being seen as an historically specific set of resources for managing the conduct of populations (Bennett 1998: 11). Bennett uses a combination of Gramsci and Foucault, contrasting 'a utilitarian calculus' with the romantic views of culture of Adorno and Benjamin. He argues that the sphere of culture has been so 'governmentalised' that we can no longer see it as a sphere outside of and in an oppositional or resistant relationship to government (Bennett 1998: 30), but rather cultural institutions such as the museum, school, library and so on, are branches of government equally involved in managing culture. For Bennett, Foucault, with his 'little struggles' which preclude society-wide revolution, offers a 'more usable characterisation of the functioning of culture–power relations in modern societies' than does critical theory (Bennett 1998: 62) and Bennett argues for a reformist emphasis in the study of cultural policy.

Does this mean that Foucault and Bennett have returned to the approach we have characterised as 'administrative theory' (see section 6.2 in Chapter 6)? Certainly Foucault's work has moved the emphasis in cultural theory away from the grand narratives of critical theory, with their rejection of a centralised locus for power. He is, however, still concerned with the exercise of power in society, aiming to produce a critique of liberal theory and liberal modes of government, while administrative theory assumed a liberal model of society in which all elements operated in some form of equilibrium, and in which media research sought to find ways of producing a more harmonious functioning of society. Beyond such a critique Foucault is concerned with an historical identification of endemic problems within liberal political thought.

If we can place Foucault within the broad field of critical theory, we can do so even more with Habermas (see also the first sub-section of section 11.2 in Chapter 11), who is generally considered to be part of the 'second generation' of the Frankfurt School, although he rejects some aspects of their work, including Adorno's pessimism. Habermas proposes that the Frankfurt School is imprisoned within the paradigm of consciousness (***ideologie kritique***) rather than a paradigm based upon communication (Brand 1989). He is broadly positioned outside the structuralist and post-structuralist frameworks. However, from an early stage in his career he also took an anti-positivist stance, seeing science and rationality in the capitalist era as producing instrumental knowledge which was hostile to, rather than emancipatory of, human beings (Lechte 1996: 187).

Drawing on the work of both early phenomenologists and Talcott Parsons, he sees an opposition between the 'lifeworld' (the 'horizon of consciousness' which includes both the private and the **public spheres**) and the 'system' (the realm of economics and instrumental reason). In his major work, *The Theory of Communicative Action* (Habermas 1987) he explored the role of language and communication within the lifeworld, as both a site of resistance and a potential to modify the system. He sees the structure and purpose of language as hermeneutic: the goal of language is understanding, leading to agreement. Ironically, however, this model is also instrumental, leading him to ignore what semioticians such as Jakobson would call the 'phatic' and the 'poetic' functions of language (Lechte 1996: 190).

One of his earliest major works on the nature and development of the public sphere (Habermas 1989) has had considerable influence in media studies, especially in relation to news media, popular factual entertainment, and the development of the internet, although it has also been critiqued, especially by feminist scholars (see, for example, Calhoun 1992; Dalhberg 2001; Lumby 1999).

8.3 Conclusion

As always, the framework(s) that have influenced the way you see the world will also shape your research. This is never a case of 'applying' a theory to your data, but of functioning within a theoretical framework right through the research process, so that all elements within it are consistent, from the initial choice of a topic to the final conclusions. Though your credibility must suffer if you try to hold two mutually exclusive positions at once, you may well find more than one intellectual framework appealing, picking and choosing elements from within several as you develop your own idiosyncratic understandings.

Censorship, for instance, looks very different through different intellectual frameworks. In researching the history of censorship, a positivist looks for the demonstrable 'facts' (following perhaps Elton, or Marx), a post-positivist seeks the most plausible explanations, while admitting that these must always be tentative and contingent (following perhaps Carr). A constructivist admits the influence of the linguistic turn in interpretation, so (like Hayden White) may adopt a post-structuralist or even (like Greg Dening) a post-modernist position. If the researcher's concern is with present censorship practices, these might be explained through Foucauldian concepts of governmentality or through Habermas's concept of the public sphere. They might also be seen as examples of social interaction (following Berger and Luckmann), or as sites for ethnographic exploration (following Garfinkel). Critical political economy might contribute to research on the economic determinations and implications of media censorship, and critical theory more generally might inform research on the social functions of censorship.

Part of the attraction of research is the sense of achievement when you reach a breakthrough in understanding, a moment of insight. Such moments arise out of the interaction of your data with your framework(s) of understanding, out of – in the broadest sense – interpretation.

PART III

RESEARCH ON TEXTS

The third of our heuristic divisions of the field of media research is texts. We could use other terms instead of 'text'. Films, television programmes, radio programmes, newspaper articles, websites, magazines, pop music and so on seem to be the items that researchers concerned with meaning(s) address directly. However, the constant repetition of such a list becomes clumsy and tedious.

The term 'products' has some appeal in a political economy perspective on the media, which recognises the role of media in the modern capitalist system. However, understanding their economic status is only one aspect of 'making sense' of the media, and cannot explain pleasure.

Applying the linear theory of communication described in the third subsection of section 1.1 in Chapter 1, we could talk about media 'messages', in which meaning exists separately from the 'encoder' and the 'decoder'. This would be consistent with the positivist and post-positivist paradigms, in which language is how humans 'refer to' and 'name' aspects of the real world, and a 'message' is like a vessel into which information, or meaning, is placed to be conveyed from one person to another. A flawed vessel may impede the process of information transfer (so that meaning is 'unclear'), but a vessel by its nature is not able to determine the information which is placed in it. This is a paradigm which is still very powerful in communication research, but has little remaining influence in media studies and cultural studies.

Literary studies traditionally referred to novels and plays and poems as 'texts', but interpreted them in a linear fashion. Under the influence of the linguistic turn in interpretation, literary studies now treat such 'texts' in much the same way as media and cultural studies, where the dominant paradigm currently accepts the view that human understandings of both the natural world and the social world are mediated through language. In this paradigm, a text is not a vessel into which meanings are poured for transmission to others, but a structure (or a 'system of signification') by which meanings are produced within a cultural context.

When we use the term 'text' as the over-riding descriptor for this section about the output of the media, we are indicating that we are broadly locating ourselves within a non-positivist research paradigm, concerned with how meaning is produced semiotically. However, we will still discuss many research traditions and intellectual frameworks, inviting you as reader to choose among the alternatives, including to decide that you do not agree with our basically semiotic approach to communication. So in the discussion which follows we will (where possible) use 'text' in speaking about semiotic views of communication and 'message' in speaking about linear views. We will consider research about the nature of texts/messages, the production of meanings by texts/messages, and the production of understandings from texts/messages by audiences, as well as providing an introduction to various methodological and philosophical approaches commonly met in the study of these questions.

It is almost impossible to talk about textual analysis without also talking about the institutions that produce texts/messages and the audiences who consume them, however we will concentrate on those research traditions that are concerned primarily with understanding texts. We cannot offer a neat model of the various threads of textual analysis, but, as we discuss textual research we will make connections with the audience model offered in the introduction to Part I.

'Content analysis' of messages is often used with effects and/or uses and gratifications studies of audience. The term can be used broadly (to refer to any examination of the content of messages/texts) or more narrowly (to refer to a particular methodology developed within social science). In the latter sense, content analysis sees messages as coded representations of the real world, fixed and knowable. The job of the researcher is to pin this meaning down, and then to interpret its implications, particularly its effects on (passive) consumers. Content analysis can be either quantitative or qualitative (or both): obviously numerical percentages imply more precision than terms like 'more' or 'fewer', but all are quantitative. For instance, you may wish to measure how much violence there is on television, to confirm 'scientifically' or quantitatively what you sense intuitively. You may be interested in how gender or race are represented on television, and whether this has changed over time: so you measure that representation now and compare it either with earlier representations or with similar studies done earlier. Or, you consider that women are not represented equitably or realistically, so you measure how they are represented and compare this to something else – an 'ideal' (equitable) representation or the real world. The more specialised forms of textual analysis within the social sciences (discourse analysis [DA] and conversation analysis [CA]) set out to analyse how audiences understand messages, that is, they are interested in the process of making meaning, rather than just in the meaning itself.

Literary criticism, which has always been part of the humanities, has not traditionally been interested in the audience, but has read texts both as messages and as aesthetic objects, the products of individual creative genius. Literary critics have traditionally assumed that meaning is inherent in a text, placed there by the author, and 'discovered' by the process of (intuitive) textual criticism, or by hermeneutics. There are clear parallels between literary theory and film theory, and film theory has in turn influenced the analysis of other kinds of media text.

But, in the push to achieve credibility within the academy, media and cultural studies wished to claim that their judgments were 'scientific', and so to replace intuitive understandings with analytic methods that could be replicable, even if not predictive. The result was the acceptance of semiotics (using the term here as a research method rather than as a communication model) and structuralism as methodologies for the analysis of texts. Semiotics sees texts as coded systems of signs, and in its early days proposed that the specific meanings of these signs could be decoded. Structuralism also sees texts as coded systems of signs, but directs attention to linguistic and cultural structures, and reaches the meaning(s) of the signs through the structures.

Despite their methodological differences, all of these textual research traditions accept a linear model of the communication process, that is they all (even – in its very early days – semiotics) assume that meaning is already there in the message/text, waiting to be uncovered. They all also grow out of the positivist or post-positivist intellectual framework, with its belief in a realist ontology, its assertion that the only true knowledge is scientific knowledge, and its faith in the growth of objective and verifiable knowledge through the scientific method (see section 1.4 in Chapter 1).

When the text is seen still as an aesthetic object, but with meaning arising out of the interaction between a creative artist and an active reader, we are beginning to shift from the linear view of communication towards the semiotic view. This is the position taken by phenomenologists, who are usually at least post-positivist in their research orientation, and possibly constructivist or associated with critical theory.

The post-structuralist endorses absolutely the semiotic view of communication, and cannot accommodate positivist or post-positivist research orientations. In this paradigm, objectivity is impossible; the value of the research lies in its descriptive power, its capacity to enlarge our horizons, without any claim to 'truth' or prediction; and the only way a researcher can 'know' the real world is through representation, through 'realism' rather than 'reality'.

Post-structuralists see texts as meaning systems constructed by the collaboration of the reader/producer with the text (seen as a system of coded signs) within a cultural context. They may use elements of the semiotic or structuralist methodologies, particularly discourse analysis and narratology. They define culture as 'a whole way of life', rather than as 'the best of artistic expressions'. Much of cultural studies uses post-structuralist methods. For cultural studies researchers, all forms of culture are 'texts', including aspects of everyday life (such as 'the beach' or 'the shopping mall'), and popular media forms such as the comic or music television (in contrast to the 'great works' studied by the literary critic).

To sum up the different approaches, we suggest some basic questions that each approach might pose in attempting to understand media texts/messages:

- Content analysis: How well does this message capture the real world through codes?
- Semiotic analysis: How does this text represent the world through codes?
- Structural analysis: How do the structures of this text create meaning(s)?
- Literary criticism: What does this text (intuitively) mean?
- Hermeneutic analysis: What did the author mean to convey through this text?
- Phenomenological analysis: What does this text mean to me?
- Post-structuralist analysis: How is the meaning of this text constructed within this cultural context?

And we remind you that some of the audience approaches considered in Part I apply again to textual research. The questions these ask may be:

- Reader-response studies: How do individual readers construct texts?
- Cultural studies: How does culture operate to produce socially differentiated readings of texts?
- Reception analysis: How do socially differentiated readers produce readings of texts within a cultural context?

Chapter 9

Researching Texts

This chapter presents a discussion of some textual research reports, illustrating the various approaches to such research (outlined in the introduction to Part III) and dividing the field according to whether the research concerns mainly the content of the text, or its structure (including its function as discourse).

In this discussion, we judge the value of such reports:

- by the clarity with which they present their case, so that the non-specialist can understand what they are saying;
- by their awareness of their methodology, and of what are acceptable standards for that kind of research;
- by the quality of their conclusions: how logically their conclusions follow from the data presented, with all inferences supported by the research.

We are not judging by the sophistication of their statistical methodology, partly because we are not particularly competent to make such a judgement, but more because if the previous criteria are deficient no amount of statistical sophistication will compensate.

9.1 Research on textual content

Content analysis

Here we are using the term 'content analysis' in its narrower sense, as a methodology developed to study media content within a social science framework, and adopting a basically linear view of communication. This position is clear in the definition of content analysis as 'a research technique for making replicable and valid inferences from data to their context' (Krippendorf 1980: 21).

The Payne Fund studies in USA in 1930 into the effects of films upon children included early examples of media content analysis, summarised by Charters (1933). The methods were more sophisticated than those of Berg on audiences (see section 3.2 in Chapter 3), and the sample was vastly larger (several hundred movies). However, there were similar unwarranted inferences from film content to psychological effects on audiences, leading to claims of moral damage.

A much better example of early content analysis was Rudolf Arnheim's 'The world of the daytime serial' (1944). In many ways a companion piece to the work of Herta Herzog (see section 3.3 in Chapter 3), the strengths of Arnheim's research are:

- the care taken in the research design to justify the size and composition of the sample, to define the units of measurement, and to ensure the systematic collection of data;
- the care taken to make the conclusions follow from the data, without distorting the data to support prejudgements;
- the attempt to be more sophisticated than simply equating content statistics with the intentions of producers or with effects on audiences;
- the recognition that some inferences are not tested, and are perhaps even untestable.

As a result of these strengths, Arnheim's results can be validly compared with later research in similar areas, and in addition can provide valuable historical information about radio serials in 1941. The main problems are the continuing difficulties of category definition, and the residual tendency to infer effects on audiences.

Since 1944, there have been many other content analyses of soap opera (see Allen 1985 for examples), but let us at this point move on to the research on news, which is our primary focus for Part III. 'News' is usually understood as a contraction of 'new information'. We are used to finding out the news through newspapers, radio, television and now the internet, but our major concern in this part of the book is with television news. There have been many institutional studies of television news – some ethnographic (examining the process of news gathering, or the interaction within a newsroom), some concerned with political economy (the ownership and control of news media), some technological (the changing role of news through different media, such as the shift from newspapers to internet news), some concerned with the function of ideology in the presentation of the news (the role of 'gate keepers' in deciding what is newsworthy).

Some of these institutional studies also incidentally address news content. For instance, Ericson et al. (1987) was a study of television news visuals: the researchers followed news crews, watching how reporters and cinematographers worked together to produce the visual component of the news. The report discusses both the content and structure of individual news items, and the process by which these visuals were selected, staged, recorded and edited, with the emphasis on the process rather than the content.

Our concern in this part of the book is with those research projects concerned primarily with news content. With potentially large quantities of data, classical content analysis has been the main research approach, particularly when the researcher wishes to measure the accuracy or bias or objectivity of news: see, for instance, the research conducted for the US Commission on Civil Rights (1975, discussed below). The major problem with this kind of content analysis is a tendency to make unwarranted inferences, to take the discussion further than the data legitimately allows. In fact, it is not possible to prove inferences made on the basis of content analysis alone, though too many research reports seem to assume that once the measurement is done the meaning is self-evident: we identified (section 3.2 in Chapter 3) a similar problem with effects studies of audiences.

There seems to be a trade-off between establishing definitions clearly enough for effective measurement, and measuring categories that are significant enough to produce worthwhile conclusions. Gerdes (1982), for instance, wished to understand what 'world perspective' was offered to television news viewers in Sydney in August 1978. His report explains his terms, describes his methods (including providing detailed category descriptions), and tabulates his results (categories of stories across the various television channels; categories of stories against the forms of presentation). His conclusion was that:

> ... television news as seen in Sydney in August 1978, was pretty parochial: it reported mainly about human life and misery from the local parish, occasionally from the diocese and once in a while, in order not to appear too narrow-minded, from the big, wide world. (Gerdes 1982: 84)

The strengths of this research are:

- It follows the rules for content analysis faithfully, acknowledging classification difficulties and explaining its processes for achieving intercoder reliability.
- It does not seek to make unwarranted inferences from the results (with occasional lapses like 'in order not to appear too narrow-minded').

However, one effect of the refusal to make larger unwarranted inferences is that the conclusions appear rather slight, given the size of the project.

That is certainly not the case with the work of the Glasgow Media Group – a huge study published in several volumes, which has become the germinal work in the field (comparable in influence to Morley's much smaller study of audiences). This work clearly links content with audience, but for our purposes we will concentrate on their analysis of the news content.

The first volume of the report, published in 1976, explained the overall intentions of the project, and its methodology in the early stages. The team had originally planned that the study would cover all BBC and ITV news bulletins for a full year, but this proved just too enormous a project. They reduced the data gathering to 22 weeks, giving them a total of 260 hours of tape, plus related current affairs programmes and a press archive for the whole period.

The researchers then did a complete computer analysis of the first three months of the television news, which enabled them to avoid 'the many problems associated with sampling in a population whose degree of differentiation and variation were not fully known' (Glasgow Media Group 1976: 48). They carefully defined story categories (listing these in an appendix) and units of measurement (including a coding sheet in an appendix).

The researchers presented a comparative analysis of the structures of the main television news bulletins on the BBC (*Nine o'Clock News*) and ITN (*News at Ten*), in terms of the length of each bulletin, the duration of items, the distribution of items by category, and the relative duration of items within each category. Variations in the categories were discussed by criteria of flexibility, time of the day, weekend variations, variations from week to week. They discovered that most news fits into one of three broad subject areas – politics, foreign, and industrial – and that the most stable of these across channels was industrial news.

The next step was a more detailed examination of the stories within this 'industrial' category, looking for principles operating in the selection of news, patterns of story coverage across industrial groups (agriculture, mining, transport and communications, etc), and a comparison between the news reports and what was happening in the 'real world'. On the latter, the conclusion was:

> There is no consistent relationship between the stoppages recorded during the first five months of 1975 ... and those reported by television news ... Further, when disputes are reported, there is no direct relation between the amount of news coverage they receive and their severity. (Glasgow Media Group 1976: 202–4)

Narrowing their focus still further, they considered the television reports of particular disputes – a Glasgow dustcart-drivers' strike and a strike at the Cowley plant of British Leyland.

This led to the second volume (Glasgow Media Group 1980), which focused on the television reporting of the economic crisis of 1975. The aural components of the news were analysed by sociolinguistics as well as by content analysis, allowing the consideration of headlines and other linguistic boundary markers, the structuring of information within items, and reported speech. The visual components were analysed for a single week only (Sunday 11 May to Saturday 17 May) because coding of the visuals was so laborious, and the team wanted a crosscheck with findings on the earlier material. From the coding categories they developed profiles for each channel, and using content analysis they developed a breakdown of the news stories on each channel for each news broadcast that week, presented in the form of tables. Semiotic analysis was then applied to selected aspects – the opening and closing routines, the visual presentation of the readers and reporters, the use of stills and graphics, the use of material from outside the studio (film excerpts, super-captions, videotape and live interviews).

By the time this second volume was in preparation, the group had survived the criticism of the first volume, so, in a final section, they addressed their critics directly – defending their use of content analysis, expressing their reservations about semiotic analysis, including a digression into regional news to fill what some critics had perceived as a gap. By the third volume, they had concluded that 'the news gives a preferential treatment to some ways of seeing in the world' (Philo et al. 1982: xi) and their ultimate aim had become clarified as identifying the ideology at work in the presentation of television news. The media, they decided, did not know how to deal with the contradictions of modern society:

> It is committed to an ideological perspective which is founded on the view of consensus, 'one nation' and 'community', while having to report phenomena which cannot be fitted easily into this framework of understanding. (Philo et al. 1982: 134)

The strengths of this research design are:

- its large initial sample (using basically quota sampling) and sensible extrapolation of smaller purposive samples from within this;
- the careful definitions of categories and units of measurement, with attention to intercoder reliability, as this study was conducted by a team of researchers;
- the willingness to use different methodologies for different purposes: classical content analysis on the large sample; interviews with participants in the events depicted on the news, and with people working in the newsrooms; a variant of conversation analysis to examine language units larger than utterances; semiotics on smaller units of text;
- the movement from the large picture to smaller and smaller units within this, allowing conclusions to be drawn about both large questions (such as the overall ideology of television news) and smaller questions (such as why a particular dispute is presented in a particular way);
- the use of appropriate presentation methods – tables and graphs for content analysis of data from large samples, and description for semiotic analysis of smaller purposive samples.

In fact, it is difficult to fault the methodology using the criteria we established at the beginning of this chapter: this research does what it sets out to do, and does it well. If you disagree with its conclusions, that will probably be because you disagree with the intellectual framework within which this research was conducted – basically a Marxist framework, which interprets ideology as an expression of economics.

Though there have been a plethora of studies of television news content since, few have been as thorough and comprehensive. Where the Glasgow Media Group derived their focus on industrial news by narrowing down from a vast amount of data, most other studies have addressed a specific issue from the beginning.

For instance, much research on the news grows out of a perception that gender differences are significant in constructing both news audiences and news content. When Gans (1980: 9) analysed the content of US television and magazine news, he discovered the following proportions among 'news makers':

- some 71 per cent were classified as 'knowns' (incumbent presidents, presidential candidates, leading federal officials, state and local candidates, alleged and actual violators of laws and mores);
- some 21 per cent were classified as 'unknowns' (protesters and 'rioters' and strikers, victims, alleged and actual violators of laws and mores, participants in unusual activities, voters and survey respondents and other aggregates);
- some 8 per cent were classified as animals and objects and abstractions.

Because so few women fit into the category of 'knowns', it is much harder for women to 'make the news' than for men, so it is not surprising that the insignificant role of women in the news has been repeatedly tested by research. Drawing on the same social science research tradition as *Bad News*, quantitative content analyses of news programs have sought to discover gender bias in employment (of news presenters) or stereotyping in representation (by the selection and placement of stories within news programmes, and by the frequency of the appearance of women as either reporters or the subjects of the news within the stories).

One early content analysis was undertaken on behalf of the US Commission on Civil Rights, on a sample of a composite television news week, covering ABC, CBS and NBC and randomly selected between March 1974 and February 1975. Under broad headings: the topic, the correspondent and the news maker, an inventory was developed for classifying how women and minorities were represented within the content of each news story. This study found that only three of the 230 news stories analysed in the sample were 'pertinent to women', and that of the 85 correspondents reporting the news only 8.2 per cent were white women and 3.5 per cent were non-white women (US Commission on Civil Rights 1977: 50). Even fewer (2.4 per cent) were non-white men, a statistic that might well concern a researcher interested in issues of race. Assuming that the major stories are presented first, the researchers concluded that it was also significant that 'Of the 45 stories which comprised the first three segments of the news for this sample, only one story (about former President Nixon's resignation) was reported by a white female':

> In sum, white males outnumbered minority and female correspondents by almost nine to one. Minority and female correspondents rarely covered crucial national stories but tended to cover issues related to minorities' and women's interests, topics which were infrequently treated in this sample. (US Commission on Civil Rights 1975: 51)

The researchers concluded from this study that the way women and minorities were depicted on television news 'suggests to the Nation that minorities and women may not matter' (US Commission on Civil Rights 1975: 55). But the national audience included those same women (and minorities), who were then confirmed in their lack of self esteem, and encouraged to assume that it was white men and their concerns that were really important.

Tuchman (1973: 170–6) sums up the research on gender representation on American television 1952–1974, and similar patterns have been repeatedly discerned by other researchers, for instance Holland (1987: 140) or van Zoonen (1988). A US content analysis study in April 1991 found that women were even more poorly represented than they had been in 1974: that television straight news stories about women declined from 10 per cent to 3 per cent and feature stories about women declined from 16 per cent to 15 per cent. Instances of reported sexism increased from 4 per cent to 14 per cent in both news stories and feature stories. The study concluded:

> When women do appear in news stories, they frequently are victims of accidents or violence, relatives of males in power, or stereotypes that trivialise any activity that might be described as productive to society. (Anon 1992: 27)

So the findings of Rakow and Kranich (1991) are not surprising. They examined one month of television news in 1990 on all three major American networks (ABC, NBC, CBS), exploring the distribution of women as news subjects and sources, and the kinds of representation offered for these women. In a move reminiscent of *Bad News*, Rakow and Kranich combined classical content analysis of large amounts of data, with semiotic concepts of 'the sign', thus avoiding a realist ontology. Their conclusions were:

> As 'signs of the times', women are used to illustrate the private consequences of public events or actions ... As 'signs of support', women are used to endorse an action or policy because of their organisational or institutional affiliations ... Like women newscasters, the women who appear in stories of this kind have their subject positions as women invoked by their appearance, but their voices as women are denied ... Those allowed to speak for women are 'unusual signs' or 'feminists' ... Because all signs are alike, only white women are allowed to signify as 'woman' ... When women's actions disrupt the social order, they are represented as part of the 'nature of the sign' – an inherent part of all women's personalities ... (Rakow and Kranich 1991: 16–20)

This leads them to an overall conclusion similar to that of the authors of *Bad News* (who might have substituted 'working class' for 'women'):

> Television news is not a reflection of society but an instance of it, locating women inside and outside the screen in a discourse that assigns the meaning of the sign 'woman' even while invoking it as if it were already there. (Rakow and Kranich 1991: 22)

This is a conclusion that draws on the data, but also applies concepts from an intellectual framework (feminism). Another way to interpret empirical evidence is to measure what has been discovered about women on television news against what is already known about women in the real world. For instance, Diana Wyndham (1984: 27) presents these statistics about women in the real world in Australia in 1983:

- less than 20 per cent of Australian families had two parents and two children;
- some 28 per cent of all Australian marriages end in divorce;
- some 41 per cent of married partners were both working.

Strengths of content analysis are:

- When applied to found text, it is inexpensive.
- It is comparatively easy to get material, including from the past. This is easier for press analysis, as complete archives usually exist: it is a little more difficult for television, which is not usually so thoroughly archived.
- It is unobtrusive, does not interfere with people's lives, so entails few ethical problems.
- It can deal equally easily with current events or past events or both (provided the evidence has survived), that is, it does not depend upon fallible memory.
- It is excellent for managing large amounts of data which can then be quantified and compared with statistics about the real world.

But it also has problems:

- Problems of sampling. It is hard to be certain that the sample studied is representative, particularly when the total extent of the phenomenon is not known (for instance, the complete range of all television news broadcasts).
- Problems of category definitions. It is almost impossible to establish watertight definitions of categories, and the principle applies that the more precise the category the less interesting/valuable is its measurement. You can recognise which people on the broadcast are female, but it is much harder to decide whether they are 'active' or 'powerful', and it is often these kinds of judgments that are sought. There is also the problem that some feminists would object to any definition of 'woman' as 'essentialist' (see the third sub-section of section 5.2 in Chapter 5).
- Problems of establishing units of measurement (and for a positivist or post-positivist, of measuring with reliability and validity). Television has both aural and visual components, which interact and change across time: how do we cut this continuum up into discrete measurable units?
- Problems of interpretation. Measuring a phenomenon (even if that can be done accurately) is not the same thing as explaining it. Content analysis

results do not tell how the content came to be that way (that can only be answered out of an intellectual framework), or what the content 'means' (that can only be answered out of a theory of communication).

Semiotics

Semiotic textual analysis began by attempting to assess how realistically a text represents the world through codes. This requires looking at news reports not as representing 'the manifest actuality of our society', but rather as reflecting, 'symbolically, the structure of values and relationships beneath the surface' (Fiske and Hartley 1978: 24). Semiotic analysis looks closely at small samples of text, so is particularly valuable in studying short, contained media texts, such as individual news stories. This is, for instance, what the Glasgow Media Group and also Rakow and Kranich did, in the reports discussed above, analysing individual stories semiotically and interpreting the results through a Marxist (in the former case) and a feminist (in the latter case) framework.

Television news is a complex text, with both moving visuals and multi-track aural components. Semiotics claims to be able to deal with all these different technical systems, by breaking each down into its component codes, then into signs. So it is useful to consider first how a less complex system might be analysed, for instance still photographs in newspapers. Hall (1972) offers a procedure for doing this, examining first the levels of signification in photographs, then the role of photographs in the news process, and finally their ideological function. This is explanation rather than action research, though he does provide worked examples that could be used as a model by other researchers. At that early stage in the application of semiotics to texts, Hall still implies that the meaning is within the sign, waiting to be decoded by the reader. However, he also recognises that not all readers decode the same way, and he suggests a reason for these variations:

> The reader may so fully inhabit the code employed by the communicator that the privileged meaning of a photograph is fluently transmitted. It is also possible for the reader 'imperfectly' to know the code in use, and here the transmission of implied meanings will be imperfect, subject to some distortion, loss of meaning, negotiation between sender and receiver. It is also possible for the reader to decode the message of the photo in a wholly contrary way, either because he does not know the sender's code, or because he recognises the code in use but *chooses to employ a different code.* (Hall 1972: 66, his emphasis)

He went on to relate these readings to their ideological context, though he still infers the readings from the text rather than testing how real people actually read in the real world. In his later work on the 'structured polysemy' of texts (Hall 1984, see section 3.5) he shifted further towards what we now think of as 'cultural studies', with their interest in the cultural context within which texts circulate. However, it was Morley's work on the current affairs programme *Nationwide* (see section 3.5 in Chapter 3) that pioneered the practice of including both semiotic analysis of the programme and research on how real audiences decoded the text. This combination of research into text and audience has since become a familiar approach within cultural studies, and has been applied to television news.

Lewis (1985) begins his report with a synopsis of a single news broadcast (ITN's *News at Ten*, broadcast 26 March 1982), and a transcript of the audio and visual elements of a single item within that broadcast (a report of a speech of William Whitelaw to the Conservative Party). He then discusses 'the audience in action', summarising his analysis of the transcripts of 54 interviews with audiences of 'decoders', representing varieties of age, gender, educational background and occupation. This research, then, applies semiotics at two levels – to the initial broadcast (his 'decoders' seek to understand the programme) and to the interview transcripts (he seeks to understand his decoders).

He developed five main categories of signification within the transcripts: units of meaning within items (called 'lexias', following Barthes 1975), themes (across the news as a whole), 'narrative contexts' (or how a lexia fits into a story), 'critical discourses' (such as 'media bias'), and 'extra-textual contexts' (all those aspects of meaning that arise from outside the text). The bulk of the report is a description of how different kinds of decoders used the categories of signification differently and combined them in different ways. He proposed that the introduction to each story – that initial statement by the anchor which is intended to 'frame' the story for the viewer – happened too briefly and quickly on television. Whereas a newspaper headline remains visible for readers to use as a framing structure for their reading of a report, the 'framing' sentence or headline disappears quickly from the television screen, leaving open the possibility that viewers may use it to 'refocus' attention from the previous story, and so 'mis-read' the story that follows. The subjects of his research often did not recall accurately, did not associate the reporters with what they had said and did not link the politicians (or other spokespeople) with their statements.

His conclusions are presented in the form of recommendations to those who construct news broadcasts – both general suggestions for improving the likelihood of viewers decoding an item in the way intended by the producers, and his own reworking of the Whitelaw item as illustration. This research seems to arise out of a critical theory approach, but its conclusions could also be read as offering administrative advice. It still, however, addresses the question we posed as typical of semiotic analysis: how does this text/message represent the world through codes? By looking at socially differentiated readings, it also locates itself within cultural studies. For a constructivist, one important part of Lewis' message is that research is always subjective and that researchers cannot subtract their own subjectivity from the process of interpretation.

Within communication and media studies, pure examples of semiotic textual analysis are now difficult to find. But the use of semiotics as an aspect of a larger project (as already discussed for Morley or Lewis) is quite common. This is because the strengths of semiotic analysis are:

- It can be applied to very small samples, and it does not require that these be representative.
- Provided the sample is small enough, it can deal with complex systems of signification like film or television, analysing both moving and still images and all the layers of sound.
- Category definitions and units of measurement can be developed to suit the material being analysed, and notions of the reliability and validity of measurement are not appropriate.

There are still difficulties that all research using semiotics must address:

- It is too time-consuming to be applied to large samples of text.
- Some problems of category definition remain: television is still a complex technical system, not easily broken down into measurable units.

But when semiotics is used within a cultural studies framework, some of the problems of semiotic content analysis are addressed. It is acknowledged that describing a phenomenon is not the same thing as explaining it, so cultural theories (Marxist, feminist, or post-colonial, described in Chapter 11) are used to explain how the content came to be that way.

Phenomenology and hermeneutics

Phenomenology and hermeneutics together constitute yet another model of analysis of content. They are not in fact the same (see the first sub-section of section 11.2 in Chapter 11), but they are related, and a number of writers (such as Stadler 1990) seem to slide between phenomenology and hermeneutics.

Although eclipsed by structuralist and post-structuralist approaches in the last three decades, phenomenology does have a long history in film study. In 1990 a special issue of the *Quarterly Review of Film and Video* was dedicated to phenomenology in both film and television. For film, Casebier (1991) claimed that objects, events, characters and stories have an existence independent of the spectator, so the film spectator's understanding is guided by 'horizons' acquired through prior experience (of the 'real world' and of film). Some people have argued that there has been a resurgence of interest in phenomenology in film study in recent years, for example Sweeney (1994) and Sobchack (1992, 2000), leading to the publication of *The Phenomenology Reader* (Moran and Mooney 2002). Stadler has argued that this resurgence is due to the recognition that earlier theories of text have tended to ignore the reader/audience (1990: 38).

In the wider field of cultural studies one recent article addresses the phenomenology of freeway travel (Wilken 2000), and some writers about television such as Scannell (1995, 1996) and Silverstone (1994) have also been influenced by phenomenology and hermeneutics. For our purposes, the most useful example is the work of Wilson (1993), who provides careful explication of phenomenological and hermeneutical terms such as 'horizon', 'lifeworld', 'familiarity', 'identification' and many examples of textual analysis using these concepts, including television news.

Wilson considers both 'horizons' within the text and the audience member's 'horizons of understanding', to examine how the viewer 'makes sense of' what she sees, through familiarity and distantiation. He analyses the ways breakfast television uses the mundane and the familiar to construct a 'lifeworld' for the viewer. Recognising that much of the everyday may be constructed from the 'discourses of oppression', Wilson seeks to show that:

> Being a member of a television audience means generating role-related, interest-driven narratives ... to bring together and make sense of events within a text, with an audience supplying speculative information of its own to remove problematic gaps. (Wilson 1993: 5)

He examines identification as 'a particular way of existing in and knowing the world' (Wilson 1993: 6) in which the viewer must appropriate the social roles of a character, along with their 'horizons of understanding', for which the experience of television's images as 'veridical' is necessary. This is akin to Casebier's notion of the film spectator being able to see through the images to the 'world' being constructed by the text. Finally, Wilson examines the various strategies, especially verbal, by which television seeks to align the viewer with a character or presenter.

The field of hermeneutics and phenomenology is fluid and diffuse. In most writing from this position, there is little sense of a 'research design' being put into practice: writers (such as Wilson or Casebier) illustrate phenomenological and hermeneutic principles through textual examples rather than seeking to demonstrate a thesis through the phenomenological or hermeneutical analysis of samples of text. In these circumstances, it is difficult to list what the strengths or weaknesses of the method might be. Clearly its practitioners prefer it over both the claims to scientific objectivity made by classical content analysis or early semiotic analysis, and the tendency of post-structuralists to overlook or under-value the affective realm. However, they are also inclined to depend heavily on intuition, making their conclusions both untestable and unchallengeable.

This dependence upon intuition is less likely to be the case when writers combine phenomenological and hermeneutic readings with more conventional research methods, such as content analysis or structuralism.

Mumby and Spitzack (1985) provide an analysis of political stories on US television news, showing that metaphors of war, sport or drama are used consistently to 'make sense' of news events. Metaphors of war present politics as a series of battles to which strategy is applied; metaphors of sport refer to winners and losers; metaphors of drama see politics as a stage on which actors perform roles. The method of gathering data here was content analysis, applied to six news stories: the interpretation is hermeneutic, demonstrating the movement of meaning between wholes (news metaphors) and parts (the presentation of individual stories and of elements within these) in a hermeneutic circle.

Because of its emphasis on the affective aspect of texts, any phenomenological analysis will also involve study of the audience. One example is Dahlgren, who examined the reception of television news through his own experience (and that of fellow-researchers), discovering that their recall was not as good as the sense of understanding at the time would have led them to expect:

> Moreover, we found that the interpretation, the 'sense' of any given story, could vary considerably between us, even after repeated study. This had to do not only with the frames of reference we applied, our different stocks of knowledge, dispositions, chains of association, and so on, but also with the 'mind sets' with which we approached the stories. (Dahlgren 1985: 237)

This required both an analysis of the content of the news broadcasts, and interviews with the analysers. The conclusions were that reception is both cognitive and affective, both active and social, and that, in Jakobson's terms (1960), the referential function (the cognitive meaning(s)) may at times be subordinate to the poetic function (the affective meaning(s)). However, the final conclusion was that television news still remains stable and conventional and relatively fixed in both structures and content.

The explanations offered by Dahlgren can be understood in phenomenological terms: his frames of reference are the phenomenologist's 'horizons of expectation', his 'stocks of knowledge' are the phenomenologist's 'lifeworld' constructed out of 'horizons of experience'. He goes on to talk about other conclusions, but the implication for researchers is very clear: your social positioning (what we have been calling your 'framework') will influence how you read any text. There are obvious connections here with researchers such as Lewis or Fiske, operating from a cultural studies perspective.

These are creative uses of hermeneutic and/or phenomenological interpretation, in the context of research projects shaped by other methodologies, making their conclusions much easier to evaluate (see Chapter 12).

9.2 Research on textual structure and discourse

Content analysis (in any form) is concerned with the meaning of textual elements: structural analysis is concerned with how these elements are combined.

One form of combination is 'genre' – the elements of style that link particular examples of representation, demonstrating family likeness. This is a concept that originated in painting, was adapted for literature (constructing, for instance, the idea of the gothic novel, or the epic poem), and adapted further to construct popular film genres such as the musical, the 'woman's film', or the western (see, for instance, Wright 1975). Feuer (1992) discusses how aesthetic, ritual and ideological approaches to genre have been applied within the study of television, using the sitcom as an example.

In one sense, our interest in television news in this part of the book is an interest in a television genre, and all research that addresses news has to address issues of genre first, because all research must define its object (see, for instance, Fiske 1987: 281–3). In the case of television news, we need to distinguish 'news' from 'current affairs' or 'documentary feature', or to distinguish major prime time news bulletins from hourly updates or special bulletins as crisis news breaks. The concept of television 'flow' (Williams 1974) is a question of genre – a recognition of the difficulty of dividing up the television programme continuum.

Auteur criticism of television is relatively rare. Like hermeneutics (with which it is often combined), auteur criticism sees meaning as placed in a text by the 'author': across the career of an author, common threads (of subject or style) can be discerned, such that any new work can be read in the light of what went before. Obviously, this is easier to do if the author is working alone – as the author of a book or a poem or a play, or the painter of a picture. Except for journalists who are given a by-line, media production is harder to attribute to a single author, so the claim of 'author' status for the director of a film is a political move, a proposal that the director has a similar relation to a film as the individual author of a book. 'Auteur criticism' arose in France, when the New Wave critics wished to make precisely that political move – to claim authorship of film for those directors whose work they particularly admired, and to dismiss the rest as 'mere hacks', following orders from the studio. Andrew Sarris (1968) offered the first major auteur study in the English language, and since then the practice of attributing a film to a director has become universally accepted in film advertising, film criticism, and by the general public who attend films. It continues to be the basis for some research and writing on film (for instance issue 10 of the online journal *Screening the Past*), despite being largely eclipsed in the academy by post-structuralist research.

It has not, however, had the same currency in the study of other media. Journalists (whether working in the press, radio or television) have avoided claiming auteur status, probably because it would be inconsistent with journalistic concepts of objectivity, claims to be simply 'speaking the truth'. Except in rare instances (the work of Lynda laPlante or Dennis Potter in television drama, for instance) other media texts are still usually presented as either anonymous or the product of a team.

For television, the reason may be that, while film study was exploring auteur and genre concepts, television was not yet a respectable object of study in the academy, and by the time that it was claiming that status post-structuralism had entered the field and was in the process of undermining earlier forms of textual analysis of media products and the notion of a single unified author.

Auteur and genre approaches arise out of the humanities, particularly studies of literature. A comparable early social science approach to the study of texts was sociolinguistics, a field which examines the rules and protocols which govern language use in social situations. In the 1990s sociolinguistic approaches have been applied to a variety of media texts.

Bell provides an introduction to the study of mass media for students of sociolinguistics, based on his own and other researchers' work on news media 'as a form of speech community' (Bell 1991: 8). The model of language used here is a variation on the communication model we have already addressed, albeit a very complex version. Bell points, for example, to the complexity of language roles in the 'author' position. Methodologically, the post-positivist framework is evident in the comprehensive discussion of sample selection: newspapers or broadcast news media; 'hard' news or 'soft'; selection of news 'outlet'. Issues here are familiar and we have dealt with them in section 4.2 in Chapter 4. Grounding his discussion in his background experience as a journalist, Bell begins with some background on news production processes indicating the importance of an institutional understanding of newsroom practices to avoid basic misunderstandings of media language.

Following a survey of the main approaches to 'media miscommunication' (content analysis, critical linguistics, and semiotics), Bell suggests studies from each point of view are too often flawed by the desire to establish bias or ideological loading. For Bell, discourse analysis provides a better grounding for the analysis of media language, through its systematic approach to data, however he expresses reservations about 'its terminological problems and attempts to encompass everything under its umbrella' (Bell 1991: 216).

Structuralism and post-structuralism

In one sense, semiotics is part of the structuralist enterprise which sought to understand the ways meanings are generated through rule-governed systems which arise within cultures, in linguistic terms with *langue*. The structuralist, then, seeks to discover how the structures of any text create meaning(s).

Though it is usually thought of as an institutional study, Galtung and Ruge's pioneering work is actually a study of the paradigmatic and syntagmatic structures of television news (Galtung and Ruge 1973): they researched how the concept of 'newsworthiness' functions to determine which items will be selected for publication and how these will be ordered. This textual concern then has implications for a study of news processes, that is of news-making as institution.

In contrast to semiotics/structuralism, post-structuralism places its emphasis on language as it is used and inflected through age, gender, race, ethnicity, class and so on (on *parole* rather than *langue*). Post-structuralists assert that viewers do not decode a pre-existing meaning, but that they actively construct meaning in the process of reading: the post-structuralist seeks to understand how the meaning of a text is constructed within a cultural context. Though television news and current affairs refer more directly than most television programming to a world outside themselves, it is quite possible that viewers attend more to the mythic elements of news stories, that (using Jakobson's terms again) they give precedence to the poetic over the referential. The more this happens, then the less predictable will be the response of any individual viewer. This is where the structuralist and the post-structuralist part company: the structuralist seeking for the meaning within the textual structure, the post-structuralist seeking the meaning constructed by the reader.

In the article on news photographs discussed above, Hall (1972) bridges these positions, claiming that the possibilities of variant readings for any one text are limited, and that one of these (the meaning encoded by the source/writer/producer of the text) is the 'preferred reading', even if this is not the way the text is decoded in practice. The more power over meaning is attributed to the reader, the closer the researcher is to the post-structuralist position. Fiske, for instance, suggests that reading against the preferred position can produce pleasure: '... reading the news cynically or angrily can deconstruct its conventions and demystify their attempted ideological practice' (Fiske 1987: 285). Jensen (1990b: 57–8) argues that it is 'the polysemy of reception, rather than the polysemy of media texts, which must be explored in order to assess concretely the relative power of media and audiences'. He links analysis of news as text with analysis of news audiences within a political (cultural) context.

These are post-structuralist readings of television news, coming to terms with the concept of meaning being inherently plural and shifting: in such research structuralist methods are employed to post-structuralist ends.

The strengths of structuralist analysis are:

- its capacity to account for large texts, seen as unified wholes (for instance, a complete film, or a week's television news programming on a particular channel);
- its attention to how small elements (the signs and codes analysed by semiotics) fall into meaningful patterns;
- its refusal to rely upon intuition in the reading of texts.

Post-structuralism developed in response to what were seen as the weaknesses of the structuralist enterprise. The strengths of post-structuralist analysis are:

- its insistence that meaning is ultimately constructed by the interaction of text with audience, rather than inherent within the text alone;
- its acknowledgement that the researcher is not an objective observer of any textual phenomenon, but actively engaged in meaning production in relation to the text.

Phenomenologists, however, are correct that both these approaches have difficulty taking account of the affective realm: structuralists simply ignore it, post-structuralists try to acknowledge it by combining their methodology with interpretive frameworks such as psychoanalysis.

Narrative and discourse

Narratological methods may be employed in their own right, or they may be employed to discourse analysis ends: again the difference lies in the researcher's view of the relation between the text and the audience.

'Narratology' is the study of the structure of narrative: seeking to understand a narrative by considering how its elements fit together. Mills (1980) sets up a complex model of how space, time and 'value' interrelate within television news. He divides 'time' into sequence ('the following of one thing after another'), duration ('the time taken for something to happen') and period: 'period' is in turn divided into interval (period of recurrence), phase ('value-time' or how we place value upon time), and tense (past, present, future). 'Space' refers to 'the distance between units and between entities within a unit': it takes into account the shape, size and position on the screen of any element within the image, as well as the way the camera positions objects within the frame (by focal length, angle, closeness, width/distance). Space and time determine value, in conjunction with the commentary/narration, which 'positions' the audience in relation to the news, like a 'priest in the pulpit', which is why Mills chooses to call news 'pulpit drama'. He then examines selected news reports using these concepts, and concludes that television news establishes 'the role of newsmen [sic] as detectives and moral guardians, as the intermediaries between the fearful world "out there" and the security of the viewers living in that world ...' (Mills 1978: 70). He extends the analogy between news reporters and detectives by examining the similarities between a news report of a murder and an episode of the television drama *Starsky and Hutch*.

The strength of this research lies in the careful definitions of terms and the rigour with which these are applied, demonstrating how narrative operates as a structure. But narratology can be applied to much less formal ends. For instance, Bird and Dardenne also consider news as narrative, functioning to create and reinforce a society's myths: 'Readers do not only consume news as a reflection of reality, but as a symbolic text that defines murder as more noteworthy than car thefts' (Bird and Dardenne 1988: 71). They provide a summary of the research reports that take this approach, including Sperry (1981).

Sperry first questions how trust in television news could rise (demonstrated by ratings research) at the same time as the public was losing faith in journalism in general. She accounts for this 'not in the literal content of television news, but in the implicit content of its architecture'. She explains that: 'Television news is a blend of traditional, objective journalism and a kind of quasi-fictional prime-time story-telling which frames events in reduced terms with simple, clear-cut values' (Sperry 1981: 297). Her basic assumptions are that every story has three elements: a teller, a tale and a listener. Every tale (both fiction and non-fiction) is not 'truth' but a selection and shaping of elements by a narrator, whose authority (and therefore credibility) is central to whether the listener will place trust in the teller. For the news, the anchor is that narrator, carrying the burden of authority. Within each news bulletin are individual 'stories', each with a hero who solves a problem or conquers a villain. Within the news broadcast as a whole the narrator serves this function, providing a point of reference, even implying that she controls the content of the stories she presents. Some stories function as metaphors, and if the audience do not recognise this metaphorical intention they may respond inappropriately. Sperry defends this thesis with examples, leading to the conclusion that deliberately altering the structure may produce more authoritative news, and weaken the distinction between 'hard' and 'soft' news. The specific change she proposes is to 'make the newsman [sic] as newsman a part of the story' (Sperry 1981: 310).

Like some of the audience studies we discussed in section 3.5 in Chapter 3 (Lopate 1977; Modleski 1982), the reader of such a research report cannot criticise the methodology, for it is hidden from us. We can only criticise the conclusions, and we have to provide our own, contrary, evidence to do this. This is sometimes easy enough to do: to provide counter-examples for the examples quoted in the report. But to do this still does not really invalidate the report, which stands or falls only on how convincingly it makes its argument from that evidence which it does present.

Research that explicitly claims to be 'post-modern' is even less amenable to rational criticism. McKie presents this abstract of his research:

> From the theoretical perspective of postmodernism's three R's (relativism, referentiality, and reflexivity), this paper contrasts television news with comedy. At this stage in eco-history it contends that, with particular regard to ethnicity and environment, the former is a dangerously exclusive area, while the latter requires more serious consideration. Questioning the truth claims of 'reality programming' and the construction of an exclusive New World Order based on an outmoded scientific world view, it concludes by advocating a greater range of knowledge traditions and a broader humour of inclusion to combat the false reassurance rituals of television news. (McKie 1993: 68)

In exemplary post-modern fashion, McKie speaks in first person, reflects upon his own methods and attitudes, deliberately transgresses generic boundaries himself as well as addressing that kind of transgression on television (in *Drop the Dead Donkey,* a sitcom set in a newsroom). Here there are no 'conclusions' for readers to evaluate: we can only judge the report by how perceptive we consider its author to be, and how well the piece succeeds in provoking new insights. That judgement will probably come out of how closely our own intellectual framework matches that of the writer.

9.3 Conclusion

Textual research may be directed at discovering the explicit (surface/denotative) meaning of the text, or the latent (underlying/connotative) meaning. Such research on television news, therefore, is often linked to a search for the ideological content. So the Glasgow Media Group identified systematic bias against the working class, writers such as Rakow and Kranich identify the operation of patriarchal values. Several of the studies discussed here (including US Commission on Civil Rights 1977) refer to the representation of race, but there is also a long tradition of studies specifically on that topic: Hall (1990) divides these representations into 'overt' and 'inferential', and Allen (1999) provides an overview of the research as well as some of his own analyses.

But when the research is directed to understanding how the news functions as discourse, it no longer seeks a meaning already in the text, but rather considers how meaning is constructed in the process of production and/or reading. This is likely to be from a constructivist or critical theory position, and using post-structuralist methods.

In the three literature review chapters (Chapters 3, 6 and now 9) we have referred repeatedly to the way research on audiences, institutions and texts bleed into each other. Much of the research which primarily addresses one of these has implications for either or both of the others, and sometimes draws attention to these implications, either in the way definitions are produced or in the way methodologies are applied – for instance in the audience implied in some content analysis, or in the concept of 'horizon of understanding' in hermeneutics, or in the notion of the implied reader in narratology. Research which deliberately addresses these interactions, however, is still relatively rare.

The Cultural Indicators (CI) programme is one of the few research streams that in principal addresses all three, and attempts to link them. However, even there the emphasis on researching audiences through cultivation analysis has overwhelmed the other two aspects. Wober (1998: 62) proposes that this imbalance may have developed out of an American reluctance to embrace the Marxist framework underlying the kind of institutional process analysis that would be necessary to fully realise CI's global aims.

But Wober also recognises that part of the reason is the sheer scope of the enterprise, and the overwhelming difficulties for a researcher of keeping all three balls in the air at once. Doris Graber (1978) was one of the first to attempt this balancing act, by linking text (content analysis of news items), audience (research into men's and women's responses to selected news items) and institution (the operation of the agenda-setting process within the newsroom). This is post-positivist research, in contrast with Valerie Walkerdine (1986), who takes a constructivist position. Walkerdine looks at herself looking at a family looking at a film, and in the process covers audiences, institutions and texts: the psychological and social positioning of herself and of the family she is watching and how these have been constructed historically as well as in the present of the research. The result is an attempt to confront the polysemy of the text (she gives a very interesting analysis of the film *Rocky 2*), to account for the variant readings of different people in terms of their personal history and their present social position, and to acknowledge the voyeuristic role of the researcher in the process.

Such complex projects are now more frequent and often more sophisticated, for instance Gripsrud (1995), Buckingham (2000) or Graber (2001). This is not surprising in a post-modern world, where intellectual boundaries are constantly under challenge. We have not provided advice on this kind of research, as it requires a range and depth of expertise that it would be unreasonable to expect of the novice to whom this book is addressed. We advise that any researcher come to grips with the research possibilities of a more limited field before trying to develop a project that requires a comprehensive knowledge of everything. So, in the next chapter (on data gathering and analysis) we will confine our discussion to texts, rather than try to consider all the methods that might link textual research with research on audiences and institutions.

CHAPTER 10

Gathering and Analysing Textual Data

Unlike much research data on audiences, media texts (such as newspaper articles, television or radio programmes, web sites) and cultural sites (such as shopping malls or beaches) usually exist before the research that seeks to understand them.

There are two families of research on texts: research concerning content and meaning, and research concerning structure and discourse. Within each of these, there are both quantitative and qualitative approaches, and considerable interaction between these. Quantitative approaches (classical content analysis and some forms of semiotic and structural analysis) seem to separate out the gathering of data from its analysis: qualitative approaches (phenomenology and hermeneutics, post-structuralist analysis, discourse analysis) elide the distinction between data gathering and analysis. To accommodate these differences, we have in this part of the book changed our format to link analysis with data gathering, rather than with interpretation. Remember to have an ethics policy in place before you begin to gather data (see section 1.5 in Chapter 1).

10.1 Gathering and analysing data on textual content

Content analysis

The term 'content analysis' implies a distinction between 'content' and 'form', and so a linear model of communication: from this position, audiences may be assumed to be undifferentiated and passive (effects studies) or socially differentiated and more active (uses and gratifications studies) but it is nevertheless assumed that they receive much the same 'message', as meaning is inherent in the text.

The search for scientific reliability and validity has led to the refinement and standardisation of techniques, but all content analysis still consists in taking a sample of media, establishing categories of content, measuring the presence of each category within the sample, and interpreting the results, usually against some external criteria.

Sampling

Content analysis is not concerned with people, so does not use the term 'population', but the principles of sampling discussed in section 4.2 in Chapter 4 still apply: if adequate sampling techniques are used, to ensure that the sample is representative, it should be possible to generalise from the results.

Sampling procedures:

- Define the parameters of the content to be sampled. This will require selection of:
  - the medium (film, radio, television, press, or more than one of these if a comparison is to be made);
  - the type of content (which might be defined generically, eg 'prime time television news' or by subject matter, for instance 'political reporting', or any other appropriate way).
- Select a method of sampling:
  Probability sampling allows conclusions to be generalised. It is particularly useful when a large amount of data is to be analysed, all of which is equally accessible, for instance if the question is the changing editorial policy in a newspaper over the whole of its life, when a complete archive exists.
  - Simple random sampling would in this case consist of assigning a number to every editorial published, and selecting numbers at random from a table.
  - Systematic random sampling would in this case consist of assigning a number to every editorial, dividing this number by the periodicity (the number of cases you have decided to use as a sample), selecting randomly a number less than the periodicity, starting at that number on the list, and then selecting systematically from that point on (remembering the risk of periodicity in the sampling frame).
  - Stratified sampling would in this case consist of defining sub-groups within the list of editorials (eg those of particular editors, or particular days of the week) and then using random or systematic sampling within each subgroup.
  - Cluster sampling would in this case consist of selecting a cluster, eg first week after Easter every year.

Non-probability sampling does not allow conclusions to be generalised, but is still useful for exploratory research before hypotheses are to be developed for more rigorous testing, or for qualitative research where the results are not necessarily intended to be generalised.

- ○ Purposive sampling is selecting a sample that will test the theory, that is perhaps deliberately extreme or deviant: if your interest was in editorial political party bias, you might select those editorials during an election campaign.
- ○ Quota sampling is selecting a sample that appears to match what is already known: one early content analysis (Arnheim 1944) assumed that the serials to be analysed were typical of all radio serials, and defended this by describing their formulaic character, and pointing out one English and two American serials as deviating from this formula and so not examined within his project.
- ○ Convenience or availability sampling is using what comes to hand, knowing that it is not representative: in some cases, for instance when archival procedures have been defective, this may be all that is possible.

Establishing categories

Setting up categories for measurement is often extremely difficult. The researcher's interest may be in political party bias in newspaper editorials, but editorials are unlikely to state: 'this paper officially supports the Democrats'. Bias will probably have to be inferred from the content and that means deciding what kinds of content might justify such inferences: Do we simply count the number of times the party is mentioned by name? Or what actions or policies of the parties were reported? Or try to measure degrees of support for the policies? Support might be measured by:

- numbers of stories. However, how will you count stories that have party implications that are not made explicit, or stories that concern more than one party?
- column inches. This allows discrimination concerning the importance given to stories, but still does not solve the problem of implicit elements;
- bias in the choice of words. How will you identify and measure 'bias'?

The more concrete you make your categories, the easier it is to define them precisely. Berger describes category labels for a study of comics like this:

> physical characteristics of heroes and heroines, villains and villainesses:
>> color of hair, color of eyes, height, weight, age, body structure, sex, race;
>
> social aspects of characters:
>> occupations, education, religion, socioeconomic class, status, role, ethnic background;

emotional nature of characters:

> warm or cold, anxious or calm, stable or unstable, authoritarian or dependent, hostile or friendly, powerful or weak, loving or hateful, individualist or conformist, vivacious or apathetic. (1991: 33)

The first group is reasonably easy to define and measure, the middle group becomes difficult in some cases (eg class), the third group involves subjective judgment and the likelihood that the categories will be blurred. And this is for a genre in which the images are still and the values simplified: forming definitions for television news is likely to be more difficult than this (see Gerdes (1982) for one solution).

In practice, the researcher is forced to compromise, making the best possible category definitions in the circumstances, acknowledging that they are always imperfect. See Sebstrup (1981) for an example of the process of refining hypotheses till they can be used as category definitions.

Measuring

Scientific experiment usually involves counting of discrete entities, or uses quantification to divide continuums (weight, height, etc). Media analysis is not dealing with quantifiable entities so, even if the categories have been well defined, measuring them is never easy.

There are specific problems of establishing units of measurement in different media. For instance, how do we accommodate movement across time in film or television? How do we measure spatial relations such as depth of field in a photograph? For newspapers, if we measure by column inches how do we weight for position on the page and vice versa? Or how do we measure the placement of photographs or the size of headlines and how do we balance one of these against any of the others? Again, these are not insoluble problems, and the researcher finds a way through them by trial and error, gradually refining the units of measurement just as the category definitions were refined. But the solutions must be recognised as arbitrary and contingent: determined by the circumstances of the research rather than by the intrinsic properties of the subject of the research.

On large content analysis projects, employing more than one researcher, the problem is compounded. The principle researcher must not only define content categories and units of measurement for her own use, but articulate these in sufficient detail that others can apply them in a consistent way. Usually the principle researcher writes down the definitions, demonstrates by example, provides practice until the other researchers are confident, and monitors the results until she is sure that the other researchers are operating in a similar fashion to herself and to each other. This is called establishing 'inter-coder reliability'. An example is the instructions given to censors: they are couched in such general language that you would not think they could be used to discriminate, but in practice the censors share so many experiences of films, and debate what they see and decide, until they can anticipate what others will say about a film and be reasonably sure that they are judging in similar ways.

Measurement is done on a standardised coding sheet, developed to suit the needs of your particular project: again, see Gerdes (1982) for the headings which may be used on such a coding sheet for television news.

The significant problems of content analysis (described in the first sub-section of section 9.1 in Chapter 9) should not stop a researcher from using the method when it is appropriate.

Hermeneutics and phenomenology

This chapter provides practical advice on research methodology. However, it is difficult to get a clear sense of what is meant by either phenomenology or hermeneutics from writing on the media (television in particular) and even harder to explain how they work as research method.

In research applying phenomenology and/or hermeneutics, data gathering, analysis and interpretation all seem to be happening at the same time. There is no standard method of sampling: however, the text samples to be analysed usually fall somewhere between the large samples appropriate to content analysis, and the very small samples usually studied semiotically. As we explained in the third sub-section of section 9.1 in Chapter 9, hermeneutics generally does not require systematic defining of categories or units of measurement, and analysis seems to depend upon intuition.

The key terms seem to be 'horizon' and 'hermeneutic circle'. The hermeneutic notion of 'horizon' (see Wilson (1993) or Casebier (1991), discussed in the third sub-section of section 9.1) can be used as an alternative to the concept of codes in semiotics (discussed in the third sub-section of section 10.1 in Chapter 10). The concept of the 'hermeneutic circle', in which meaning arises out of the cyclical interaction between the work as a whole and its constituent parts, has been applied for instance by Mumby and Spitzack (1985) to television news (see the third sub-section of section 9.1). However, Mumby and Spitzack used content analysis as their basic methodology, and applied hermeneutics as a method of interpretation of the results.

In the absence of a prescribed methodology, instead of offering you instructions on how to 'do' hermeneutics or phenomenology, we recommend that, if you wish to use these approaches, your research design must arise out of a thorough understanding of their philosophical principles. This places a heavy burden on the researcher – one that novices may feel reluctant to take up. Our discussion in the third sub-section of section 9.1 and the first sub-section of section 11.2 in Chapter 11 should be enough for you to at least recognise and evaluate other people's research done from a hermeneutical or phenomenological position, even if you do not choose these approaches for your own research. You might, of course, still choose to use hermeneutic or phenomenological principles to interpret data gathered by other methods.

Semiotic analysis

One of the attractions of semiotics has been its attempt to provide a more systematic methodology, which does not simply rely on intuition. We have used the term 'semiotic' in two senses – to refer to a model of communication in which meaning is constructed in the process of the circulation of signs, and to refer to a method of textual analysis which is based upon this communication model. It is the second sense which concerns us in this chapter, 'semiotics' as the systematic study of signs.

Semiotics initially paid attention primarily to the text, attempting to eliminate the subjective, to make conclusions testable because reproducible: like classical content analysis, theoretically anyone who did the same exercise equally thoroughly would come to the same conclusion. But this required a method that completely accounted for everything within the system to be analysed, which proved an impossible goal, even though semioticians selected texts of limited size and looked closer and closer at the smallest elements of meaning within the text.

Semiotics starts with the assumption that all communication occurs by the exchange of signs, each of which has at least one **signified** (a mental concept) and at least one **signifier** (a physical aspect). The signifier 'cat' (a word, written on a page or spoken) brings signifieds to the reader's mind (associations which draw on previous experience).

The sign 'cat' and the sign 'bat' have both different signifieds and different signifiers. However the word 'cat' and a drawing of a cat, though different signifiers, seem to suggest the same signified (a furry, four-legged, domestic animal that purrs). If this were so, then it would follow that each signifier has only one signified; that signifieds refer to something in the real world; that each signified is fixed, inherent in the sign, just waiting to be discovered; and that therefore signs continue to exist outside the communication process. This is where the science of semiotics began, and why at this level it must be identified as a methodology which operates with a linear model of communication. However, there are very few examples of such 'pure' semiotics, and none that we know of in research on television news as text. These mostly accept a far more sophisticated view of semiotics, which we can demonstrate if we consider our example further...

- If each signifier had only one signified, then 'cat' could not mean all the different things we make it mean (not only furry domestic animal, but also furry wild animal, nasty woman, whip with multiple tails, sailing boat with double hulls, etc). Even for signs which appear to have only one meaning (signified), you cannot be sure that my meaning is the same as yours: do we really have the same idea of 'thickness' or 'democracy' or 'wild' or 'red'...?
- Sometimes we communicate actual objects in the real world. If you give me flowers it is a communication (of friendship, of thanks, of sympathy, etc); that is, the flowers function both as material object and as sign. But

most of the time we do not exchange objects, we only exchange signs, and in these cases the sign does not refer directly to something in the real world, but goes through a mediating process in our minds. So the referent of the sign is a mental concept, something that links the sign and the real world: in the case of our sign 'cat', the referent is not any real furry object, but rather our mental concept of 'catness'.

- So, because we must take into account the mental concept as referent, and this is dependent on the particular mind engaged in the communication, our understanding of communication must include a place for the producer and the receiver of the sign (who may or may not be the same person). Some signs actually change their signified: the personal pronouns are called 'shifters' because their signified is determined by who uses them. But even for signs that do not shift in that way, the producer of the sign has chosen a particular signifier (rather than any other), and both the producer and the reader of the sign will select from among the many possible variations of signified, so the meaning(s) will be constructed by the interaction between the sign and the user(s).
- Finally, because meaning is not fixed and inherent within the sign, and because signs construct meaning only as they circulate within communication, and because the signs refer only to mental concepts rather than to referents in the real world, then they also necessarily refer only to other signs, in what has been called an endless 'play of signification'.

This leads us to amend the simple diagram presented in Chapter 1 (Figure 1.2), to place the real world outside the communication event, though still connected to it, as shown in Figure 10.1.

Theoretically, every time we try to explain the meaning of something we simply restate one of the possible meanings, without ever reaching 'the' meaning. In practice, we usually agree enough for communication to continue, provided we share enough of the culture/ideology which contains the communication. However, it is no longer possible to talk about the 'meaning of the sign', only about how signification operates, and one of the chief ways it does this is through simultaneous similarity and difference.

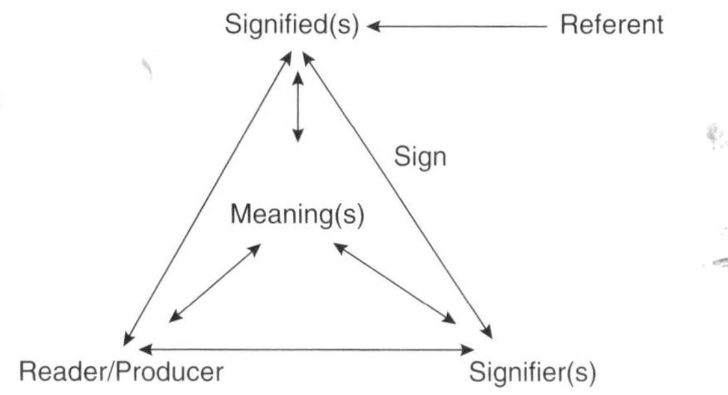

Figure 10.1 Signification of a sign

For instance, one code of linguistic signifiers is grammar: any word functions within this code (that is how they are similar), but they all function differently ('I' is a pronoun and 'run' is a verb; 'run' is present tense, 'ran' is past tense, etc.). One code of visual signifiers is colour: all colour has depth and texture and affects the retina in specific ways that make the members of the code similar, but our minds register differences that we label with different names (this is another example of how one sign – a colour, refers us to or is referred back by another – a word, in an endless cycle).

Colour is a good example of how signs operate at two levels:

- **denotation**, as near as possible to a literal meaning, though in practice only highly specialised systems of signs like mathematics can produce completely denotative statements like 6 + 2 = 8;
- **connotation**, the value added to the literal meaning.

For instance, 'green' denotes a particular colour response of our retinas, and connotes nature, permission to move forward, the Irish, jealousy, illness, etc. You can change the connotation of a sign by changing the signifier while retaining the signified (for instance, a photo of the same girl in clear light and hard focus or in dim light and soft focus). Ultimately, it is culture which organises our responses to signs, and this process can be represented diagrammatically as in Figure 10.2.

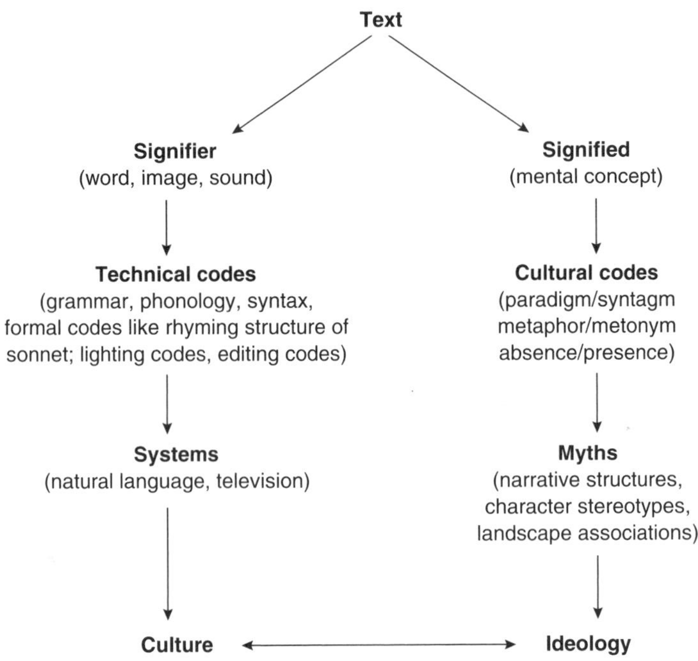

Figure 10.2 Signification of a text

Every text is composed of signs, which all have both signifier(s) and signified(s). Signifiers (which in media are most likely to be words, images or sounds) are organised through technical codes (words organised through the codes of grammar, phonology and syntax; images through lighting and editing codes, etc) into systems (such as television) which operate within a particular culture. Signifieds are organised through cultural codes (such as the binary oppositions found by structural analysis) into myth, which operates within ideology (see the first sub-section of section 11.2 in Chapter 11). Signifieds are always related to other signifieds, through codes of presence (metonymy, **syntagm**, organisation) or absence (metaphor, paradigm, selection).

Every signified is one of a set (a paradigm) of similar signifieds, and our selection of one necessarily excludes every other one of that set: if we make our cat all black it cannot also be all white, if we make our pet a cat the same pet cannot also be a goldfish. This is a relation of absence, a relation to all the other possible signifieds that have been excluded. Black and white are members of the paradigm of colours, cats and goldfish are members of the paradigm of domestic pets.

Every sign is placed in a text syntagmatically, in relation to other signs (a relation of presence). In the photograph of our black cat, she is eating from a bowl, and standing beside our Labrador dog; this photograph is placed in our album before the one of our white cat and after that of the Labrador as a puppy; or this photograph is a still from a moving picture sequence in which she eats her dinner and then jumps out the window.

Traffic lights are part of the paradigms of traffic signals (along with flashing lights at level crossings, stop signals, arrows painted on the road) and of coded colour relationships (red for danger, green for safety); they are displayed syntagmatically (spatially with red above orange above green, and temporally with each flashing in a particular pattern).

Paradigms and syntagms are culturally specific, and they fall into patterns which produce the myths for that culture (narrative structures, character stereotypes, associations attached to physical features like landscape, and relationships among all these). This is a view of 'myth' which comes from anthropology and sees myth not as falsehood but as social explanation. Within this view, myths contribute to ideology, to the unconscious set of values and beliefs which provide frames for our thinking and so help make sense of the world in which we live (see the first sub-section of section 11.2 in Chapter 11).

This long explanation is necessary because, though semiotic analysis is still a form of content analysis (in the broad sense) it produces a very different result from classical content analysis (in the narrow sense), and its procedures are rather different. In fact, like hermeneutics and phenomenology, there are no fixed (or even generally agreed) procedures: you are left to derive your own procedures from basic principles, and your success will be judged by how convincing you are rather than how well you meet scientific criteria of reliability and validity (see Chapter 12). So we recommend that you read widely what others have done using these principles, and we offer a starting point for this in the research discussed in Chapter 9. You might also consider the questions and exercises posed by Hartley (1982: 154–87), or the example analysed by Fiske (1987: 296–308). Bignell (2002) has a chapter on television news, in which he provides examples of semiotic analysis using the narrative functions proposed by Hartley (1982: 118–19): 'framing', 'focusing', 'realising' and 'closing'.

Most reports of good semiotic analysis cover similar ground to classical content analysis, starting with a literature review, a definition of terms, a question to be answered, and a description of the research design. The sample is usually a single example (or a small range) of text, selected purposively: for instance it may be a single item in a news report, selected to illustrate how women are presented in news stories. To extract this single item from the television continuum, the researcher may just use common sense to locate the first words uttered by the presenter about this item and consider the sequence ended when the first words are uttered about the next item: or she might use narratology (see the second sub-section of section 10.2 in this chapter) to locate a sequence structurally.

You can then make a careful shot listing of the sequence: a coding sheet for this purpose is likely to have a column for the time (in seconds), a column for a description of the visual content (or more than one column for complex visuals, such as embedded or superimposed images or titles), a column for a transcription of the words of the presenter or reporter, and a column for other sound (diegetic – that is, obviously emanating from what you can see in the image, or non-diegetic – that is, with no obvious source within the image).

From this description of the sequence, you will extract smaller units of measurement, defined by examining the signifiers, and the technical codes into which these fall. The images may be a combination of studio footage, location footage, and fixed images (such as inserts, maps, intertitles). For live action (both in the studio and on location), editing codes break down the sequence further, into shots. Camera codes can be considered – both the position of the camera in relation to the action (close-up to wide shot), and the movement of the camera. Speech codes may be aural (words spoken) or visual (words printed on the screen), they may be synchronised or voice-over, they may support or contradict other sound.

The coding categories come from the signifieds – from cultural codes or from ideological concepts. If your concern is with the representation of gender, you will be looking at the people: not just the raw numbers of men and women which might be addressed by classical content analysis, but more subtle matters, such as who speaks and for how long and to whom, how people present themselves (through codes of dress, makeup, hair, voice), how they relate to each other (closeness and distance, tone of voice), how the camera treats them (coming in close, looking up at them or down on them)...

As you work, you may try to link the coding of signifiers and signifieds. You may need a separate sheet for the coding of the signifieds, and possibly others that connect the two axes. It might, for instance, be worth extracting the dress codes for men and women across the different visual signifiers: you might construct a grid with signifieds on one axis (men's and women's dress codes) and signifiers on the other (across the various codes, such as editing, lighting, colour).

Obviously, these subtle matters are not reducible to measurable entities, so 'measurement' in semiotic research is unlikely to be statistical: your coding sheets are intended not to produce scientifically reliable and valid claims, but rather to help you find those connections and relationships that might otherwise not be noticed. The relationships that you discover by this process are then interpreted through the kinds of frameworks of understanding discussed in Chapter 11. Results, in the form of conclusions reached partly by induction and partly by intuition, are usually presented discursively – in descriptive prose.

The differences between this and classical content analysis are matters of attitude rather than of process: you might compare, for instance, the analytical categories used for content analysis by Gerdes (1982) with those for semiotic analysis discussed by Fiske (1987: 283–93).

10.2 Gathering and analysing data on textual structures

Structural analysis

The 'structure' is what holds the parts of something together. Structural anthropology assumes that meaning arises from the relationships among social elements, rather than being inherent in the individual elements themselves (Leach 1976). Similarly, textual analysis can be a search for what holds the whole text together: some grid that explains the rules operating within the textual structure. Like early semiotics, structuralist textual analysis started within a linear model of communication, looking for syntagmatic or paradigmatic structures within texts.

Paradigmatic structures

One of the commonest paradigmatic structures identified within texts is binary oppositions, coming from the tradition particularly associated with Swiss structural anthropologist Claude Lévi-Strauss. He hoped to discover human nature, across cultures, so he analysed two aspects of primitive societies:

- the rules governing marriage and inheritance and family responsibility (kinship systems);
- the stories passed on within the society to explain the world around them, both natural phenomena and social customs (myths).

With myth, his method was to divide each story into segments according to relations and statuses, compare these segments with each other and with those of other stories to find the common elements, show these elements as transformations of other elements, and trace the rules governing these transformations. He found that myths were similarly structured across many different cultures, and worked within patterns of parallels, oppositions and inversions, all based on dichotomies, which could be presented diagrammatically, for example as pairs or consonant triangles. The basic oppositions he discovered were nature/culture, and man/woman and the rest flowed from these (raw/cooked, good/bad, etc) (Lévi-Strauss 1955).

But Lévi-Strauss was interested not only in finding out such underlying structures, but in explaining why humans choose to use such stories, instead of just saying what we mean directly. He concluded that myths are coded statements, expressing unconscious wishes which are inconsistent with conscious experience. One such universal myth is the Oedipus story: sons 'kill' their fathers and 'marry' their mothers. The attraction of structuralism for psychoanalysis (and vice versa) should be obvious – they are both concerned with something going on below the level of consciousness, and each can support the other's argument (see the second sub-section of section 11.2 in Chapter 11).

Lévi-Strauss, as an anthropologist, studied primitive societies: he believed that in modern times myth had been replaced by history and science. However, Russian folklorist Vladimir Propp applied structuralist methods to the Russian fairy tale – a form still circulating at the time of his research (the 1920s, though his work was not translated into English for 30 years). Like Lévi-Strauss, Propp analysed these tales according to relations and statuses. The statuses were the characters, who fell into various categories according to their relation to other characters: hero, villain, donor, dispatcher, false hero, helper, princess and her father (Propp 1975: 79–80). He found a limited number of recurring patterns, and this work has been taken as a model by some film theorists (eg Will Wright's 1975 structural study of the western), though it has also been criticised (Bordwell 1988; Jameson 1981).

The methods pioneered by Lévi-Strauss and Propp were seen as scientific (reliable because replicable) and have been applied widely across media research: they can still be used as models for positivist and post-positivist research. For instance, if your concern was gender representation within news reports, you might use Propp's character relations as coding categories for either content analysis (of a large sample of news items) or semiotic analysis (within a single news item). You could also develop your own coding categories, seeking binary oppositions: male/female, dominant/subordinate, and so on. You would, of course, still need an intellectual framework (Chapter 11) within which to interpret your results.

Both early semiotics and structuralism have been criticised by post-structuralists, who are usually located within a critical theory or constructivist paradigm. Post-structuralists deny that meaning is inherent within signs, and so deny the possibility of adequately categorising or measuring the signs and structures within a text. Post-structuralist textual analysis, like hermeneutic analysis, does not have a set of rules to follow. Instead it has a philosophical position, which is put into practice through each piece of textual analysis, establishing techniques appropriate to the question being explored, while sharing certain attitudes:

- The position of the researcher is acknowledged as a part of the research, from asking the initial question to final conclusions.
- The result of the analysis is description (a restating of the content of the signs, or the underlying structures), not prescription (talking about what 'ought' or 'should' be in the sign or structure).
- Such description from a viewing position is always and necessarily contingent and relative, never objective, fixed, permanent.
- But it is still valuable, adds to the sum total of knowledge and understanding of the world: the fact that 'truth' is an impossible goal does not prevent us from seeking it.

The post-structuralist may use techniques already discussed to understand signification (through semiotics) or paradigmatic structures (through structuralism), or may be more interested in the analysis of syntagmatic structures (through narratology and discourse analysis).

Narratology and discourse analysis

Syntagmatic structures

To understand the syntagmatic structures, we need to understand the relationships of one signifier to another. There have been many attempts to apply to the audio/visual media the equivalent of grammar (the inflected relation between words used in speech or writing) or syntax (the functional relation between words used in speech or writing): see, for instance, the discussion in Metz (1974: 31–91). So far, none has managed to account for all the elements in such a complex spatial and temporal field, which is not divided neatly into clearly bounded signs. A related difficulty is that grammar accounts for words and syntax for sentences, but neither can account for larger structures like paragraphs or chapters in a novel: for television news, these larger structures are daily broadcasts within a particular timeslot, one news slot with another on the same day, news programming schedules within the institution of television programming.

Tzvetan Todorov (1981: 48–53, originally published in France, 1968) has proposed one way of analysing the syntagmatic structure of literary texts, that we have found useful for 'texts' of all kinds, shown in Figure 10.3.

We have adapted Todorov's terms here: our thanks to William D. Routt for discussions many years ago which resulted in this model, though its flaws are our own responsibility. Our model proposes that texts are composed of sequences, which contain propositions. Propositions have two elements: actants

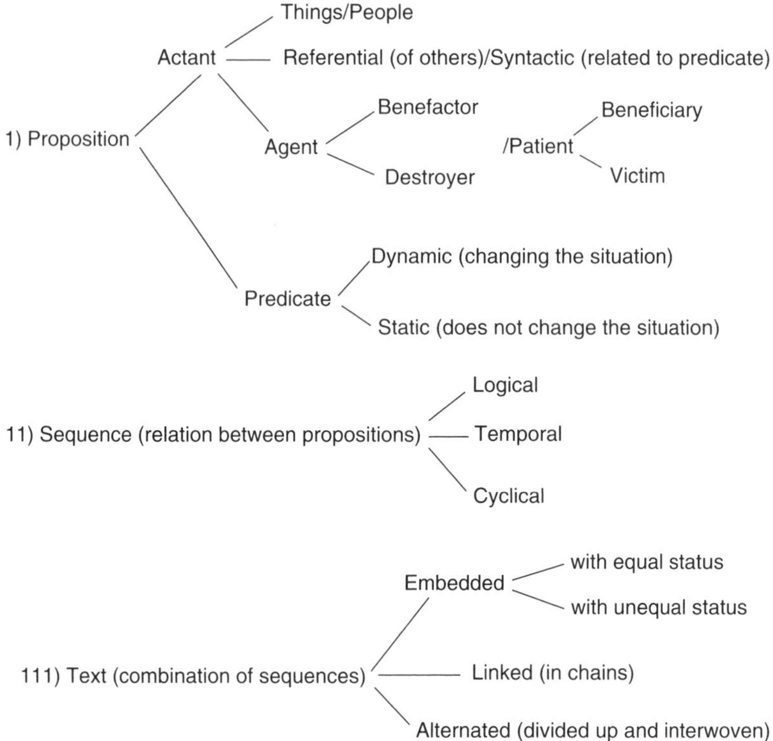

Figure 10.3 Todorov's model for analysing the syntagmatic structure of literary texts

and predicates. Actants can be further distinguished in several ways: as things or people; as referential (related to other actants, including outside the text) or as syntactic (related to the predicate, always within the text); as agent (influencer/benefactor or corruptor/destroyer) or patient (beneficiary or victim). Predicates are either dynamic (changing the situation) or static (not changing the situation). Sequences relate propositions to each other, either logically, temporally or cyclically. Texts are composed of sequences, either linked (in chains, one event of a story following another), alternated (divided up and interwoven with each other, as when a story has several threads on the go at once, and moves between them), or embedded (inside another sequence, either with equal status or with unequal status, as in a flashback or flash forward within a story).

Todorov was speaking about a particular kind of literary text – classical narrative, which he thought of as mythological, chronological and causal. But we have found this model useful much more widely, in understanding any text, at any level. For instance, with literature the text may be a sentence, or a paragraph, or a chapter, or a novel or the body of work of an author. For media, we can think of a day's television programming as a text, with our television news broadcast as a sequence. Or our television news programme as a text, with individual stories within it as sequences. Or each individual news story as a text, with each shot (the part of the track between two editing marks) as a sequence. This can be a very helpful tool for a television researcher, who needs to locate the signifiers for semiotic analysis, or to break up the television continuum for structural analysis. For instance, it may be that the news anchor is a referential actant (a person, whose relation to the other actants and to the predicate is only as commentator), the news item relates the anchor logically to the events being described in the story, and this story is linked in a chain with other stories within the news broadcast.

This does not solve all the problems of dividing up the television continuum, but it does provide a systematic way to select text for semiotic study, provided the text uses narrative in some way. 'Narrative' is, at its simplest, a chronicle of how something gets from A through B to C: it has been described as consisting of an initial equilibrium, which is disturbed and then through the course of events restored, though always in a way that makes the place where the narrative ends slightly different from the place where it began (Todorov 1977: 11). To analyse television news this way, you would select your news broadcast (or item), identify the actants and predicates, then consider the syntagmatic structures which organise these as signifiers. For instance, your item may include a presenter (an actant) located where an action occurred (a predicate): the relation between the two is established syntagmatically through sound (she talks about the location and the events that occurred there) and image (she is standing next to a pile of weapons captured in the event, talking to another actant who took part in or witnessed the event). The narrative structure can then be identified: relating the sequence of events in the real world to the telling of a story about these events, embedded inside another structure of 'news-gathering' as process.

To explain the 'structuration' of narrative (the process by which narrative acts as structure), Roland Barthes (1915–80) developed a schema of five narrative 'codes', derived from and demonstrated in his analysis of Balzac's novella *Sarrasine* (Barthes 1975). The 'symbolic code' organises binary oppositions (like those identified by Lévi-Strauss). The 'semic code' creates characters and settings, by attaching elements of meaning ('semes' such as, for people, facial features, habitual gestures, clothing, actions) to a figure within the narrative. In this sense, a 'figure' is an immediately recognisable (because culturally coded) 'type', which may be a person (like Propp's character types) or another element within the narrative (a setting like 'the beach', or an object like 'a top hat'). The 'referential code' is what connects elements of meaning to existing knowledges, that is to other concepts rather than to any 'real world' outside the codes. The 'proairetic code' relates any action within the narrative to what we know of other actions (such as 'falling in love' or 'declaring war'). The 'hermeneutic code' controls how the elements of the narrative fit together to provide us with an understanding of why things happen and how problems will be solved: Barthes proposes stages in this process, analogous to Propp's narrative functions.

Applying Barthes' codes to television news, it is:

- the symbolic code that attaches significance to the gender of the news anchor (the binary opposition of man/woman);
- the semic code that organises the signs by which we identify her femaleness (dress, hair, makeup, all within culturally coded standards for television news);
- the referential code that helps us to understand the relation between what she says and what we have heard other news anchors say in similar broadcasts about this event;
- the proairetic code that connects the events in the story she is narrating to other sets of similar events;
- the hermeneutic code that proposes perhaps that this is a 'good news' story that will end happily or perhaps that it is an ongoing element of one of the larger 'problems' that the news brings to us each night.

So, if our question concerns the structure of this particular news item (or its syntagmatic relation to others within this broadcast), we will find Todorov's model useful. If our question concerns '**intertextuality**' (the relation between this item in this broadcast and other items in other broadcasts), then Barthes' model may be more useful.

This shifts our attention from the structure, to the discourse of the text. Narrative is **diachronic** (taking place over time), so, it has a beginning, middle and end. Because television, unlike newspapers or even books, moves forward inexorably, there seems to be a natural connection between television and narrative, which is the primary structure of ALL television: not just fiction, but also game shows, advertisements, news... However, no two tellings of any story, even in the most 'formulaic' of television, are ever quite the same. We are talking here about the difference between story and discourse, and so about narrative theory or 'narratology'.

The distinction between story and discourse has been made by many theorists in different ways (Aristotle's *mythos/logos*, the Russian formalists' *fabula/szujet*, Claude Bremond's *récit/raconte*). The particular usage we are employing derives from Seymour Chatman (1978), who proposes that narrative must have both story (its content, the events and existents it talks about, the 'what'), and discourse (the way in which it is told, the selection and ordering of the events and existents, the 'how'). For, though a narrative must have a beginning, a middle and an end, they need not always be presented in that order. From this perspective, story is potential, discourse is actual; story elements (plot functions, characters) are predictable (as demonstrated by Propp's work on fairytales), whereas discourse provides variety/surprise.

The story is transformable from one medium to another. When a novel is transformed into a BBC television series, for example, most of the basic story elements remain the same: most of the characters feature in both novel and TV series, many of the events and locations will be in both. However the differences between the novel and the TV production (such as the condensing of several characters into one, the elimination of some locations and the moving of events from one location to another) make up what Chatman calls 'discourse'.

Such a view allows us to think of all media texts as discourse, as constructions of a particular telling from a vastly larger potential story, and this puts all such tellings initially on the same plane, as equals, rather than setting up an originating 'truth' against which later tellings are measured. In this view, for example, there is no point in claiming that the novel is the definitive text against which the film or television series is measured: we can discuss the range of potential meanings constructed by one discourse and those produced by another without necessarily valuing one over the other. An example might be the various re-tellings of the Ned Kelly story ranging from *The Story of the Kelly Gang* (produced in 1906) to the several made in the 1920s and the 1930s to the version starring Mick Jagger (Richardson 1970) and finally the version starring Heath Ledger (Jordan 2003, adapted from Robert Drewe's 1991 novel *Our Sunshine*) or the international best selling novel by Peter Carey (*True History of the Kelly Gang*, 2000).

For television news, the events (with their existents – the places and people involved) constitute the story, the telling of them in a particular way by a particular news crew for a particular broadcast constitutes the discourse.

In a discourse analysis of news, therefore, a researcher might, following Propp, assign the people on the news to character types: hero, villain, donor, dispatcher, false hero, helper, princess and her father. It is these characters which provide the variety on television news, as the events are repetitive and therefore predictable: on television news, we constantly see stories of strikes, scandals, disasters... and each time we read the new example through our experience of earlier examples. We may also read the news story through the 32 narrative functions identified by Propp, or Barthes' five codes. We may be interested in understanding the principles operating within a single news broadcast (or item) to construct its discourse, or to compare the way two or more broadcasts (on different channels or on the same channel at different times) construct the discourse around a single story.

A key to understanding discourse is to understand the processes of enunciation: that is, who is speaking and to whom. Chatman explains this process by a model, which he applies to both film and literature, and which can be extended to other forms of text. However, because literature is written by authors (that is, usually individual people) it is easier to start there, and consider later how it may apply to other media texts (often produced by a team of people). In Chatman's model there are six 'positions':

- 'real author' (the person who wrote the book, real flesh and blood, never known to the reader who has only the text as evidence);

- 'implied author' (the person whom the text invites the reader/viewer to construct as author);
- 'narrator' (the character from whose viewpoint the text is constructed, who may, or may not, be explicitly present in the text as a speaking character 'I');
- 'narratee' (the character in the text to whom the narrator speaks, whether implicitly or explicitly);
- 'implied reader' (the person whom the text implicitly addresses);
- 'real reader' (you or me, real flesh and blood people, never known to the real author, except in the rare cases when an author and a reader are both present at the same time).

One of the ways the writer of fiction may play with the reader is to disguise these functions or to move them around. Non-fiction texts are less likely to do this. On television news, for instance, the real author is the news team, or (for an individual story within a bulletin) the journalist who researches and presents the story. We, as viewers, can never know these as people, only as implied authors, whom we can construct from the evidence of the text (by both how they look and what they say). The presenter (who may or may not also be the implied author) is the narrator, explicitly providing voice-over. The implied reader is usually the narratee of the programme, unless there is someone inside the programme to whom the text is spoken (whether implicitly or explicitly). The implied reader/narratee is constructed as a particular sort of person with views about the subject being presented in the news item. The real reader is us, the viewers in their lounge-rooms, and the real authors cannot be sure that we do in fact have the values they have constructed for us.

Sometimes real authors try to control the response of real readers through the narrator, who provides a frame through which readers view/understand the story. So, one way to understand the narrative structure is to consider who the narrator is, and how she functions within the discourse. Kozloff (1992: 81–5) describes these functions as:

- inside or outside the diegesis (that is, part of what is happening, or not part of it);
- telling the whole tale or telling only part which is embedded within a larger story;
- far away in space and time from the story or near;
- supporting the point of view of the discourse or detached and/or ironic;
- reliable or unreliable (that is, telling or not telling the 'truth');
- omniscient or fallible (that is, knowing or not knowing the 'truth').

A convention of television news is to place the reporter on the spot where the events took place – even when no sign of the events remains: this positions the reporter inside the diegesis. It also makes claims to authority, by locating the reporter close in space (even if not in time) to the event. The broadcast often slips between the presenter in the studio (controlling the overall report) and the reporter in the field (presenting that aspect of the report). News narrators always claim to be reliable – that is another accepted convention of news. But they may not always claim to be omniscient: they are often reporting before the events have ended and with no way to be able to predict an outcome.

Another way to approach discourse analysis is to consider how time operates within the discourse:

- the order of events (their relationship to chronology);
- the sequence of events (their relationship to each other);
- the use of flashback or flash forward or simultaneity of events;
- the duration of events and the relation between story time and discourse time, which might be summary (discourse time shorter than story time), ellipsis (discourse time zero), scene (story time and discourse time equal), stretch (discourse time longer than story time), pause (story time zero, for instance freeze frame);
- the frequency of the representation, which might be singulative (one telling of what happened once), repetitive (n tellings of what happened once), or iterative (one telling of what happened n times);
- the liveness of the representation, which might be simultaneous with the event, or after the event.

All these concepts (and how they may be applied within textual research) are considered in detail by both Chatman and Kozloff. Studying discourse by examining the role of the narrator, or the function of time within the narrative, or the enunciation, is very different from the kind of discourse analysis proposed in the second sub-section of section 5.1 in Chapter 5, as the term 'discourse' is always slippery (see the Glossary).

Much textual research within cultural studies is done by a 'mix and match' of methods. For instance, structuralist methods of breaking a text down into manageable pieces may be combined with semiotic methods of analysing the processes of signification in operation within a small text sample, or with discourse analysis of who is speaking and to whom and within what time-scale.

10.3 Conclusion

You may see your research as producing understanding of the meaning/content of the text (content analysis), of the meaning constructed through the fusion of horizons of understanding between text and reader (phenomenological/hermeneutic analysis), of the signification processes at work in the text (semiotics or structuralism), or the discourses operating within the text (post-structuralism, discourse analysis or narratology). The positivist or post-positivist is likely to prefer content analysis, because this is the method that achieves results that can be rigorously tested; the critical theorist can choose any of the above methods, provided the results of the research can be directed towards improving the social world; the constructivist is likely to use semiotic and/or structuralist and/or hermeneutic methods to post-structuralist ends, or possibly to use discourse analysis or narratology; the participatory action researcher's primary concern is to involve participants in the research, no matter what research methodology is applied.

Much textual data gathering results in a new description of the content of the text, that is, it is a combination of data gathering and analysis, but it still requires interpretation through a framework of understanding, which we will discuss in the next chapter.

CHAPTER 11

Interpretation of Textual Data

Because the gathering and analysis of textual data so often occur simultaneously, we covered both together in the previous chapter. We choose to discuss interpretation separately, even though it is all-pervasive, throughout your research, from the very beginning to the writing of the last word of the report. Though your framework has been operating all along, it is more immediately apparent in textual research, concerned directly with 'meaning'.

If you believe that the meaning is in the text, just waiting to be recognised, you may read the text either as a representation of the real world or as symptomatic of some more complex and underlying reality. To interpret your textual data, then, you will need a theory that accounts for the relationship between the real world and representation. You may find this in the theory of realism, or in explanatory concepts such as gender, class, nation or race.

If you believe that the meaning is constructed in the course of the reading you will be interested in theories that account for the relationship between the reader and the text. You may find this in phenomenology or hermeneutics, or in psychoanalytic theories or in the concept of post-modernism, though you may still apply explanatory concepts such as gender, class, nation or race.

The various theories are not necessarily mutually exclusive: you may well use more than one of these, or shift about among them during the course of your research.

11.1 Theories of the relationship between the real world and representation

Realism

Arguments about the representation of reality and definitions of 'realism' are basic to the study of the media, beginning early in the study of film, when two conflicting ideas were posited simultaneously: that the camera cannot lie (film is truth 24 times per second) and that all film is illusion or artifice. The argument between these positions continues to the present day: it underlies the debates concerning the epistemological status of documentary films and 'reality' television, as well as many developments in cultural theory.

Though photography, radio, film and television give us the feeling that they have captured reality (that they are 'accurate' or 'authentic'), they are at best two-dimensional analogues of aspects of the real world. The media regularly report cases of viewers who fail to make that distinction: these are the people who send baby clothes to the actress who plays the role of an expectant mother in a soap opera, or (to take a more spectacular example) who firebomb William Boyde's car because he plays a rapist in *Eastenders* (*Age*, 26 January 1989). These people have confused realism with reality, but given the pivotal role realism plays in how we read all forms of representation this is not particularly surprising.

Raymond Williams (1988: 257) provides a history of the term, an etymology. For him, realism became an identifiable movement in the history of literature around the eighteenth century, with a shift towards depicting the lives and actions of people of lower as well as higher social ranks. A later shift made the action contemporary, rather than historical or legendary, and at the same time secular rather than metaphysical. He proposed that, from the late nineteenth century, a distinction was made between realistic detail (realism as method, increasingly called naturalism) and realism as attitude towards reality (the search for a larger realism of which the 'surface' details are a minor part). At the turn of the twentieth century all these attitudes were apparent, and film found its place among them. As film developed out of vaudeville, realistic subject matter was further extended from the middle classes to the working class, and a new element was added: the presentation of events and actions from a particular viewpoint.

Film theorist Colin MacCabe (in Bennett et al. 1981: 216–21) took up this last point. Drawing on theoretical understandings of realism in the nineteenth century novel, he defined a 'classic realist text' as one which, by its use of a meta-language (voice-over narration or camera point-of-view), constructs a particular position for the spectator in relation to 'reality', but disguises the text's status as 'construction', presenting it as 'natural' or 'transparent'. This focuses attention on the 'spectator' constructed by the text (a potential or abstract entity), rather than on the 'viewer' who sits in the audience (an actual, flesh-and-blood person): textual analysis can uncover the former, while audience research (as discussed in Part I) is concerned with the latter.

Considerable debate about spectator positioning followed, particularly over whether the inevitability of closure in the classic realist text (the habit of making the end of the narrative implicit in the beginning) made such texts inherently politically conservative. It was argued that the constriction of the spectator's position had the effect of preventing the viewer from taking any other ideological position than that of the dominant discourse within the film (see, for instance Bennett et al. 1981: Part IV).

Such debates make clear that realism can be found right across the film spectrum, both fiction and non-fiction. It can also be found in radio and television, for instance in the claims to accuracy/objectivity ('showing it like it is') made by broadcast news. Ien Ang (1985, see section 3.5 in Chapter 3) found notions of realism central to her study of soap opera: she coined three terms for different kinds of realism, all of which may be present in any single text. For her, 'empirical realism' is the denotative match of the representation against our experience of the real world; 'emotional realism' is the connotative match of the representation with our emotional experience; and 'classical realism' (MacCabe's 'classic realist text') is the pleasurable illusion of an internally consistent world presented transparently.

In Western culture, 'realism' has become a criterion of value: we are encouraged to like those representations which are realistic, and to use lack of realism as a justification/explanation for not liking others. In academic circles, much of the responsibility for this rests with F. R. and Q. D. Leavis, and the revolution they produced in the 1920s and 1930s at Cambridge University in the teaching of English literature (Eagleton 1983: Chapter 1). In the Leavisite project, the role of the literary critic was to save civilisation by the preservation of English culture through the study of the greatest works of literature. The Leavises established 'realism' as the primary moral criterion, and the techniques of realism as the most valuable literary skills. These attitudes passed across from literature into film study, and indeed into all forms of textual criticism. For film and television, the skills most valued within this framework cover writing (sensitivity of characterisation, unity of structure, realistic dialogue); directing (artistry of lighting, symbolic use of camera movement and angles and lenses, evocative power of sets and locations); acting (power to convince and move the audience, depth of characterisation) and a sense of moral value (power/energy/life).

These skills are obviously found in fiction, but can be located also in documentaries. It is harder to recognise them in those forms of television which make a claim to be simply recording the real world: game shows, sport, 'reality' programmes, current affairs or news. But once a viewer recognises that a boundary does exist between the real world and representation, they soon also realise that there are conventions governing that representation. In the case of news, we do not see unmediated reality, but a representation using conventions such as a studio presenter, reporters in the field, intercutting between live action and the studio, written inter-titles and sub-titles, flashbacks to earlier reports, and so on. These conventions arise (referring back to Figure 10.2 in Chapter 10) partly out of technical codes (culture) and partly out of cultural myths (ideology).

Ideology

We began the discussion of this complex term in the second sub-section of section 5.2 in Chapter 5, with Marx and Althusser. In recent years the term has broken away from its Marxist roots, to circulate in general discourse. Again,

Williams (1988: 153) provides a valuable etymology, proposing at least three different uses: any set of coherent ideas (any '-ism', whether or not the speaker agrees with the ideas, so all ideologies are potentially true), a set of ideas which the speaker believes to be false (so you hold to ideology, I know the truth), or the invisible set of ideas and values which enable us to function within our world (so you and I may or may not share ideology/ies).

The term also appears in our model of signification (Figure 10.2). There we proposed that the paradigms and syntagms that we find by semiotic analysis are culturally specific: they fall into patterns which construct and are in turn constructed by the myths for that culture, using 'myth' here in the sense of social explanation. In this sense (which we will use for the rest of this chapter), any aspect of your life which seems obvious, natural, just common sense, is probably constructed in ideology, making it difficult to recognise, unless we have had some reason to distance ourselves from it. As time passes, some ideas that were once completely 'obvious' and 'natural' have to be argued for, and eventually may shift value completely: for instance, few people now accept the once common belief that usury (charging interest on the loan of money) is immoral.

Within any community (unless we are engaged in civil war) we need to rub along together, so at any one time there will be a 'dominant ideology' – a set of ideas that are coherent with each other, and to which most people within that community subscribe. Because of the connection between culture and ideology, it is likely that popular cultural products such as television will usually express that dominant ideology, since that is what will make television programs most 'popular': commercial television needs to sell eyeballs to advertisers, and the advertisers need to sell their products to consumers. However, because no culture/society is ever entirely homogenous, and because commonly held ideologies lose or gain ground over time, we are likely also to find other less powerful and possibly conflicting ideological positions. When something irritates you on television, it may be expressing an aspect of ideology with which you are not sympathetic: when it is expressing something with which you are sympathetic, you will not even notice it.

One ideological position enshrined in our television, to the point where we are no longer aware of it, is the endorsement of individualism: viewers are expected to identify with the protagonists in drama, in news stories, in sport, and in game shows... As ideology circulates within systems of signification such as television, it is reconfirmed: signs and the ideology to which they contribute are constantly being communicated, exchanged and accepted/negotiated/rejected again.

From this perspective, ideology both shapes the researcher's approach (determining what she will look for), and is embedded within the text, waiting to be recognised. The process of recognition is in two stages: analysis (redescription of the content) and interpretation (relating the content to ideology). White (1992) provides a useful introduction to ideological interpretation of television content, including many examples. We have already considered how ideologies of class (see the second sub-section of section 5.2 in

Chapter 5) and gender (see the third sub-section of section 5.2) have operated within media audience research, and they can be applied again to the interpretation of texts, though inflected differently.

A Marxist is likely to ask questions about how class is represented within the text, and how this contributes to or challenges the dominant ideology: researchers from different Marxist positions will take up different aspects of these questions. But class may also be of concern to non-Marxists, and explorations of its representation in texts may also be combined with explorations of other issues within representation. An example is David Roediger's *The Wages of Whiteness: Race and the Making of the American Working Class* (1991).

A feminist is likely to ask questions about the role of women within society. In the third sub-section of section 5.2, we proposed different segments within feminism, and each of these has its own particular 'take' on the interpretation of texts, as Kaplan (1992) explains. Liberal feminists tend to prefer quantitative content analysis, either measured against the 'real' or the 'ideal', leading to the idea of 'positive' and 'negative' images of women (Kaplan 1992: 254–5, discussing the work of Diana Meehan; also see Franzwa 1974). Early Marxist feminists also tend to prefer quantitative content analysis, but in order to demonstrate the production of woman as consumer, and to encourage social solutions (Kaplan 1992: 257–9, discussing the work of Lillian Robinson). Radical feminists tend to prefer more qualitative and descriptive textual analysis, focusing on difference, aiming to reject the male symbolic order, and to encourage women to 'find themselves' and their own individual solutions (Kaplan 1992: 259–60, discussing the work of Lopate, also discussed in section 3.5 in Chapter 3). Post-structuralist feminists often use psychoanalytic methods to discuss the construction of subject positions through language (Kaplan 1992: 264–7, discussing the work of Modleski and Brunsdon, also discussed in section 3.5). Recently, these feminists have been interested in the representation of embodiment and its connections to how women speak within texts (for instance, Thornham 2003).

Feminist research may also be interested in explorations of the representation of nation or race – an ideological force field which we have not yet discussed.

'Nation' and 'race'

These terms are interdependent. Once loyalty to the place where we were born was an accepted fact of life: we were born into a nation, took our nationality very seriously, expressed it in continuing national culture, in taking part in the national political system, and in being willing participants in patriotic wars. Racial identification was a part of this nationalist sentiment. Now we are seeing several concurrent ideological shifts worldwide: the dominant Western nations (the prosperous ones like the USA, France, Britain) are moving towards internationalism (the European Union, the North American Free Trade

Agreement, the World Bank). The breakup of large empires (Britain, Spain, France) over the twentieth century, and in the last few years the breakdown of the socialist nations into their constituent parts, has produced 'new' nations in Africa, South America, and central Europe, with bitter internecine struggles for national identity, including 'ethnic cleansing', as ideologies of racism shift with national aspirations. Clearly, this has real effects on the lives of real people, but it is also something that is being played/fought out within representation... (Morley and Robins 1999; Wollen 1991).

Benedict Anderson proposed that a nation was 'an imagined political community' (Anderson 1983: 15): geography may provide natural boundaries (rivers, mountain ranges, the sea), government may provide political structures, but it is the way a group of people identifies with a nation that ultimately determines its survival. Some nations (the USA for instance) feel completely confident in their identity, but others seem compelled to argue endlessly about who they are. Canada, always positioned against its more powerful neighbour, devotes a journal to theorising nationalism: *Canadian Review of Studies in Nationalism.* Australia sustains a rich literature on just what constitutes Australian national identity, and has done so since the first settlement (see Dixon 1999; White 1981): the place of media representation in that construction has also been thoroughly explored (see Turner 1993).

As part of the argument about national identity, former colonies (such as India, Australia or New Zealand) often position their sense of nationhood in resistance to their colonial origins: this has been theorised as post-colonialism (see Ghandi 1998). A foundation text was Edward Said's *Orientalism*, first published in 1978. Said proposed that Western culture (particularly in Britain and France) had constructed the Orient within discourse, 'politically, sociologically, militarily, ideologically, scientifically, and imaginatively during the post-Enlightenment period'. As a result, 'European culture gained in strength and identity by setting itself off against the Orient as a sort of surrogate and even underground self' (Said 1991: 3). The thesis is still compelling, though Said later developed and revised his views (see Kennedy 2000; Said 1993).

The construction of the Orient as an Other of Western culture has been vigorously debated, across a range of positions. MacKenzie (1995) reviews this debate, and Mongia (1996) and Macfie (2000) both provide extracts from some of the participants. The application of these concepts to media texts can be found in Shohat and Stam (1994) and in Kaplan (1997).

The establishment of a nation has often been at the cost of the displacement of an earlier culture, and one way to justify this has been an assumption of racial superiority: issues of race and racism and of the connection of this to national identity and post-colonialism have also been widely discussed (for instance, Fanon 1970; Jackson and Penrose 1993). This has been developing in tandem with studies of media representations of race, of non-whiteness (Bhabha 1983; Daniels and Gerson 1990; Dates and Barlow 1990).

In recent years it has been recognised that Euro-centric racism is based on the naturalisation of whiteness: that white people do not even see that 'white' is a race marker, as much as any other skin colour (see, for instance, Hill 1997, or – linking whiteness and gender – Frankenberg 1993). In media studies, Dyer has provided foundation texts, arguing in an influential article (Dyer 1988) and a later book (Dyer 1997) that whiteness is 'a culturally constructed category' (Dyer 1988: 44) within representation. This concept is argued further in Bernardi (1996, 2001) as it applies to early American cinema, and by Fiske (1996), who links American politics to the representation of race and gender in the American media.

One influential theorist who links questions of class, race and gender provocatively is Gayatri Spivak (1988). Drawing on Derrida, Foucault, Marx, Deleuze, Freud and Said, she addresses what she calls 'the subaltern female subject', that is non-white women, concluding that 'the subaltern cannot speak' (Spivak 1988: 308).

All these theorists and commentators can be useful in providing models and approaches for the interpretation of textual data as representations of either the real world or of ideology. They can also be useful in conjunction with theories of the relationship between the reader and the text.

11.2 Theories of the relationship between the reader and the text

Phenomenology and hermeneutics

> Phenomenology is a philosophical endeavour concerned primarily with perception and structures of experience … The phenomenological enterprise entails describing the perceptual act, or the relationship between perceiving subject and what is perceived, as it is perceived. (Bennington and Gay 2000)

We can approach phenomenology through Descartes' assertion that 'I think therefore I am': he then distinguished between the subject (that which is doing the thinking) and the object (that which is thought about). Writing early in the 20th century, Edmund Husserl (1859–1938) rejected this positivist position, and focused upon the act of experiencing rather than on what is being experienced – on subjectivity, the process of the subject's experience of the object. He rejected 'false rationality' (the positivists' assumption that the world of experience is only an illusion behind which lies the real world measurable by science – Cooper 1997), but he still saw 'pure' phenomenology as a 'rigorous science' seeking to establish knowledge of the essences of phenomena. This was to be achieved by an insistence on the primacy of 'fundamental description' and a return to the 'things themselves'. However, as our thinking as humans contains common theoretical assumptions and prejudices there was a need to 'bracket', or put aside for the time being, the observer's taken-for-granted orientation to the world (Holstein and Gubrium 1998: 263). Within an Althusserian framework (discussed in the second sub-section of section 11.1 in this chapter), this taken-for-granted orientation would be seen as 'ideology', impossible to put aside in this manner. But phenomenologists consider they can step aside from their own world-view, while seeking the essential properties of that which is observed: some, for instance, seek to determine the ontology or essential properties of film, or television (see, for example, Lipkin 1990; Wood 2001). One of the elements of the process which Husserl sought to 'bracket' was ourselves: in the process, we are 'reduced' to 'pure subject' or the transcendental ego (Cooper 1997: 402), leading to Husserl's version of phenomenology being termed 'pure phenomenology' (Cooper 1997) or 'transcendental phenomenology' (Eagleton 1983).

Central to phenomenology is the notion of 'intentionality', which is quite different from the notion of authorial intention in literary criticism. Phenomenology argues that many of our actions and mental states are directed, or 'intended', towards objects: it is argued, for instance, that a film 'intends' a world which the spectator is able to see as meaningful, even when that world is fictional. Phenomenology (like post-structuralism) seeks to address perceived weaknesses in semiotics – that semiotics tends to privilege text at the expense of the reader; that it deals only with an idealised model of language, rather than language as it is used in everyday life; and that it downplays the experiential and affective aspects of language use. Phenomenology seeks to address feelings as well as cognition – the subjective and intersubjective significance that people experientially attribute to the media. Phenomenology has been particularly attractive to critics such as Casebier (1991) who has built upon Husserl's work in seeking to understand the role of emotion and value in the experience of watching film, and to writers such as Cavell (1979) who seek to develop an aesthetics of film. Underlying both of these goals is the desire to produce a hierarchy of value in film, which is no doubt a significant reason for the neglect of popular film and television by such critics.

Phenomenology is built upon the concept of the 'lifeworld' (see the discussion of Habermas in the second sub-section of section 8.2 in Chapter 8): those conceptions of the world around us that we share with others. At any moment we experience a number of related 'lifeworlds': of a student, a son or daughter, a member of a religion or of a political persuasion, a sports player, and so on. Within each of these we play roles, and have goals, allowing us all to see aspects of the same world from different perspectives. These perspectives arise out of the hermeneutical concept of 'horizon' (of experience or of expectation). From experience we learn to anticipate. It is a cognitive 'horizon of expectation' that leads us to assume that a door can be opened and will reveal something on the other side: we have seen many other doors, and this one shares its 'doorness' with all those others. All this is completely familiar and ordinary to us (again, rather like the taken-for-grantedness of ideology), and it is by the interaction of what is familiar and what is strange in the media that we incorporate what we see and hear in audio/visual programmes into our experience, and so into our lifeworld.

Martin Heidegger (1889–1976) was a disciple of Husserl, although he rejected some of Husserl's central tenets, such as the transcendental ego. For Heidegger, who has been labelled an existential phenomenologist, the subject is produced through and by language and culture, within a reality which includes both subject and object, indivisible and full of meaning. Heidegger also developed the notions of the everyday and the familiar which are so important to media theorists such as Scannell (1995, 1996) and Silverstone (1994).

Maurice Merleau-Ponty (1908–1961) is also sometimes called an existential phenomenologist, in contrast to the transcendental phenomenology of Husserl. One problem identified within phenomenology (Rothfield 2002, 2003) is a tendency to focus on the universal, leaving little space for the particular and specific (for instance, Casebier 1991). Merleau-Ponty recognised that one way in which the specific enters into a consideration of subjectivity and consciousness is through a consideration of the body: 'people's experience of the world occurs through and because we are material, bodily beings' (Rothfield 2003).

This recognition of the role of embodiment in human perceptual experience, and of the particular in phenomenological investigation underpins much of Vivian Sobchack's work on film. Sobchack has sought to construct a phenomenological theory of film experience, placing considerable emphasis on 'the material and carnal foundations of language', or the 'embodied' foundations of the film experience. She is seeking to address the 'semiotic and hermeneutic questions posed by the medium of cinema' while insisting that the viewing subject has a material existence in a world of bodily experience (Sobchack 1995: 36).

Hermeneutics is related to phenomenology. It was first developed as a tool for authenticating early biblical texts, but it was later carried over into literary and historical interpretation, seeing works (and by extension, media texts) as aesthetic wholes, which cannot be reduced to a logical system as claimed by semiotics or structuralism. Like ethnography, which relates parts and wholes (Baszanger and Dodier 1997), hermeneutics asserts that meaning arises out of what has been called the 'hermeneutic circle': the cyclical interaction between the work as a whole and its constituent parts.

Wilhelm Dilthey (see Nash 1969: vol. 2) made a fundamental distinction between explanations (sought by science) and understandings (sought by the humanities), and positioned hermeneutics firmly as a quest for understanding. In this quest, the text is central, but the experience of the author and of the reader may also be implicated. Hans-Georg Gadamer (1973), for instance, was prepared to accept that culturally determined shifting meaning is actually an integral part of the text itself. The role of the interpreter is, therefore, to track down the (historical and cultural) influences at work in a text (the 'horizons' of meaning, see the third sub-section of section 9.1 in Chapter 9). E. D. Hirsch (1976), on the other hand, distinguished meaning (fixed, what the author intended) from significance (shifting, what the reader values): he considered that meaning was willed, and the author was the only compelling normative source of that meaning. Paul Ricoeur (1976) denied any privileged position for the author, and described interpretation as arising out of the interaction between sense (ideal, inside the text) and reference (real, outside the text), event (actual and transitory) and meaning (potential and propositional).

Phenomenology and hermeneutics position texts (and their meaning(s)) in relation to authors and (even more) to readers, though different theorists do not agree on a formula for such relations.

Psychoanalysis and analytical psychology

A very different way of conceptualising the relationship between the text and the reader is to propose a 'theory of mind' – of how we think about the world. Psychoanalysis, which began as a branch of science (medicine, psychology), was the first such theory to have its principles adapted to apply to the interpretation of texts and has often been used in conjunction with post-structuralist methods.

Sigmund Freud (1856–1939)

Freud was in his lifetime ridiculed and condemned, his ideas kept afloat by a loyal band of devoted followers; then he became the new guru and his theories the basis for radical change in philosophy as well as in medical practice; then they became so naturalised as to be invisible. The terminology specific to psychoanalysis has likewise moved from being esoteric into being simply a part of everyday speech ('egotistical', 'libido', 'repression', etc).

Freud's major psychoanalytical writing was done 1896–1930: for the novice, Storr (2001) is a helpful introduction. Freud's theory starts from the proposition that all human life is based on the conflict between two major motivations – the pleasure principle (*eros*, sexual desire) and the reality principle (*thanatos*, the death wish). These create 'drives', the most basic of which is sex: one of his most controversial propositions was that sexuality is established in infancy. He divided human development into stages: the first three of these are the oral stage, the anal/sadistic stage, and the phallic/libidinal stage, in which the Id (made up of our instincts, our drive towards physical pleasure) is formed.

The Ego (the sense of self) is formed in the next stage, through the process of 'identification' – our relation, both conscious and unconscious, to other people. The little boy starts by loving his mother and identifying with his father (who also loves his mother). As his sexuality develops, he becomes jealous of the father, and fears the father will punish him (by castration) for his incestuous love of the mother. The Oedipal moment is the boy's rejection of the mother and the consequent acceptance of the father's authority, which leads into the dominance of the Superego (conscience, the acceptance of patriarchal law). Freud's explanation for little girls is that they begin by identifying with the mother, then become jealous of the mother and wish to displace her to seduce the father. Though both sexes form new attachments outside the nuclear family, these always somehow repeat and return to the original attachments to the mother and father – that is what makes us all 'split subjects'. The formation of the Superego is a compromise between the pleasure principle and the reality principle, at the cost of repressing much of our drives into the unconscious.

The unconscious is that part of our mind which is normally out of our reach, but occasionally spills over into our conscious experience, and so can be reached indirectly, through dreams (which function by displacement, and condensation, which are the equivalents of metonymy and metaphor in language) and parapraxes (jokes, slips of the tongue, misreadings, mislayings, failure of memory...). The unconscious is most active when disturbed, producing neurosis (obsessional, hysterical or phobic – the result of the repression of desire when sublimation is not possible) or psychosis (paranoia, schizophrenia – delusions, as the link between the ego and the external world is severed). Freud claimed that psychoanalysis can cure these disturbances, through transference (the 'talking cure'), using the analyst as a substitute.

Where Marx saw economics as the base on which life was built, Freud saw sex as a universal explanation. This makes his theories normative and prescriptive, but also constructed from within his own (limited) social experience: he broke with accepted ideas of childhood, but seemed bound inside the ideas of class and gender which ruled in his social world, and unaware that he was transferring these values into his case histories.

How does all this apply to media study? A very good introduction is provided by Charles Altman, in his review of a 1975 issue of the French journal *Communications.* Altman provides an example of Freudian 'symbol-chasing', in the comment by Raymond Bellour in his analysis of *North by Northwest* that: 'The miniaturization of the razor and the shaving brush suggests that the penis risks being reduced' (Altman 1985: 529).

But a more sophisticated application of psychoanalytic principles to understanding textual content is through Freud's theory of dreams as coded ways of understanding our experience. Of all the media, the analogy works best for film. This is partly because of the physical circumstances in which films are viewed: our isolation, passivity and immobility as spectators in the dark, with our senses heightened as a result. But it is also more than this physical aspect. In his section on 'Film/Dream', Altman (1985: 524–7) introduces Suzanne Langer's point that films are always 'now', in the present as dream is, and Jean-Louis Baudry's suggestion that while we watch we temporarily regress. He explains how Metz goes further, suggesting that the dependence of film on narrative (that is on fiction), is analogous to Freud's ideas of the dependence of the human mind on fantasies, and that films (or at least the classical Hollywood narrative film) function as dreams do by a process of secondary elaboration (that is, by seamless editing, motivated action and camera movement, absence of unexplained activity). Finally, he summarises Thierry Kuntzel's application to film of Freud's idea of how dreams function by condensation, displacement and symbolisation. Freud considers that the content of dreams comes from the dreamer's 'daily residue', and as the film is not about us how can we read any film as our 'daily residue'? Kuntzel's explanation is that films set up in the pre-credit sequence an expectation which the rest of the film satisfies, and suggests that (for a spectator) the pre-credit sequence is the equivalent of a dream's 'daily residue'.

Eagleton (1983) suggests that psychoanalytic literary criticism in general can set out to analyse the author, the character(s), the form of the work, or the reader. Freud is most helpful with the first two of these. The first is what Freud himself did in his study of Leonardo da Vinci: other examples would be any of the psycho-histories, perhaps Spoto's (1992) biography of Hitchcock. An approach through the characters within the text, however, is more common than the analysis of authors: tracing the relationships formed by characters in narratives with 'mother figures' and 'father figures', representing that perpetual slide within the human psyche between the id and the ego, back and forth between childhood and adulthood. In much fiction (whether in literature, film or television) we have main characters who are still in the process of reaching maturity, and the main part of the story concerns their journey towards it, interrupted by mistakes and false starts (so-called 'rites of passage'). Alternatively, this search for the 'self' can be pursued through Foucauldian concepts discussed in the second sub-section of section 8.2 in Chapter 8.

Freud is less helpful when it comes to analysing the form of the work, or the reader. It is certainly possible to compare a media text with dreams, searching for the signifieds behind the signifiers. For film and television, this requires a conception of the screen as a window (the realist position) or as a frame (the formalist position), through which we can reach these signifieds. But the Freudian system cannot cope with interpreting the processes of signification (the production and consumption of the signifiers) and so cannot analyse texts in which the process of signification has become one of the meaning systems, that is, modernist, reflexive texts. As such texts have become increasingly important in recent years in all media, if psychoanalysis was to continue to be a useful interpretive system it had to be modified to cope with them.

Jacques Lacan (1901–1981)

The psychoanalytic theories which best coped with the form of the text are those of Lacan. The novice is recommended to approach Lacan through commentaries, starting again with Altman (1985), who provides a concise and useful summary. Lacan accepts the Oedipal moment as determining, but describes it rather differently. For Lacan, the 'imaginary' is that (pre-Oedipal) period when the child cannot recognise the boundaries between himself and the rest of the world. (The use of the male pronoun is not accidental – Lacan, like Freud before him, accepts the male as the normative example of humanity.) The 'mirror phase' is when the child begins to see a whole self as possible, though not yet putting up barriers between himself and the rest of the world: it begins when he sees the image of self in the mirror, without recognising the differences between the signifier and the signified. The 'symbolic' is when the barriers are recognised and established through language, which is based upon difference (as in the 'fort-da' game described by Freud). In this process, the Law of the Father divides the child from the mother by its prohibition of incest, thereby driving desire underground into the unconscious. The phallus (which for Lacan is not simply equivalent to the penis) denotes sexual difference. Our self-concept is always vulnerable, at risk of being overthrown by the Other (particularly parents, or the Law).

For Lacan, language is composed of signifiers, rather than of signs: desire is 'the potentially endless movement from one signifier to another' because language only works by division/articulation/lack/absence/difference. This means that 'to enter language ... is to become prey to desire' (Eagleton 1983: 167), but language is also always slipping away from us. This constructs two positions which are important in the interpretation of texts: the 'subject of the enunciation' is the person posited by the speech act (spoken to or about), the 'subject of the enunciating' is the person speaking: they often appear to be identical, but in fact never are (cf Chatman's narrators and authors, see the second sub-section of section 10.2 in Chapter 10).

Conventionally, literary enunciation is presented to us as anonymous (like Hollywood classical narrative), but modernist texts draw attention to their enunciation (for instance, the plays of Bertold Brecht). This brings us back to the inadequacy of former conceptions of the screen as a frame or a window: Lacan sees the screen as a mirror, setting up an Imaginary relationship between the spectator and what she sees on the screen. This is not merely that we 'identify' with what we see (that is, that we temporarily pretend that it is 'us'), nor that we carry over into our real life characteristics associated with what we have seen on the screen (like little girls wearing copies of Britney Spears' clothes). Rather it is that in the dream-like circumstances of the viewing experience (darkness, solitude, passivity, etc) we regress to the Imaginary stage of our development, losing our grip on the distinction between the Imaginary and the Real. In the film viewer, a dialectic is established between a subject and its mirror-image: the viewer sees that what is on screen is at the same time identical with reality (in shape, colour, etc) and different from it (merely an image, representation). Metz describes this process thus: '... to understand the film (any film) I must perceive the photographed object as absent, its photograph as present, and the presence of this absence as significant' (Metz, in Altman 1985: 523). Altman further explains: 'Fiction films mean nothing if we refuse to take them – at least provisionally – as reality. On the other hand, they cannot achieve their true status as fiction if we hold permanently to that illusion' (Altman 1985: 523). This shifts the central issue from the signified to the signifier, from the text as reflection of reality to the text as mental operation, that is to the process of signification, to analysing textuality rather than texts.

Where a simple Freudian reading forces us to limit our analysis to that of the author or of characters within the text, a Lacanian approach opens up the other areas of analysis posited by Eagleton – that of the form of the work, and of the audience. The form of the work can be studied through an analysis of the relationship of the reader to the enunciation. The audience can be studied through the idea of film as language, and of the viewer (now called the spectator) as a subject constructed in language. This opens up the concept of the sub-text: that which is not spoken, that which is omitted, can be very important in constructing what is spoken. Metz (1983) explored at length the concept of 'the Imaginary signifier' in film. These theories, and the interpretive methods which have been built upon the theories, have been extremely influential in film theory, and can also be applied to other media texts (particularly fiction). In feminist film theory, Lacanian analysis was at first a great leap forward, explaining the mechanisms of patriarchal oppression in a way that previous systems had not done. But it was also pessimistic – the only response it opened up for the female social subject was to read from a male gaze (and so be complicit in the objectification of women) or to refuse to watch at all (and so deny herself pleasure). But pleasure is increasingly a valued effect of cultural products, and the issue of how pleasure is constructed is increasingly an issue within cultural studies.

One response has been to consider the formal differences between film and television, and to conclude that the television spectator is not as 'determined' as the film spectator: where the film spectator has been said to 'gaze' (Mulvey 1975), the television spectator has been said to 'glance' (Ellis 1992). Sandy Flitterman-Lewis (1992) accepts Mulvey's Lacanian view of how film operates to construct spectators, but insists that television operates differently. Extending the idea of television form (and particularly the soap opera, which is also endless), as imitating/reflecting women's work patterns, Flitterman-Lewis speaks of television as threatening the male control of the gaze, by decentring the spectator through multiple identifications, lack of closure, and a proliferation of stories. These modified psychoanalytic approaches require at the same time a certain essentialising (and therefore simplifying) of television form.

One way to avoid the problems for feminists that the approaches of both Freud and Lacan produce is to find a different route through psychoanalysis. Nancy Chodorow's book on mothering (1978) offers such an alternative. She changes the emphasis by acknowledging the primary importance of the mother as the first cathexis object for the infant, and seeing the break from the mother as paramount in shaping personality.

Gaylyn Studlar (1984) interprets the pre-Oedipal phase as absolute identification with the mother, in which the mother is defined not as lack (per Lacan) but rather as plenitude, to which we spend the rest of our lives seeking (inevitably unsuccessfully) to return. In this scenario, the film represents a dream/screen, an excuse to repeat the phantasy of being reunited with the mother, making the female the controlling gaze. Identification is therefore through masochism (following Deleuze rather than Freud and Lacan and Mulvey) and particularly through phantasy, which is multiple and fluid and cross-gender (so women in the audience can identify with either men or women on the screen). Fantasy theory builds on a different Freudian scenario than that so far discussed. In place of the 'fort-da' game, it proposes as founding scenario 'a child is being beaten': this scenario has three elements (the one being beaten, the one doing the beating, and the observer) instead of two, allowing the subject to choose one of the three positions, or to oscillate between them.

Carl Jung (1875–1961)

Jung provides a different way of understanding the relation of viewers to texts. Like Freud, Jung's ideas have been naturalised and his specialist terms have entered the language (introvert, extravert, complex, persona...). In 1906, Jung, already a training psychiatrist treating dementia praecox (schizophrenia) at the Burgholzi Psychiatric Hospital (Zurich), began to correspond with Freud, whom he believed supported his ideas on repression, dreams, and, in particular, complexes. In 1913, at Freud's instigation, their intense intellectual, professional and emotional relationship ended, after Jung had questioned Freud's insistence that the unconscious housed only repressed, once conscious material. Jung renamed the domain for repressed psychic matter the *personal unconscious* and defined the *unconscious* as culturally collective and positive in nature. He also believed that Freud's concentration on the libido as the primary cause of neurosis and psychosis was over-emphasised and misplaced. To distinguish his own work from Freudian 'psychoanalysis', Jung called his approach '**analytical psychology**'.

Jung's idea that there exist collectively inherited psychological motifs was developed from his analysis of patients, and of his own psychotic episodes precipitated by the break with Freud. He wrote of images arising from the unconscious, that constellated into patterns similar in content to myths and fairy tales (compare this with Lévi-Strauss and Propp, discussed in the first sub-section of section 10.2 in Chapter 10): initially (in 1912) he called this phenomenon 'primordial images', and later 'archetypal patterns'. He wrote of them, not as aspects of personal memory, but as patterns of thought and behaviour universally common and recurring – present in dreams, as well as in works of art and literature.

Among the dominant archetypal patterns are the concepts of anima (the patriarchal/authoritarian/rational) and animus (the matriarchal/democratic/intuitive). Jung was ahead of his time in insisting that these patterns are innate to both genders, and must be equally attended to for psychic health: unlike much Freudian thought, women were never regarded as 'other' to the male norm. Another archetypal pattern is the shadow, often understood to be the dark side of our individual and collective selves. It is most obviously expressed during periods of war, racism, sexist behaviour, religious intolerance, etc, via irrational projections onto those assumed to be 'the enemy'.

Jung's ideas, particularly archetypal theory, provide a way to interpret textual content. So far such interpretations have been largely confined to the fictions of film and television rather than to non-fiction formats, but there is no logical reason why his ideas cannot be applied to all visual and literary texts. For instance, Siegfried Kracauer (1947) read German films of the period between the wars as symptoms of the German collective unconscious: he suggested that if viewers had been perceptive enough it was theoretically possible to read from these films the likelihood, even the necessity, of the rise of a dictator like Hitler within Germany. Joseph Campbell's hero quest theory (Campbell 1973, first published 1949), inspired by Jungian thought, has been widely applied in textual analysis. Rushing and Frentz (1991) analyse the way in which the heroes of Hollywood films struggle with shadow material. Hockley (2001, 2003) or Hauke and Alister (2001) offer more contemporary readings of Jung in relation to film and television, while Izod (2001) is one of the few to examine non-fiction, with a chapter on the archetypal hero in televised sport.

You can keep abreast of debates among the followers of Jung, and of the application of his ideas across many spheres (including textual analysis) on the *C. G. Jung Page* (www.cgjungpage.org).

In David Bordwell's (1996) overview of grand theories of film one alternative proposed to psychoanalysis is 'cognitive theory', which is concerned with the spectator's rational processes, as opposed to unconscious responses to cinema (Peterson 1996: 115). Cognitive science seeks to understand how the human mind functions, drawing on linguistics, cognitive psychology, artificial intelligence, ethnography, literary theory and the philosophy of language (Branigan 1992: xii).

Post-modernism

Most recently, post-modernism has challenged all interpretation of texts. There is still fierce debate about just what constitutes 'post-modernism' (summed up in Collins 1992). From a rigidly linear model of communication, which sees meaning as encoded by the sender of the message, and the responsibility of the reader to lie in accurately decoding that same meaning, variant readings are simply 'mistakes'. One alternative is to recognise the polysemy of texts, and the role of the audience in the construction of a meaning out of that polysemy. This is a post-structuralist position, which sees the real as a construct and the search for meaning as always relative to the circumstances of the reading. Post-modernism starts at this point, but can go much further (as we have already discussed for history and historiography, in the first sub-section of section 8.2 in Chapter 8).

Despite the widespread use of the term, available definitions of 'post-modernism' are still vague, so once again we resort to etymology. Historically, the term arose in counterpoint with modernism, which arose in counterpoint with aesthetic realism. Realism we discussed earlier as an ideology which values authenticity and verisimilitude. This was challenged by modernism, which spoke through fantasy, through distortion, attempted to capture states of mind rather than external reality, addressed form rather than content in art. Raymond Williams would call these alternatives 'naturalism' (the imitation of reality, mimesis) and 'realism' (the representation of a deeper reality, diegesis). Post-modernism, with its denial of all 'grand narratives', rejects not only realism and naturalism, but also any other '-ism'.

According to Hal Foster (1985: ix–x), the techniques of post-modernism share one intention – to critically deconstruct tradition: the post-modernist insists that criticism is not about 'works' (unique, symbolic, visionary) but about 'texts' ('already written', allegorical, contingent). At the extreme, some post-modernists claim not only that all meaning is relative (like Derrida) but that the search for meaning is itself pointless: Baudrillard (1983), for instance, claims that television (simulation of the real) has replaced/displaced reality. For some post-modernists, therefore, we live in a world without meaning, in which there is nothing new: everything is created out of parody (ironic re-circulation of signs), repetition (the 'already said'), and pastiche (the juxtaposition or *bricolage* of the 'already said'). The pessimistic view of this world is the end of 'meaning': anything can 'mean' anything we want it to. But in practice, most of us are more optimistic than this: we not only continue to seek for meaning, but also seem to agree much of the time about what texts may 'mean', even if we also accept that meaning can be inherently plural and shifting. Frederic Jameson interprets post-modernism through Marxist economic views, concluding that it is driven by the 'logic of late capitalism' (1991: 16–25), which fetishises the commodity culture.

The arguments surrounding post-modernism are far from over, including the debate about whether post-modernist relativity implies a joyous breaking of old boundaries which have enslaved culture, or the pessimistic acceptance that we are eternally caught in a cycle of signification that defies all opposition and makes political action pointless. There have even been tentative propositions of what will follow post-modernism (Lopez 2001).

11.3 Conclusion

All these (and many other) frameworks of interpretation are potentially available to a researcher. An extreme post-modernist will deny any point in the search for meaning within texts: from any other position discussed in this chapter, the search for meaning is both appropriate and intriguing. Those concerned to identify the workings of ideology might seek evidence of the representation of nation/race, class or gender, using content analysis, semiotic/structuralist analysis or narratology/discourse analysis. Those interested in how texts work to produce representation will probably start with theories of realism, and apply methods that expose these workings (content analysis, semiotics/structuralism, hermeneutics/phenomenology, post-structuralist narratology or discourse analysis). Those interested primarily in how the minds of readers/viewers work to produce meaning may apply Freudian/Lacanian psychoanalysis, Jungian analytical psychology, or new developments in cognitive theory to their analysis of texts. There are also, of course, ways of linking more than one of these into a matrix of interpretive strategies.

Only wide reading of both the theorists themselves, and of research reports building upon these theories, will help you to work out your own preferred framework. Clearly, the writers of this book have their preferences, but we also consider that providing novices with a map of the field, and encouragement to explore, is more useful than prescribing what theory/ies they 'ought' to accept.

We hope that students will use the basic materials provided in the methodology chapters to shape the mechanics of their early ventures into research, but that they will also (even if this has to be postponed till postgraduate study provides more opportunities) explore for themselves more widely than this, and into areas in the theoretical chapters that may seem too esoteric for the novice.

Chapter 12

Reaching Conclusions, Evaluating the Research, Writing the Report

The matters discussed in this chapter apply broadly, to all media research – across audiences, texts and institutions and the connections between these. This broad application, however, does not make decisions easy: putting principles into practice according to the researcher's personal intellectual or philosophical framework(s) always requires care and attention to detail. In a book such as this it is difficult to cover all the possibilities across so wide a field.

12.1 Reaching conclusions

This is a surprisingly ambiguous phrase, once again context-specific and dependent upon your intellectual framework. It may simply mean coming to the end, deciding there is no more to be gained by continuing, even if you have not arrived where you expected to when you set out. People 'finish' research in this sense for any number of reasons: they run out of time and money, lose interest, find that the research setting is no longer open to them, discover that their intellectual position has altered so much that they are no longer comfortable doing what they planned, fall ill, fall in love, go off to a South Sea island to find adventure in the real world...

However, most researchers persevere, till they come to a point when they decide to stop adding to the research, and present the findings in some form for others to read. The last element of the research report is then the 'conclusions'. For the positivist or post-positivist, these 'conclusions' are the results reached by the analysis and interpretation, often presented in terms of a probability statement about the original hypothesis. For the critical theorist or participatory action researcher, the conclusions may be a statement of present activity or future policy. For a constructivist, the conclusions may encapsulate their current thinking on a subject. In all cases, there may also be a discussion of what has *not* been achieved – the questions that remain unanswered or the new questions that have arisen.

Conclusions arise out of analysis and interpretation: by applying thought to your data, you decide (in the terms we set up in Chapter 1) what new knowledge you have produced, and how this fits into old knowledge. To do this, you will need to have standards, that you apply all through the project, both to what you have read of the work of others, and (hopefully) also to your own work.

12.2 Meeting standards

Issues of rigour (how well standards have been met) are yet another instance of the circularity of the research process: they appear to be something that you consider at the end of your research, but they are actually controlling factors in all phases of the process.

Positivist framework and quantitative methodology

This position requires what Denzin and Lincoln (2000: 872) call 'foundational' evaluative criteria (validity, reliability and objectivity). The positivist aims to speak from a neutral position, outside the research, and to reach conclusions that can be claimed to be objectively 'true'. Even with empirical data, disagreement about conclusions is always possible (remember the blind men and the elephant), but as the data and methods of analysis are refined then the likelihood of agreement increases.

From this position, 'error' is the difference between your results, and the results that would have been obtained if the research was flawless: in fact, the use of the concept is a recognition that flawless research is impossible. The 'standard error' (see the first sub-section of section 5.1 in Chapter 5) is a measure of how accurately your sample represents the population from which it was drawn, and hence with what level of confidence you can generalise to that larger population.

'Reliability' is a measure of stability. The reliability of data is judged by the replicability of the project: the likelihood that similar data would be gathered if the same researcher conducted the research again on another representative sample, or on the same sample at another time, or if similar research was conducted on a similar sample by another researcher. This is hard to achieve with questionnaire and survey data, both because of the influence of interpretation in the construction and administration of questionnaires and because of lack of comparability between answers, and a resulting lack of reliability in the quantified responses (see Cox 1996: 34–8).

The reliability of the analysis depends upon the researcher ensuring that procedures for coding and interpreting the data follow standard principles, so that the same researcher would always produce the same result: if several analysts are working on the same data, 'inter-coder reliability' is the measure of likelihood that all the coders would produce similar results from the same data. High reliability is easier to achieve for analysis than for data, because statistical procedures exist to measure the reliability of numerical calculations: consult the statistics textbooks for the required formulae. Problems of reliability lead also to problems of validity (see Wentland 1993).

In the data collection phase, 'validity' is often used as a synonym for 'accuracy', judged by internal consistency (within your own data) and external consistency (between your data and other available data). At this point, much depends on the adequacy of sampling techniques (Grosof and Sardy 1985: 187). The validity of analysis is usually measured statistically, with the ultimate aim of achieving correlations that are statistically significant and that avoid spurious cases (consult the statistics textbooks for procedures).

However, validity is also a measure of the logic of an argument, rather than the truth of a statement. A valid argument is one in which the conclusions MUST be true provided the premises are also true (Collinson 1987); for instance, the following syllogism:

Premise 1: All dogs have four legs
Premise 2: This animal is a dog
Conclusion: This animal has four legs

This would be a valid conclusion to draw, however it may still be untrue, for instance if the dog had had a leg removed after an accident, so Premise 1 was untrue.

So, before you can claim that your conclusions are valid, you must demonstrate both that your data is factually valid, and that your argument is logically valid, within the overall aim of external validity (generalisability) and internal validity (truth).

All through this book we have been arguing both that the positivist framework is itself flawed and that these standards of error, reliability and validity are not achievable in research on the social world. As we have also said before, this is not an argument against the use of quantitative methods: used sensibly and appropriately, they can be really valuable. If they *are* used, then measures of error, reliability and validity are appropriate, and should be employed. What should be avoided is blind faith that such measures give an objective picture of the 'truth' of the conclusions: from a post-positivist position, probable truth can be postulated, but from other positions these standards are not measures of truth, but simply of how rigorously the methods were applied.

Such basic disagreements make the issue of standards very controversial. Nevertheless, these positivist standards have had a huge influence on how research – from whatever framework it is conceived – has been evaluated.

Positivist or post-positivist framework and qualitative methodology

In research on the social world, post-positivists prefer to use qualitative methods, and even positivists have sometimes admitted that such methods can be valuable. However, the concept of 'standard error' cannot be applied to the non-probability sampling techniques common in qualitative research. In fact, in most respects it is impossible for qualitative researchers to achieve the standards expected for quantitative research.

One response to this dilemma is to adapt research procedures, but continue to apply the standards of reliability, validity and objectivity devised for quantitative methods, acknowledging at the same time that expectations must be modified. Peräkylä, for instance, discusses various ways to improve the reliability and validity of conversation analysis of tapes and transcripts, in an effort to enhance objectivity, 'to assure the accuracy and inclusiveness of recordings' and 'the truthfulness of the analytic claims that are being made about these recordings' (Peräkylä 1997: 201). Webb et al. (1966: Chapter 7) are at pains to enhance the reliability and validity of their 'unobtrusive measures', and to encourage the use of methods (such as triangulation, discussed below) to control stability of both data and interpretation.

Qualitative research, by its very nature, often has low reliability. For instance, focus group interview data is inherently non-replicable, because it can be reasonably assumed that no two groups will ever produce the same discussion, even if the groups are homogeneous and discussing the same topic. However, one way to decide how many focus groups to conduct is to keep repeating the task with different groups, until the same issues begin to arise repeatedly, that is, until a level of reliability has been reached related more to the principle of diminishing returns than to the replicability of results. The qualitative researcher would defend focus group data, despite its poor reliability, because it provides much richer data than the more rigorous experimental and survey methods that produce a technically higher measure of reliability.

The validity of qualitative research is even more difficult to judge than its reliability. Two widely discussed techniques of validation for qualitative research are respondent validation and triangulation.

Respondent validation

Respondent validation is taking tentative conclusions back to the research subjects for their response. This is an extension of the usual assumption that research subjects know more than the researcher, so their judgments should be given more weight. This may well be true; it is, after all, why we asked the research subjects in the first place. However, there is logically no way of proving this. Just as we may get two different perspectives by observing behaviour and by asking people about their actions, we may well get a different perspective by taking our research conclusions back to the research subjects: but in both these cases (observation versus asking; our research conclusions versus the subjects' conclusions) there is no telling which should be given more credence, as logically neither can be expected to be inherently more 'truthful'.

Triangulation

Triangulation is the use of two or more (usually three) different research approaches (of data gathering, or of analysis and interpretation) to the same question. Employing more than one method is time-consuming and requires mastery of several research techniques: it may well be better left to the experienced researcher. But, more importantly, it may still not provide the validation you seek:

- There is a logical fallacy in the idea that if two or more people say something it is more likely to be true than if only one person says it: after all, they may have all obtained their information from the same false source. It follows that, if validity exists at all, it is inherent in each piece of research, independent of every other piece, so triangulation will just require the researcher to test the validity of three separate pieces of research – added work for no measurable increase in confidence.
- Most social science and humanities research constructs its object of study and context in the course of the research. Under these circumstances, there is no external standard of 'truth', against which the research conclusions can be measured.
- The argument would hold only if the different methods were measuring exactly the same thing, but different measures and methods are used precisely because they add new dimensions to the research.

In both these cases (respondent validation and triangulation), this is not an argument against the method, which can certainly produce new insights into any research problem. Rather it is an argument against depending on such methods as a measure of validity. How, then, can qualitative researchers enhance the validity of their conclusions? Silverman (2000: 177–85) suggests five ways:

- 'The refutability principle' requires that the researcher deliberately seek out non-conforming cases, in order to preclude later refutation by others.
- 'The constant comparative method' requires that the researcher start with testing a small part of the data and expand this slowly by constant comparison, revising categories to account for new information as it arises.
- 'Comprehensive data treatment' requires that all available data be examined, rather than only a sample, thus allowing generalisations just as valid as those arising from statistical correlation.

- 'Deviant case analysis' requires that any deviant cases that arise from comprehensive data treatment are fully explored and integrated into the conclusions.
- 'Using appropriate tabulations' requires that qualitative researchers acknowledge that quantification is sometimes appropriate and employ it when it is sensible to do so.

Although Silverman is still using the language of positivism, he is also moving away from Denzin and Lincoln's (2000: 872) 'foundational' criteria of evaluation and towards their 'quasi-foundational' criteria. These use a vocabulary different from the foundational criteria: internal validity becomes credibility, external validity may still be generalisability but it may rather be transferability, objectivity becomes internal **reflexivity**. In a similar spirit, Miles and Huberman (1994: 278–9) propose that internal validity (whether the conclusions seem to 'make sense') may be called 'credibility', and external validity (whether the conclusions may be applied more widely than the present study) may be called 'transferability' or 'fittingness'. These terminological shifts express the post-positivist doubts about both the objectivity of the researcher and the absolute truth of the conclusions.

They also imply changes in procedures. Miles and Huberman (1994: 263) suggest the following ways to test or confirm findings:

- test data quality by:
  - checking for representativeness;
  - checking for researcher effects;
  - triangulating;
  - weighting the evidence;
- examine exceptions:
  - outliers from the pattern;
  - extreme cases;
  - surprises;
  - negative evidence;
- test explanations by:
  - asking 'if … then …';
  - ruling out spurious relations;
  - checking rival explanations;
  - getting feedback from informants.

These arguments about standards for qualitative research continue in the social sciences: see, for instance, the summary by Potter (1996: 194–6) of eight different positions taken in relation to evaluation. Gergen and Gergen (2000: 1031) prefer to reconceptualise the validity of qualitative research, to encompass the concerns of the non-positivists.

Non-positivist framework

The non-positivist is likely to use mainly qualitative methods, but may also sometimes use quantitative methods. In either case, there are no standard methods of evaluation of the results.

The post-structural linguistic turn has denied absolute correspondence between the word and what it represents (see the first sub-section of section 10.2 in Chapter 10), which leads to the proposition that 'the warrant for scientific validity is lost, and researchers are left to question the role of methodology and criteria of evaluation' (Gergen and Gergen 2000: 1026). Smith and Deemer (2000: 878) propose that relativism is now 'our condition in the world', and that it is necessary to 'change our imageries and metaphors from those of discovery and finding to those of constructing and making'. In such a relative world, where there can be no permanent and universally agreed standards, 'truth' is either considered impossible to locate or is accepted to be a construct rather than an objective goal. Under these circumstances, the extreme view is that objective research standards are neither possible, nor necessary: in practice, most researchers (even post-structuralists or post-modernists) hold a much less extreme position, continuing to judge what they read. But they cannot continue to use the positivist concepts of error, validity or reliability.

Validity, in the broad sense of avoiding conceptual or logical blunders, remains a goal, but success cannot be quantified: the term may not even be raised within the non-positivist research report. However, it is assumed that best practice has been followed throughout the research, and it is left to readers to judge for themselves (among other things) whether the data gathering methods have been appropriate to the questions asked, whether the instruments used (such as survey questionnaires or oral history interviews) have elicited accurate information, whether they agree with the definitions employed, how far they are willing to accept an argument from a single case or a small range of cases, whether ethnographic field work has fallen into the traps of skewed sampling or of anecdotalism, or to what extent the conclusions reached would hold over time or could be applicable in other situations (transferable).

It remains the responsibility of the researcher to provide the reader with the information necessary to make such judgments: with clear definitions, justifications for the procedures adopted, explanations of the principles and theories that have shaped the research. If the reader comes from a different intellectual framework, and disagrees with the basic principles employed within the research, then there are only two possibilities – to reject the research entirely, or to judge it by its own internal criteria. For instance, critical theorists may judge the value of their research by how useful it could be in shaping policy, particularly in helping to change (improve) the social world (Miles and Huberman 1994: 280): a reader from a different position might consider this irrelevant, but might still be interested in the results of the research from their own perspective.

In the social sciences (sociology, psychology, education), where the non-positivist frameworks are relatively recent, there is still much debate about what standards should be applied and how these should be implemented. This is what Denzin and Lincoln call the 'non-foundationalist' approach to criteria of evaluation, contending that there is no value-free knowledge, and that criteria are actually moral and political rather than epistemological: they flow from 'a feminist, communitarian moral ethic of empowerment, community, and moral solidarity' (Denzin and Lincoln 2000: 872). An early expression of this position is Lincoln and Guba's discussion of standards of 'trustworthiness' and 'authenticity' (1986), which included standards of 'tactical authenticity' (in whose interests the research was conducted). One complete issue of *Discourse Studies* (vol. III, issue 4, December 2001) is devoted to the discussion of 'Authenticity in media discourse'. This debate about evaluation is happening in parallel with the debate about new forms of writing (Richardson 2000) and about the identification and explication of frameworks (Lincoln and Guba 2000).

All these debates are also influencing the humanities (literature, history), but not usually in such an explicit fashion as in the social sciences. Traditionally, there has been an absence of standardised methods for judging the worth of humanities research, but scholars have still not hesitated to criticise those who fail to convince.

In the twentieth century, the main debate within historiography concerned whether or not history was a science (for instance, Hughes 1964). This debate centred on the definition of historical 'fact', and the consequent issue of whether objective and true knowledge of the past was ever possible. Because history concerns the specific and individual event, it does not usually seek to generalise, although historians may suggest that a number of instances constitute a 'trend'. There is no way to know even whether any 'trend' will continue, and certainly not to predict other individual instances.

Though this debate comes out of the positivist paradigm, a majority of historians in that period always judged the value of research by what we would now think of as post-positivist criteria, requiring the historian to seek the truth, even while recognising that the best that could be achieved is interpretation – contingent and incomplete.

So debates among historians have always concerned how to deal with contingency: for instance, how reliable can conclusions be if they are drawn from incomplete evidence? or how far can causation be implied in the relationship between events and their antecedents? or how far can we understand the past from a perspective within the present? Gottschalk (1969, first published 1950), whose writings provided the basic training for several generations of practising historians, devotes a chapter to 'The problem of authenticity, or external criticism' and another to 'The problem of credibility, or internal criticism'. More recently, Startt and Sloan (1989: 42–5) discuss the criteria of 'good history' under the headings: topic definition, bibliographic soundness, research (locating the evidence), accuracy (establishing the authenticity of evidence), explanation (offering credible generalisations and interpretations), historical understanding (capturing the spirit of the past) and writing (of narrative). The terminology used by these writers is clearly commensurate with that of the post-positivist social scientists. So, standards are important to historians, even though they have never agreed on standardised methods of testing for authenticity or credibility, so they have no way of measuring success. In the absence of objective standards, historians can only set out to produce 'a significant, convincing, honest, authentic, and engaging product' (Startt and Sloan 1989: 12).

The standards applied to the historical research discussed in Chapter 6 come out of this post-positivist paradigm. However, there are also influences there from constructivism (denying the possibility of establishing 'truth' and seeking rather what is useful or enlightening) and critical theory (judging the value of history to the project of social change). Those historians who have embraced post-modernism (such as Jenkins 1991, 1997) are still not able to explicate alternative standards for judging the success of post-modern history.

To sum up, there are two different kinds of question to be asked, when judging the standards of research:

- How valuable was it to ask the original research question? (judging the appropriateness of goals and intentions)
- How well has the researcher done what they set out to do? (judging the rigour of procedures)

As always, the answers will be dependent upon the intellectual framework within which the researcher is operating. A positivist will expect low levels of error and high levels of reliability and validity: a post-positivist will tolerate higher levels of error and lower validity and reliability, and a non-positivist may decide that such concepts are not relevant at all to this project. The latter decision does not mean that you, as a researcher, can do what you like: it simply means that you will have the responsibility of convincing a reader of the value of your research, without recourse to these formal concepts. It is in the presentation of your report that you provide a reader with the information to make this judgment.

12.3 Report writing

As you begin to prepare your report you need to consider:

- Who is your audience?
- What content is it essential/important/advisable to include?
- What is the best format for presentation?

Once again, 'appropriateness' is the main criterion in each case. So let us consider this in relation to the possible audiences that you may be addressing.

Audience

Examiners and thesis assessors within an academic context

Academic institutions aim to pass on the skills of a field to novices, and the sort of research that we have been describing usually comes towards the end of that process, as a final year project or a postgraduate thesis. Good teachers will have made clear at all stages of the course what is required from students, and report and thesis writing is just another of these hurdles. If you have not been given a written explanation of the requirements, then you have every right to ask for them.

Your assessment will then be a judgment of how well you have met the requirements. Internal assessors have the advantage of knowing something about your other work, but an external assessor has only the finished product and a copy of the requirements: you have to expect that she will follow these to the letter, so you have to do so too. This may sound pedantic, but academic research (and, in particular, the thesis component) is considered to be the equivalent of a trade apprentice's 'masterpiece', the piece of work that proves skill in the craft worthy of acceptance as an 'expert' in the field.

The minimum requirements will be:

- adequate and accurate citation (see Chapter 2);
- a table of contents, which ideally could be read as a summary of the thesis;
- chapters roughly equal in size and importance, demonstrating a capacity for organisation and structure;
- the problem or field of enquiry set out in the introduction, and returned to in the conclusion, leaving no loose ends or irrelevancies;
- a writing style appropriate to the content (probably drier, less ornamented, than other kinds of reports);
- a bibliography/reference list, in the format related to your citation system.

But the final judgment of your thesis or report will cover much more than these minimum requirements: it will evaluate the whole process of your research, hopefully from within an intellectual framework sufficiently similar to your own that the assessor can be sympathetic with what you are trying to do and will criticise only how well you have done it.

Peers in the research community

Along the way (for instance, while you are doing your doctoral research, before submitting the thesis) you may decide to submit an article for publication in a journal, or present part of your research as a conference paper. Certainly, after your thesis has been examined, you may choose to present parts of your research to a journal or conference. In this case (unless you have been invited to present – and possibly even then), you will be writing for peer assessment, that is, your article or paper will be sent out to recognised experts in the field for comment, and a judgment of both its appropriateness for the purpose and its intellectual and stylistic quality. This is academic 'quality control', designed to weed out the second-rate.

Except for house style, there will be no written requirements for passing this hurdle, so you must simply learn from experience. We advise:

- Have your paper or article read informally by colleagues (or former lecturers or thesis supervisors) before submitting it formally for peer review. Sending anything in draft form, no matter how willing you are to revise at a later date, is unnecessarily increasing the risk of rejection.
- Look closely at the subject matter of articles or papers from previous journal issues or conferences, to ensure that you have chosen your outlet appropriately.
- Look closely at the style of presentation of journal articles, and follow house style (the form of citations, the use of italics, etc), even if that requires considerable adaptation from the way you presented it (or plan to present it) in your thesis.
- Keep your language judicious and measured, no matter how strongly you feel on a subject. Remember that you will not know to whom your report is being sent for review, so make sure you would not be embarrassed if it went to the person whose research you are criticising or superseding. This is not a suggestion that you should tone down your findings, only your language.
- Do not lose heart if you are rejected. If you have followed the advice above, your work will be worth the time of a reviewer, and you can hope that the comments they make will enable you to rewrite and improve, ready for later resubmission either to that outlet or to another, more appropriate one.

The organisation that commissioned (and possibly funded) the research

Institutional report writing is very different from academic essay or thesis writing:

- It is usually much shorter. These readers are not judging *you* from this report: they have already done that before they decided to allow or to commission you to do the research. They are interested only in the results of your research, and they want these presented as succinctly as possible.
- Provide an 'executive summary' as the first element of the report. This is a complete summary of the conclusions and recommendations for action, preferably in not more than one page. The rest of the report expands on this.

- There is no single format, but using a numbering system, for example one similar to the one used in this book can help a reader to navigate through the content. In particular, if these numbered headings are listed in the table of contents, a reader can both see at a glance how the argument is constructed and easily locate the section(s) of special interest to them.
- Start with a statement of the problem/issue being addressed, preferably in point form. Return to this in the conclusion, preferably addressing each point from the initial statement in a comparable point in the conclusion.
- Use diagrams and charts whenever these can usefully summarise information, and not only for numerical data. Miles and Huberman (1994) stress the value of data displays, as a way of presenting findings visually, and give very useful advice on constructing these.
- Attach large documents (such as interview transcripts, or financial reports) at the end. You can quote from these or refer to them in detail (by page and paragraph) along the way.

What this means is that you may have to do two reports – one for your academic supervisors and one for the institution which has allowed or commissioned the research.

The general community

Writing for newspapers and general (rather than academic) journals is yet another ball game. Again, the best advice is to read widely, finding the outlets that are most likely to be interested in what you have to say. This kind of writing can be very satisfying, particularly if you wish to affect community attitudes or change political or social practice, but it seldom wins brownie points within the academic world. The general community has the right to be kept informed of what is being done in its name, but no matter how brilliantly you do that, it will not help you to get a job or a promotion, unless you stick at it long enough to become a recognised 'public intellectual' with a profile that cannot be ignored.

Content and form

Different kinds of research produce different kinds of results, and consequently require different kinds of presentation. Some forms of research have conventions for their presentation, that act like templates. For instance, Spradley (1979: 212–16) advises on the 'Steps in writing an ethnography', which assumes a particular format for presentation. Such templates are required by positivists, still used by post-positivists, but are unlikely to be used by non-positivist researchers.

For, even at the stage of reporting, it is the intellectual framework within which the researcher operates that determines practice. If you are a social scientist, working within a communications studies department, with a positivist bent and a preference for quantitative research, you are likely to present your findings as far as possible in the form of graphs, tables and charts. If you are an historian working within a media studies or cultural studies department, with a constructivist approach and a preference for qualitative methodology, you are likely to present your findings in discursive forms, most commonly as essays.

Qualitative research produces much more variety of reporting than does quantitative research. Potter (1996: 172) proposes that:

> There are five basic purposes that qualitative researchers can exhibit when writing up their reports: description, interpretation, explanation, criticism, and action advocacy. Authors almost always exhibit more than one of these types in their writing, but there is usually one that predominates ...

He then explains (Potter 1996: 175–6) how such purposes can be identified:

- through the form of expression chosen (he proposes five alternatives: interpretive realist tale, mainstream realist tale, critical tale, confessional tale, literary tale);
- through the locus of the argument (on authority, logic, evidence or emotion);
- through the degree of contextualisation of evidence;
- through the degree of self-reflexivity.

If you are a student, presenting a research report or thesis for examination, you must consider the expectations of your department. Once you are qualified, you can seek out academic departments or commercial fields where you can employ your own preferred format and/or style.

Style

'House style' refers to the system in place in an institutional context, governing the presentation of papers, reports or theses. An academic department will have a preferred method of presentation, covering everything from citation style to the size of pages and whether you are permitted to print on both sides of the paper. A journal or conference will have its own method, usually controlling whether papers are accepted in hard copy or on computer diskette or as email attachment, and what word processing package(s) is/are acceptable, as well as what citation style is required and what formatting is allowed (for instance, underlining or italics).

But 'style' is much more than any of these. It is the way your own personality is expressed through your writing, and it can vary enormously both between individual writers and within the work of a single writer depending on the audience being addressed. Your writing style in a thesis will be very different from your writing style in a book (even if it is derived from the thesis): your writing style in an article for an academic journal will be very different from your writing style in an article for a popular magazine. Partly, you adapt your writing style to the expectations of your audience, partly you choose your audience to fit the kind of style you prefer – back to the circularity of the research process.

The range of stylistic options open to the discursive presentation of research is constantly widening. Providing it is consistent with your intellectual framework, you might use emotive and personal reports, diaries, poetry or drama scripts. For instance, the editors of the Ethnographic Alternatives Book Series say:

> Ethnographic Alternatives will emphasise experimental forms of qualitative writing that blur the boundaries between social sciences and humanities ...
>
> We are interested in ethnographic alternatives that promote narration of local stories; literary modes of descriptive scene setting, dialogue and unfolding action; and inclusion of the author's subjective reactions, involvement in the research process, and strategies for practising reflexive fieldwork. (Ellis and Bochner 1996: facing front page)

They later demonstrate what they mean (Ellis and Bochner 2000) in a piece that shifts between their own voices and that of a student, and between exposition and narrative. There is also the possibility of presenting your discursive report in a non-written form – as a performance, or as a film, radio or video production (see Gergen and Gergen 2000; McCall 2000). Whatever style you choose, the key is to provide all the information that a reader needs, and in language that a reader can follow. The use of long words, convoluted sentences and jargon is to be deplored: it is not a sign of your sophistication, but of your insecurity.

Key aspects of style are voice, emotion, tense, and organisation.

Voice

Grammatical 'voice' is divided between active ('I did it') and passive ('It was done'). But we are using the term 'voice' in a different way, to cover both the degree to which the writer is visible within the text (first or third person) and how actively the implied author 'speaks' within the text (direct or indirect speech).

It was once completely unacceptable to use the first person in a research report: from a positivist or post-positivist perspective, the third person was considered to give necessary objectivity and distance, and to ensure the respectability of the report. This was so important that when early ethnographers wrote about their own experiences in the field, in the form of memoirs, they often used a pseudonym (see the examples quoted by Tedlock 2000: 460–1). Now such subterfuges are unnecessary: for instance, Tulloch (2000: 1–5) opens his account of audience research with a personal history of his own interest in audience research methodology. From a critical theory or constructivist perspective, ethnographers deal reflexively with the data they have gathered. This means they openly depict the interaction between themselves and the cultural context: instead of having to choose between writing a memoir or autobiography centring on the self or a life history or standard monograph centring on the other, the ethnographer can present both self and other together within a single narrative form that focuses on the process and character of the ethnographic dialogue (Tedlock 2000: 465).

From a participatory research perspective it is more important to allow the research subject to speak. One way this has been done is by what has been sometimes called the 'ethnographic novel', the writer depicting the individual research subject's story like the protagonist of a novel, but within an accurate cultural context (Tedlock 2000: 461). Another is the *testimonio*, which reads like an autobiography, in the first person, spoken by the research subject (Beverley 2000; Tierney 2000).

Even within first-person narratives, there are other choices to be made. Ellis and Bochner (2000) shift between a dialogue style (in direct speech, identifying each of the writers as participants in an exchange, and later exchanging in a similar way with members of their audience in a research colloquium) and an expository style (expressing what one of them thinks in what they label 'the handbook genre': Ellis and Bochner 2000: 735).

It is also possible to use multiple voices, to allow more than one perspective to be presented within a single report, though hierarchising of these is still likely, giving precedence to the nominal 'author' (Gergen and Gergen 2000: 1028–9).

It is all these styles of writing that draw attention to the subjectivity of the person and the person written about (whether or not these are the same person) that Denzin (2000: 899) calls 'intimate', providing examples of newly emerging forms such as performance ethnography, and new developments in older forms such as film and video production. Richardson proposes that such writing is actually a 'creative analytic practice' (2000: 929) – that in such cases the act of writing becomes part of the process of analysis and interpretation.

Emotion

Science once required not only objectivity (and so third person narration) but also neutrality (the absence of emotion). Positivists and post-positivists consider emotion unscientific, and therefore unacceptable within academic discourse. Non-positivists accept that emotion may have a place in research, though they may still choose not to express their own emotions in any report.

Once emotion is admitted within writing, the moral position of the writer becomes obvious. Brady calls for anthropologists to think poetically, that is both to study the cultural place of language, literature and theatre and to think about these in forms that admit of emotion:

> Through poetic portrayal, although perhaps fictional at the level of precise time and sequence of events, anthropological poets often attempt to convey the

> cross-cultural circumstances and events of their fieldwork in an authentic and penetrating way ... By varying their forms of expression to include poetry, anthropologists attempt to say things that might not be said as effectively or at all any other way. (Brady 2000: 956)

Tense

Science required report writers to write always in the past tense: that was what a 'report' was, a description of what had already been done/achieved/learned. Non-positivist research no longer requires this: 'Immediacy draws the reader into the story. A story occurring in the present as if now unfolding draws the reader in' (Charmaz 2000: 527).

Organisation

Even when the language is emotive or poetic, or the style is creative and innovative, you have a responsibility both to your readers and to your material – a responsibility to make your meaning clear. A report is aimed at assisting a reader to understand, so it should present both your findings and the processes of your thought. You can provide this kind of assistance by addressing your material through one or a combination of several forms of organisation:

- by chronology (linear direction, possibly themes within this);
- by theme (possibly chronological development within each);
- by logic (listing causes, describing stages...).

None of the above is intended to be prescriptive: you do not have to adopt the new ways any more than you have to accept the old ones. The only legitimate limits on your choices are those imposed by the context within which you write (audience expectations), and your own intellectual framework.

12.4 Final evaluation

The standards you wish to meet should be implicit in your research all along and constantly monitored, in the same way as, when you read someone else's research report, you have the right to expect 'best practice'. As discussed in section 12.2 in this chapter, your intellectual framework will shape how you make these judgments. However, there is a form of evaluation that really does come at the end of the process, and applies to all the research paradigms.

Here is a checklist that you can apply in this final stage (whether to your own research process, or someone else's):

- The question/hypothesis: Was this a reasonable question to ask (one for which it is possible to find an answer)? Was the question worth asking (will

finding the answer be valuable, either to help in future practice or just to enlarge the available knowledge of a worthwhile subject)?
- The methodology: Were the broad methodology and the specific research techniques chosen appropriate to the question being asked?
- The data gathering process: Were all terms carefully defined, and the definitions scrupulously and consistently applied? Was the position of the researcher within the project appropriately allowed for in the data gathering process? Were sampling and selecting procedures appropriate to the question and to the methodology? Were ethical issues adequately taken into account? Was data gathered with due diligence?
- The analysis of data: Was the form of analysis appropriate to the type of data gathered? Were analytic procedures (all of them, not just statistical procedures) rigorously and accurately followed?
- The interpretation of data: Was the data allowed to determine the interpretation (not gathered to allow a predetermined interpretation)? Did the researcher acknowledge the position from which the data was being interpreted? Was the position appropriate to the interpretation of the kind of data that had been gathered? Was the data strong enough to support the interpretation being offered?
- Conclusions and reporting: Were the data, and its analysis and interpretation, sufficient to support the conclusions? Were limitations to the research process, the data gathered and the interpretations offered all acknowledged? Was the report clear and judiciously argued? Did the conclusions and the report as a whole adequately address the initial question? Do you still think it was a reasonable question, worth asking? What could/should have been done differently?

Media research (like all social science or humanities research) does not produce fixed, permanent and absolute conclusions. The good researcher does the best she can under the circumstances, acknowledges weaknesses, and looks forward to even more interesting or compelling results in the next project. If you can answer all the evaluation questions without prevarication or embarrassment, you have done well. And hopefully, along the way, you will have experienced some of the joys of original research – exploring the world of ideas with an open mind. The possibilities continue to expand:

> We occupy a historical moment marked by multivocality, contested meanings, paradigmatic controversies, and new textual forms. This is an age of emancipation; we have been freed from the confines of a single regime of truth and from the habit of seeing the world in one color. (Denzin and Lincoln 2000: 162)

12.5 Conclusion

The research the current writers value is that which asks questions that we consider important enough to take up time and energy, chooses a methodology appropriate to answer those questions, and then does the best it can within the constraints of the chosen methodology, acknowledging its inherent limitations. The researchers that we most respect are those who understand and acknowledge their own intellectual framework(s), but do not demand that everyone else must agree and do likewise. If you can locate yourself within an ideological and cultural and social position, and never forget it while you are doing your own research, then you are on the way to being a good researcher. Compared with that – the mechanics is easy…

Glossary

Unless otherwise noted, these definitions are specific to media studies, and may therefore differ from general dictionary definitions. They should be regarded as a starting point, not as final definitions. Terms marked * also appear elsewhere in this glossary.

Administrative research: research aimed at assisting an institution to develop and implement policy, and often funded by that institution. The term originates with Paul Lazarsfeld, who pointed out that good administrative research depends also on the concepts generated by *critical research.

Aesthetics: the principles of taste, usually associated with the arts.

Analysis: the process of breaking down into component parts, or systematising data, to make patterns within the data more evident (see *interpretation).

Analytical psychology: after Jung, a theory of human development and subjectivity which posits both a personal and a collective unconscious (see also *psychoanalysis).

Anthropology: the study of how a society or culture functions, originally applied to the study of primitive societies, geographically and culturally distant from the anthropologist's own society (see *ethnography).

Audience: the receiver(s) or consumer(s) of a text.

Authenticity: a standard applied

1. by historians, in judging the trustworthiness of evidence, particularly documents;
2. by post-positivists, in judging the trustworthiness of research findings.

Authority: a non-positivist research term referring to the degree of trust which a reader accords to a text (comparable to the positivist's *reliability).

Behaviourism: a positivist intellectual *framework which seeks to understand human behaviour by observing and quantifying how real people act and interact, and from this to establish predictive rules.

Case study: the detailed and intensive study of a single case, usually by a combination of methods (such as document analysis, interviews, observation or participant observation), and often resulting in *thick description.

Censorship: official or unofficial practices which limit public access to texts.

Channel: a term from the process school of communication, referring to the route of transmission of a message (physical: voices or bodies; technical: telephone, television; social: schools, media).

Citation: acknowledgment of sources.

Class:

1. a highly contested term within social theory, referring broadly to social divisions based upon the ownership of property;
2. *Marx postulated the divisions to be: the proletariat (working class), bourgeoisie (middle classes) and ruling classes (the owners of the means of production).

Code:

1. within the semiotic school of communication theory, a term referring to any organising system for signs (technical/cultural);

2. within the process school of communication, a term referring to shared rules for creating meaning within messages (see *encode/*decode).

Communication theory:
1. linear (or process) theories of communication postulate messages passing between a *sender and a *receiver;
2. semiotic theories of communication postulate texts circulating within a context.

Concept: an idea which is derived from a *model, and defined specifically within that model (for example, 'patriarchy' from/within feminist theory).

Connotation: a term from the *semiotic school of *communication theory, referring to the kinds of social meanings that become attached to signs over time, in the process of *signification, overlaying their reference to the real world in the process (for instance, 'green' connotes safety; a fox is a pest in Australia, to be exterminated, but a native animal in Britain, to be hunted or protected from hunters). See *denotation.

Constructivism:
1. one of the five research frameworks proposed by Lincoln and Guba (2000), each with its own *epistemology, *ontology, *methodology and *ethics (see also *positivism, *post-positivism, *participatory action research, *critical theory);
2. an *epistemological position, which maintains that all knowledge is constructed, and therefore subjective (see *realism, *idealism).

Consumer: within media studies, the individual to whom a media text is addressed.

Content analysis: a form of textual analysis in which units of measurement are defined which can be applied to a text, and the resulting data can be interpreted quantitatively (and sometimes qualitatively).

Convergence: the process of two or more concepts or activities moving closer together. In media studies the term is used
1. institutionally to refer to the increasing vertical and horizontal ownership and control of media, telecommunications and computer companies;
2. textually to refer to the increasing integration and sharing of media 'content' across media, telecommunications and computer mediated forms so that media forms are increasingly becoming 'hybrids';
3. in terms of audience the development of patterns of use of media, telecommunications and computers in relatively 'seamless' ways.

Conversation analysis: a form of analysis developed within social science, to understand the interpersonal interactions between speakers talking together (often abbreviated to CA).

Covert research: research conducted without the subject's knowledge or consent.

Critical:
1. broadly, pertaining to the practice of criticism;
2. more narrowly, taking the pessimistic view of society and culture, assuming (and finding) the least hopeful prognosis, and favouring political action to remedy social ills (see *critical theory and *critical research).

Critical research: following the Frankfurt School, research aimed at exploring the social and cultural context and developing conceptual tools for this purpose, contrasted with *administrative research.

Critical theory:
1. one of the five research frameworks proposed by Lincoln and Guba (2000), each with its own *epistemology, *ontology, *methodology and *ethics (see also *positivism, *post-positivism, *participatory action research, *constructivism);
2. following the Frankfurt School, theory critical of 'instrumental rationality' as practised by positivist natural (and social) science, and leading to critical research.

Cultivation analysis: that aspect of the Cultural Indicators (CI) programme which measures long-term changes in beliefs, opinions, attitudes and behaviours attributable to television viewing.

Cultural studies: a field of study leading to a research approach which asks how culture operates to produce socially differentiated readings of texts.

Culture: a particularly difficult concept, used in broadly two ways to mean

1. the most valued artistic and literary expressions within a society (from *aesthetics);
2. a whole way of life, including all customary behaviours and generally accepted ideas (from anthropology/sociology) (see *material culture).

Decode/decoder: a term from the process school of communication, meaning to read/the reader of a message in the light of the rules of *encoding (shared codes).

Deduction: the process of reaching conclusions by applying theories or principles to the data (see *induction).

Demographics: measurements of the qualities of *populations (age, gender, etc).

Denotation: a term from the *semiotic school of communication theory, referring to the kinds of meanings that become attached to *signs, in the process of *signification, by reference to the real world (for instance, 'green' is simply a colour, a fox is a four-legged furry animal). See *connotation.

Diachronic research: investigating a single *variable (which may be a theme or a place or a person or a civilisation or any other concept) across time.

Discipline: a division (by subject matter and research methodology) within intellectual life, identified by the naming of university departments, the existence of professional organisations and the circulation of publications such as journals.

Discourse analysis: although this term has specialised uses in linguistics and cognitive psychology, in media studies its main uses are

1. broadly, any form of analysis of talk and text;
2. more narrowly, a form of analysis developed within sociology, to understand how talk and text structure (rather than merely represent) reality (usually referred to as Discourse Analysis or DA);
3. from a *Marxist position, an analysis of the hierarchies established within communication, allowing some levels of communication (usually those of the dominant *ideology) to take precedence over others in any social context.
4. from a *rhetorical position, a set of rules and procedures developed for the *phenomenological analysis of talk and text;
5. from a *structuralist position, the analysis of what is absent from a text, to expose the ideological content hidden within its structure.

Documentation: written forms of *material culture.

Effects studies: research which seeks to measure the effects of the media upon audiences.

Empirical research:

1. research by experiment, based on the model of *scientific experiment on the physical world;
2. research based upon data gathered by systematic observation of the material or social world.

Empiricism: seeking to explain and predict by generalising from experience and discovering necessary relationships among phenomena. (In this book, we propose that it is not accurate to use the term to cover all theoretical frameworks that support empirical methods.)

Encode/encoder: a term from the process school of *communication, meaning to compose/the composer of a message in the light of shared rules (codes).

Epistemology: a theory of how knowledge (as opposed to belief) is constructed by human subjects, answering questions of 'how do we know what is?' (see *ontology, *constructivism, *realism).

Error: a statistical measure of the accuracy of data and analysis (see *standard error).

Ethics: a set of standards by which a group of people seek to regulate their behaviour, drawing on the moral dimension of human character and conduct.

Ethnography: a research procedure used by sociologists, anthropologists and those engaged in cultural studies. Ethnographers attempt to understand how a *culture operates by close observation. The term originated with the anthropological study of remote communities, and in media research has been applied to the study of how families watch television in their own lounge-room, or how a media organisation, such as a radio station, functions.

Ethnomethodology: a methodology which constructs understandings of the everyday world ('reality') through *hermeneutic interpretive procedures (such as *conversation analysis) that acknowledge participants' understandings of their own world.

Factor analysis: a statistical procedure to measure what associated *variables (factors) can produce a result, or a range of possible results, including reducing many measured variables to a much smaller number of latent (not measured) underlying variables.

Falsification: the method, associated with Karl Popper, of testing a proposition by seeking the cases that do not fit: as opposed to *verification.

Feedback: a term from the process school of *communication theory, referring to the response of a *decoder to a message, allowing modification of the next message.

Feminism: an intellectual framework that assumes that women are at least equal to men (the complexities of the term are discussed in detail in Chapter 5).

Field research: a systematic study of a phenomenon in its own social setting. Sometimes equated with *ethnography.

Framework: a view of how the world operates (see *paradigm 1).

Generalisability: a *positivist term to indicate how far the conclusions reached for a sample may (within acceptable levels of *error, *validity and *reliability) apply to the wider *population from which the *sample was taken.

Genre: a covering term for a group of texts of similar subject matter and style.

Grounded theory: a method of *inductive analysis developed by Glaser and Strauss and used extensively within social scientific research.

Hegemony: Gramsci's term for the capacity of the state to achieve the co-operation of its citizens, by a mix of force and consent.

Hermeneutics:

1. a method of interpretation of texts, which sees all meaning as constructed from the interaction of parts and wholes, in a movement called the 'hermeneutic circle', potentially infinite;
2. a theoretical and research perspective seeking to understand human activity (including all forms of *culture) in a similar manner to the interpretation of texts, by locating them within a social or intellectual context.

Heuristic: assisting in finding out, by tentatively applying principles derived from past experience.

Historicism:

1. initially, the interpretation of human experience through the concept of historical change;
2. as defined by Karl Popper, the attempt to understand the patterns of the past in an effort to predict future developments;
3. more recently, the study of the past as a means to understand the present;
4. in contemporary conservative political *rhetoric the judgement of the past by the standards of the present.

Historiography:

1. the practice of the writing of *history;
2. the study of how history has been written.

History:
1. the events of the human past;
2. the surviving record of the human past;
3. writing about the human past, derived from study of the surviving record.

Humanist/Humanism: the philosophical position which values the diversity of human experience, and places this value above that of God or nature.

Humanities: the academic *disciplines which study the uniqueness of human experience, but within its social contexts (specifically literature, history, languages).

Hypothesis: within *positivism a proposition which a particular piece of research sets out to prove or disprove (see also *null hypothesis).

Idealism: an *epistemological and *ontological position, holding that reality ultimately comprises ideas, and that nothing exists independently of our thinking about it. When translated into research, idealists deny the value of *scientific method for studying human behaviour, and prefer research to be descriptive and interpretive rather than explanatory (see *positivism, *materialism, *realism).

Ideology:
1. broadly, a system of ideas;
2. from a *Marxist position, 'false consciousness', or the acceptance of the system of ideas favourable to the ruling *class;
3. from an Althusserian position, those ideas which are so naturalised as to appear self-evident.

Induction: the process of reaching conclusions through the accumulation of supporting data (see *deduction).

Industry: within media studies usually applied to the institutional structures within which media texts are produced.

Institution:
1. a set of rule-governed practices (eg censorship);
2. an organisation which implements institutional practices within social and physical contexts (eg board of censors).

Interpretation: the process of understanding or seeking for meaning, by relating information to a broader intellectual framework, or *paradigm (cf. *analysis).

Intertextuality: the creation of meaning through the relation of one text to an/other text(s).

Interview: a research method involving purposive conversation with respondents (cf. *observation).

Marxism: the intellectual framework derived from the teachings of Karl Marx.

Mass culture critique: the view that popular *culture (including television) is a debased form of culture, because it is mass-produced and aimed at the lowest common denominator (the public as 'mass').

Material culture: those aspects of *culture which take a material form (books, videotapes, films in cans, household objects, etc.).

Materialism:
1. from an *ontological perspective, the view that the world exists independently of its observation (see *idealism, *realism);
2. from a *Marxist position, 'dialectical materialism' is the view that the world exists independent of our observation of it, but that it is constantly changing in a pattern of action and reaction.

Medium: a term from the process school of *communication, referring to the physical or technical means of converting a communication *message into a *signal (spoken language, television).

Message: a term from the process school of *communication, referring to meanings *encoded and transmitted between a *sender and a *receiver.

Meta-analysis: the integration or comparison of many studies, and/or the analysis of how earlier studies have analysed their data.

Method: a specific, orderly research procedure (such as questionnaires, oral history interviews).

Methodology:
1. a coherent set of *methods and techniques which are used together, to enable the conduct of research (eg *field research, *case study);
2. the systematic study of methods.

Model:
1. a conceptual tool to sort and order data;
2. an intellectual framework (see *paradigm 1).

Modernism (cf *post-modernism):
1. a movement within the arts, literature and architecture which placed emphasis on rationality and questions of form;
2. developing in the period in European history since the Enlightenment, the relatively unsystematic set of ideas and values associated with scientific and social progress, and economic expansionism.

Multiple regression analysis: a statistical procedure which measures the nature of the impact of the combination of two or more *variables on some outcome.

Multivariate analysis: a statistical procedure which measures the strength and direction of the associations between two or more dependent *variables across two or more groups of subjects.

Narrative: a sequential verbal or written presentation, consisting of story elements (the fundamentals that are there in every recounting of the narrative) and *discourse elements (those specific to this particular telling of the story).

Noise: a term from the process school of *communication, referring to any interference added to the *signal between the *encoder and *decoder, making decoding more difficult (mechanical noise: static on radio, snow on television, a stutter; semantic noise: jargon, tones of voice).

Non-positivist research: a term used in this book to cover those frameworks which position themselves against *positivism: *post-positivism, *constructivism, *critical theory, and *participatory action research. These imply that knowledge can be increased by *qualitative methods as well as *quantitative methods, that description and interpretation are acceptable methods of data analysis, and that *objectivity is not possible.

Normative analysis: statistical procedures which test data against a norm (or external standard).

Null hypothesis: an *hypothesis that any difference in results between two samples within a *population is due entirely to sampling *error.

Objectivity: a claim to truth based upon factual accuracy and lack of bias. Objective research claims that the researcher stands outside the project, having no influence upon the data being collected, and interpreting the data without being influenced by her own prior experience or values. Objectivity remains a goal for *post-positivists, even though they do not believe that it is achievable, but it is rejected by *non-positivists.

Observation: a research method involving purposive looking (cf *interview).

Ontology: the nature of what exists, and what can be examined by research (answering the question 'what is?') (see *epistemology, *idealism, *materialism).

Paradigm:

1. within research generally, a framework of knowledge which allows some questions to be asked and denies the validity of other questions (sometimes called a *'model');
2. within *semiotics, a structure of meaning, in which *signs are related to other signs through relations of absence (the present sign being chosen from a larger number within the paradigm and implying the existence of the other signs in that paradigm).

Participant observation: an *ethnographic research method, in which the researcher engages in the behaviour or the social situation under study.

Participatory action research: one of the five research frameworks proposed by Lincoln and Guba (2000), each with its own *epistemology, *ontology, *methodology and *ethics (see also *positivism, *post-positivism, *constructivism, *critical theory).

Phenomenology:

1. a research approach which claims to be *objective, by the researcher standing outside the research but viewing from the position of the research subject, while deciding how that subject constructs meaning (through language and interaction);
2. a way of understanding the affective aspects of *audience members' experience of texts.

Plausibility: a term from the *non-positivist research approach, implying the degree of confidence which a reader may have in the truth of data or analysis (comparable to the *positivist's *validity).

Pleasure:

1. in everyday language, what is pleasant;
2. in *psychoanalytic (Freudian) terms, all experience is ultimately attributable either to the pleasure principle (ruled by Eros and constructed through sexuality) or the death wish (ruled by Thanatos and constructed through masochism).

Polysemy: the potentially multiple meanings of a text.

Population: a term from social science research, meaning the totality of possible cases (which may be, but is not necessarily, limited to human beings) to which the research study relates (see *sample).

Positivism:

1. a research approach from a *realist perspective, which maintains that objective knowledge (explanations of human behaviour) can be gathered from observable evidence, and that the *validity and *reliability of any conclusions reached from that evidence can be measured (see also *idealism, *non-positivist research);
2. one of the five research frameworks proposed by Lincoln and Guba (2000), each with its own *epistemology, *ontology, *methodology and *ethics (see also *constructivism, *post-positivism, *participatory action research, *critical theory).

Post-modernism: an ontological and epistemological term, covering a *constructivist and contextualist view of the modern world, which celebrates diversity and creativity, and breaks down boundaries between social concepts and within language. The optimistic version sees a flowering of creativity in this chaotic cultural landscape: the pessimistic version sees the end of all 'meaning'.

Post-positivism:

1. the approach, growing from Popper's critique of *positivism, which seeks objective truth by *scientific method, but evaluated by *falsification (rather than *verification). This is how the term is used in this book, and also how it is used by Lincoln and Guba (2000), as one of their five research frameworks, each with its own *epistemology, *ontology, *methodology and *ethics (see also *constructivism, *positivism, *participatory action research, *critical theory);
2. any methodological approach which challenges *positivism (in this book, we call this *non-positivist research).

Post-structuralism: a set of *epistemological frameworks which are both developments of and reactions against aspects of *structuralism, and which see language-in-action as determining human cultural and social practices.

Primary source: a term used in *historiography to refer to documents which contain first-hand accounts and which are therefore considered to be relatively *authoritative.

Profile: a general description of a research *subject or *population.

Psychoanalysis: after Freud, a theory of human development and subjectivity which posits a determining role for desires repressed in the unconscious (see also *analytical psychology).

Public sphere: that area of the social world not encompassed by private life or established institutions, where ideas circulate freely, leading to the formation of public opinion.

Qualitative research: research which is primarily based on description rather than on measurement.

Quantitative research: research which is primarily based on measurement rather than on description.

Questionnaire: a research method, involving asking questions of respondents, requiring either oral or written answers.

Ratings: the measurement of audiences and their demographic composition.

Reader:
1. a real person within the social world who (literally) reads a written text, or (metaphorically) 'reads' an audio/visual text;
2. within the semiotic school of *communication, the position within *signification from which meaning is constructed (in contrast to the *decoder of the process school).

Reader-response studies: a field of study leading to a research approach which asks how individual readers construct texts.

Realism:
1. an *epistemological and *ontological position which maintains that the world exists independently of its observation (see *constructivism, *materialism);
2. a philosophical position which maintains that explanations of how the world operates can only be obtained by studying the underlying mechanisms and structures that connect phenomena (for instance, Marx claimed that the system of social class was based upon relations of production).

Receiver: a term from the process school of *communication, referring to the *decoder of a *message.

Reception analysis: a research approach which asks how socially differentiated readers produce readings of texts within a cultural context.

Referent: a term from the semiotic school of *communication, referring to that to which *signs refer (whether in the real world or other signs).

Reflexivity:
1. a research strategy in which the researcher reflects upon the process of research itself within the *methodology;
2. a textual strategy within film and television in which the maker reflects, within the text, on the process of textual production.

Relativism: an *epistemological and *ontological position, which proposes that what we know and how we know it is relative to our position in the world.

Reliability: a *positivist term to indicate the stability of data and analysis.

Research: the systematic process of asking questions and finding answers.

Rhetoric: in general use, language designed to persuade or impress.

Rhetorical analysis: a form of textual analysis that identifies the formal techniques of *rhetoric, as described first by Ancient Greek orators.

Sample: within social science research, a number of cases selected to be representative of a larger *population (see *standard error).

Scientific method: a loose and contested set of empirical approaches developed in the physical sciences to measure phenomena and to quantify the effects of *variables upon these phenomena in order to develop predictive theories.

Secondary source: a term used in *historiography to refer to evidence which is not first-hand and which is therefore considered to be less *authoritative than *primary sources.

Semiotics: the study of how *signs signify (of how meaning is constructed socially through signs).

Sender: a term from the process school of *communication, referring to the *encoder of a *message.

Sign: the basic term of *semiotics, referring to an element of a meaning-system, having no inherent meaning itself but contributing to meaning by its relations (*paradigmatic or *syntagmatic) to other signs.

Signal: a term from the process school of *communication, referring to the physical form of a communication (a Morse code bleep, printed marks on a page, etc).

Signification: a term from the semiotic school of *communication referring to the process by which meaning circulates through *signs.

Signified: a term from the semiotic school of *communication, referring to the mental concept invoked by a *sign.

Signifier: a term from the semiotic school of *communication, referring to that aspect of a *sign which has physical qualities, perceived through our senses (a sound, an image, etc).

Social sciences: the academic *disciplines which seek to find the principles by which human society operates (specifically psychology, sociology, education).

Spectator: the viewing position constructed by a text (in contrast to the *'reader' or viewer in the social world).

Standard error: within *quantitative research, a measure of how closely the *sample matches the *population which it claims to represent, and therefore what degree of confidence can be placed in generalising the conclusions from the sample to the population (see *error).

Structural-functionalism: an intellectual framework which links the *structure of society (how the elements of social systems combine) with its functions (the use-value of human activity).

Structuralism: an *epistemological framework which seeks to scientifically analyse the underlying *structure of *culture and of individual cultural products.

Structure: the principles underlying the organisation of essential parts into wholes. Structure can be identified within anything that is capable of being observed and analysed, from individual texts to *culture.

Subject:
1. within media research, a single case, which may be studied on its own (as a *case study) or in conjunction with other subjects in a *sample;
2. within philosophy, a person with a sense of self(-identity).

Subjectivity:
1. the viewing of data from a perspective influenced by the viewer's personal experience (the opposite of the *objectivity desired by *positivists);
2. within philosophy, the sense of self that identifies (creates identity for) a *subject.

Survey: systematic collection of data.

Synchronic research: investigating one or more *variables at the same specified 'moment' in time (which may, depending on the research problem under examination, be defined variously, as a minute, a day, a generation, a year, a century, etc).

Syntagm: a structure of meaning, in which *signs are related to other signs through relations of presence and combination (each sign contributing meaning to all the others in the syntagm).

System: anything composed of parts organised into a whole.

Text: a term from the semiotic school of *communication, referring to any complex communication, that is, a signifying *structure composed of many *signs.

Textual analysis: interpretation of the meaning(s) of texts through a *system (see *content analysis, *hermeneutics, *phenomenology, *psychoanalysis, *semiotics, *structuralism, *post-structuralism, *discourse analysis).

Theory: a set of *concepts, derived from and contributing to a *model, which together explain a phenomenon or practice.

Thick description: a term used initially by anthropologists to apply to the description of data obtained by thorough and detailed investigation of a single case, a narrow set of examples, or a *synchronic moment.

Transferability: a *post-positivist term to indicate how effectively research conclusions can be assumed to apply to a wider range of cases than those studied within the current project, and dependent on information being available about both contexts.

Triangulation: the use of more than one (usually three) form(s) of evidence, in order to test an observation or *hypothesis.

Uses and gratifications studies: a research approach which asks what audiences do with the media.

Validity:

1. broadly, a measure of the truth of a statement;
2. within *quantitative analysis, a statistical measure of the internal and external consistency of an argument;
3. within *rhetoric, a measure of the logic of the argument. A valid argument is one in which the conclusions MUST be true provided the premises are also true: an argument may be valid in form and still untrue, for instance a syllogism with one false premise.

Variable: an element of a situation which can be varied and the variation quantified.

Verification: the method of testing a proposition by demonstrating that it fits all possible cases.

Bibliography

Adorno, T. W. and Horkheimer, M. *The Dialectic of Enlightenment*, trans. J. Cumming (London: Verso, 1979).

Adorno, T. W. 'Culture industry reconsidered', in *The Culture Industry: Selected Essays on Mass Culture* (London: Routledge, 1991, first published 1963).

Agresti, A. and Finlay, B. *Statistical Methods for the Social Sciences*, 2nd edition (San Francisco: Dellen Publishing Company, 1986).

Alasuutari, P. *Rethinking the Media Audience* (London: Sage, 1999).

Aldgate, A. 'Defining the parameters of "quality" cinema for the Permissive Society: the British Board of Film Censors and *This Sporting Life*', in A. Aldgate (ed.) *Windows on the Sixties* (London: Tauris, 2000) pp. 19–36.

Allan, S. *News Culture: Issues in Cultural and Media Studies* (Buckingham: Open University Press, 1999).

Allen, R. C. *Speaking of Soap Operas* (Chapel Hill: University of North Carolina Press, 1985).

Allen, R. C. (ed.) *Channels of Discourse Reassembled: Television and Contemporary Criticism*, 2nd edition (London: Routledge, 1992).

Allor, M. 'Relocating the site of the audience', *Critical Studies in Mass Communication* V (1988) 217–33.

Altheide, D. L. 'The news media, the problem frame, and the production of fear', *Sociological Quarterly* XXXVIII, no. 4 (1997) 647–68.

Althusser, L. 'Ideology and ideological state apparatuses', in *Lenin and Philosophy and Other Essays*, trans. Ben Brewster (London: New Left Books, 1971).

Althusser, L. and Balibar, E. *Reading Capital*, trans. Ben Brewster (London: New Left Books, 1968).

Altman, C. 'Psycho-analysis and the cinema: the imaginary discourse', in B. Nichols (ed.) *Movies and Methods*, vol. 2 (Berkeley: University of California Press, 1985) pp. 517–30.

Alvarado, M. and Buscombe, E. *'Hazell': the Making of a TV Series* (London: Routledge, 1978).

American Psychological Association. *Publication Manual of the American Psychological Association*, 5th edition (Washington, DC: American Psychological Association, 2001).

Anderson, B. *Imagined Communities: Reflections on the Origin and Spread of Nationalism* (London: Verso, 1983).

Ang, I. *Watching 'Dallas': Soap Opera and the Melodramatic Imagination* (London: Methuen, 1985).

Ang, I. *Living Room Wars: Rethinking Media Audiences for a Postmodern World* (London: Routledge, 1996).

Ang, I. and Stratton, J. 'The end of civilization as we knew it: *Chances* and the postrealist soap opera', in R. C. Allen (ed.) *To Be Continued ... Soap Operas Around the World* (London: Routledge, 1995), pp. 122–44.

Angrosino M. V. and Mays de Pérez, K. A. 'Rethinking observation: from method to context', in Denzin and Lincoln (eds) (2000) pp. 673–702.

Anon. 'Media report to women, Summer 1992', *Gender and Mass Media Newsletter* XIII (Nov. 1992) 27.

Arnheim, R. 'The world of the daytime serial', in P. F. Lazarsfeld and F. Stanton (eds) *Radio Research 1942–3* (New York: Essential Books, 1944) pp. 34–85.

Atkinson, P. and Coffey, A. 'Analysing documentary realities', in Silverman (ed.) (1997), pp. 45–62.

Australian Broadcasting Authority. *Investigation Into the Content of On-Line Services: Report to the Minister for Communications and the Arts* (Sydney: Australian Broadcasting Authority, 1996).

Bailey, C. *A Guide to Field Research* (Thousand Oaks: Pine Forge Press, 1996).

Barker, M. 'Critique: audiences "R" us', in R. Dickinson et al. (eds) *Approaches to Audiences: a Reader* (London: Arnold, 1998) pp. 184–93.

Barr, T. *newmedia.com.au*. (St Leonards: Allen and Unwin, 2000).

Barthes, R. *S/Z* (London: Cape, 1975).

Baszanger I. and Dodier, N. 'Ethnographhy – relating the part to the whole', in Silverman (ed.) (1997) pp. 8–23.

Battistuta, S. and Duncan, S. *Accounting for Non-Accountants* (South Melbourne: Nelson, 1998).

Baudrillard, J. *Simulations* (New York: Semiotext(e), 1983).

Baym, N. K. *Tune In, Log On: Soaps, Fandom and Online Community* (Thousand Oaks: Sage, 2000).

Beere, S. 'Women's viewing patterns', *Annual Review of BBC Broadcasting Research Findings* XVII (1991) 51–62.

Beilharz, P. (ed.) *Social Theory: a Guide to Central Thinkers* (North Sydney: Allen and Unwin, 1992).

Bell, A. *The Language of News Media* (Oxford: Blackwell, 1991).

Bell, D. *The Coming of Post-Industrial Society: a Venture in Social Forecasting* (New York: Basic Books, 1976).

Beman, L. T. *Selected Articles on Censorship of the Theater and Moving Pictures* (New York: H. H. Wilson Co., 1931).

Bennett, T. et al. (eds) *Popular Television and Film* (London: BFI Publishing/Open University, 1981).

Bennett, T. *Culture: a Reformer's Science* (St Leonards: Allen and Unwin, 1998).

Bennington, T. L. www.ascusc.org/jcmc/vol5/issue4/bennington_gay.html (2000: visited 19 November 2002).

Bennington, T. L. and Gay, G. 'Mediated perceptions: contributions of phenomenological film theory to understanding the interactive video experience', *Journal of Computer Mediated Communication* 5, no. 4 (June 2000) www.ascusc.org/jcmc/vol5/issue4/bennington_ gay.html

Berger, A. A. *Media Analysis Techniques* (London: Sage, 1991).

Berger, D. E. et al. *Applications of Cognitive Psychology: Problem Solving, Education, and Computing* (Hillsdale: L. Erlbaum Associates, 1986).

Berger, P. L. and Luckmann, T. *The Social Construction of Reality: a Treatise in the Sociology of Knowledge* (Harmondsworth: Penguin Books, 1979).

Bernardi, D. *The Birth of Whiteness: Race and the Emergence of U.S. Cinema* (New Brunswick: Rutgers University Press, 1996).

Bernardi, D. *Classic Hollywood: Classic Whiteness* (Minneapolis: University of Minnesota Press, 2001).

Bernstein, M. (ed.) *Controlling Hollywood: Censorship and Regulation in the Studio Era* (New Brunswick: Rutgers University Press, 1999).

Bertrand, I. *Film Censorship in Australia* (St Lucia: University of Queensland Press, 1978).

Bertrand, I. 'What we are allowed to see: censorship in Australian cinema', in J. Sabine (ed.) *A Century of Australian Cinema* (Melbourne: William Heinemann Australia, 1995).

Bertrand, I. 'Education or exploitation: the exhibition of "social hygiene" films in Australia', *Continuum* XII, no. 1 (April 1998) 31–46.

Beverley, J. '*Testimonio*, subalternity, and narrative authority', in Denzin and Lincoln (eds) (2000) pp. 555–65.

Bhabha, H. 'The other question ...', *Screen* XXIV, no. 6 (Nov.–Dec. 1983) 18–36.

Bignell, J. *Media Semiotics: an Introduction*, 2nd edition (Manchester: Manchester University Press, 2002).

Bird, S. E. and Dardenne, R. 'Myth, chronicle and story: exploring the narrative qualities of news', in J. W. Carey (ed.) *Media, Myth and Narrative: Television and the Press* (Thousand Oaks: Sage, 1988).

Bordwell, D. 'ApProppriations and ImPropprieties: problems in the morphology of film narrative', *Cinema Journal* XXVII, no. 3 (Spring 1988) 5–19.

Bordwell, D. 'Contemporary film studies and the vicissitudes of grand theory', in D. Bordwell and N. Carroll (eds) *Post-Theory: Reconstructing Film Studies* (Madison: University of Wisconsin Press, 1996) pp. 3–36.

Bourdieu, P. 'The aristocracy of culture', *Media, Culture and Society* II, no. 3 (1980) 225–54.

Bournemouth Media School, Centre for Creative Media Research. *Projects* (Online home page) 2003. Available from www.artlab.org.uk/projects.htm (accessed December 2003).

Boyd-Barrett, O. and Newbold, C. (eds) *Approaches to Media: a Reader* (London: Arnold, 1995).

Brady, I. 'Anthropological poetics', in Denzin and Lincoln (eds) (2000) pp. 949–80.

Brand, A. *The Force of Reason: an Introduction to Habermas' Theory of Communicative Action* (Sydney: Allen and Unwin, 1989).

Branigan, E. *Narrative Comprehension and Film* (London and New York: Routledge, 1992).

Brody, S. R. *Screen Violence and Film Censorship: a Review of Research* (London: HMSO, 1977).

Brown, M. E. *Soap Opera and Women's Talk: the Pleasure of Resistance* (Thousand Oaks: Sage, 1994).

Brunsdon, C. *The Feminist, the Housewife, and the Soap Opera* (Oxford: Oxford University Press, 2000).

Brunsdon, C. and Morley, D. *Everyday Television: 'Nationwide'* (London: BFI, 1978).

Buckingham, D. *The Making of Citizens: Young People, News and Politics* (London: Routledge, 2000).

Buerkel-Rothfuss, N. L. and Mayes, S. 'Soap opera viewing: the cultivation effect', *Journal of Communication* XXXI (Summer 1981) 108–15.

Burgess, R. G. *In the Field: an Introduction to Field Research* (London: Routledge, 1993).

Calhoun, C. *Habermas and the Public Sphere: Studies in Contemporary German Social Thought* (Cambridge, MA: MIT Press, 1992).

Campbell, J. *The Hero with a Thousand Faces* (Princeton: Princeton University Press, 1973).

Carmen, I. *Movies, Censorship and the Law* (Ann Arbor: University of Michigan Press, 1966).

Carr, E. H. *What Is History?* (Harmondsworth: Penguin Books, 1961).

Casebier, A. *Film and Phenomenology: Toward a Realist Theory of Cinematic Representation* (New York: Cambridge University Press, 1991).

Castells, M. *The Rise of the Information Society* (Oxford: Blackwell, 1997).

Castro, E. *HTML for the World Wide Web*, 4th edition (Berkeley: Peachpit Press, 2000).

Catterell, P. and Jones, H. *Understanding Documents and Sources* (London: Heinemann, 1994).

Caulley, D. N. 'Ethics: examples of informed consent for interviews', *Evaluation News and Comment* VII, no. 1 (1998) 15–23.

Cavell, S. *The World Viewed: Reflections on the Ontology of Film* (Cambridge, MA: Harvard University Press, 1979).

Charmaz, K. 'Grounded theory: objectivist and constructivist methods', in Denzin and Lincoln (eds) (2000) pp. 509–35.

Charters, W. W. *Motion Pictures and Youth: a Summary* (New York: Macmillan (now Palgrave Macmillan), 1933).

Chatman, S. *Story and Discourse: Narrative Structure in Fiction and Film* (Ithaca: Cornell University Press, 1978).

Chen, P. and Hinton, S. M. 'Realtime interviewing using the World Wide Web', *Sociological Research Online* IV, no.3 www.socresonline.org.uk/socresonline/4/3/chen.html (accessed 30 September 1999).

Chodorow, N. *The Reproduction of Mothering: Psychoanalysis and the Sociology of Gender* (Berkeley: University of California Press, 1978).

Christians, C. G. 'Ethics and politics in qualitative research', in Denzin and Lincoln (eds) (2000) pp. 133–55.

Collingwood, R. G. *The Idea of History* (Oxford: Clarendon Press, 1946).

Collins, J. 'Postmodernism', in Allen (ed.) (1992) pp. 327–53.

Collinson, D. *Fifty Major Philosophers: a Reference Guide* (London: Croom Helm, 1987).

Compesi, R. J. 'Gratifications of daytime serial viewers', *Journalism Quarterly* L (1980) 155–8.

Cooper, D. E. 'Phenomenology', in M. Payne (ed.) *A Dictionary of Cultural and Critical Theory* (Oxford: Blackwell, 1997) pp. 400–5.

Corner, J. 'Meaning, genre and context: the problematics of "Public Knowledge" in the new audience studies', in J. Curran and M. Gurevitch (eds) *Mass Media and Society* (London: Arnold, 1991) pp. 267–84.

Corner, J. *Studying Media: Problems of Theory and Method* (Edinburgh: Edinburgh University Press, 1998).

Couvares, F. G. (ed.) *Movie Censorship and American Culture* (Washington, DC and London: Smithsonian Institution Press, 1996).

Cox, J. *Your Opinion, Please! How to Build the Best Questionnaires in the Field of Education* (Thousand Oaks: Corwin Press (Sage), 1996).

Dabbs, J. M. Jr 'Making things visible', in J. van Maanen et al. (eds) *Varieties of Qualitative Research* (Beverley Hills: Sage, 1982).

Dahlberg, L. 'Computer-mediated communication and the public sphere: a critical analysis', *Journal of Computer Mediated Communication* VII, no.1 www.ascusc.org/jcmj/vol7/issue1/dahlberg.html (2001).

Dahlgren, P. 'The modes of reception: for a hermeneutics of TV news', in P. Drummond and R. Paterson (eds) *Television in Transition: Papers from the first ITSC* (London: BFI, 1985) pp. 235–49.

Danaher, G. et al. *Understanding Foucault* (St Leonards: Allen and Unwin, 2000).

Daniels, T. and Gerson, J. *The Colour Black: Black Images on British Television* (London: BFI, 1990).

Dates, J. L. and Barlow, W. *Split Image: African Americans in the Mass Media* (Washington, DC: Howard University Press, 1990).

de Certeau, M. *The Writing of History*, trans. T. Conley (New York: Columbia University Press, 1988).

de Grazia, E. and Newman, R. K. *Banned Films: Movies, Censors, and the First Amendment* (New York: R. R. Bowker, 1982).

Dening, G. *Mr Bligh's Bad Language: Passion, Power and Theatre on 'The Bounty'* (Melbourne: Cambridge University Press, 1992).

Denzin, N. K. *Symbolic Interactionism and Cultural Studies: the Politics of Interpretation, Twentieth-Century Social Theory* (Oxford: Blackwell, 1992).

Denzin, N. and Lincoln, Y. (eds) *Handbook of Qualitative Research* (Thousand Oaks: Sage, 2000).

Devol, K. S. *Mass Media and the Supreme Court: the Legacy of the Warren Years*, 2nd edition (New York: Hastings House, 1976).

Dixon, M. *The Imaginary Australian: Anglo-Celts and Identity – 1788 to the Present* (Sydney: UNSW Press, 1999).

Docherty, D. et al. *The Last Picture Show? Britain's Changing Film Audience* (London: BFI, 1987).

Doherty, T. P. *Pre-code Hollywood: Sex, Immorality, and Insurrection in American Cinema, 1930–1934* (New York: Columbia University Press, 1999).

Dworaczek, M. 'Censorship on the internet: a bibliography', Marian Dworaczek's home page, www.library.usak.ca/~dworacze/ (updated 13 November 2001, visited 11 January 2002).

Dwyer, T. and Stockbridge, S. 'Putting violence to work in new media; policies, trends in Australian internet, computer game and video regulation'. *New Media and Society* 1, no. 2 (Aug. 1999) 227–50.

Dyer, R. 'White', *Screen* XXIX, no. 3 (Autumn 1988) 44–64.

Dyer, R. *White* (London: Routledge, 1997).

Eagleton, T. *Literary Theory: an Introduction* (Oxford: Blackwell, 1983).

Electronic Frontiers Australia. 'Comments on mandatory filtering and blocking by ISPs', www.efa.org.au/Publish/ispblocking.html (updated 18 March 2003, visited 20 March 2003).

Ellis, C. and Bochner, A. P. *Composing Ethnography: Alternative Forms of Qualitative Writing* (Walnut Creek: Altamira Press, 1996).

Ellis, J. *Visible Fictions*, 2nd edition (London: Routledge, 1992).

Elmer-Dewitt, P. 'On a Screen Near You: Cyberporn', *Time* (domestic) [US] www.time.com.time/magazine/archive/1995/950703/950703.cover.html (updated 3 July 1995, visited 12 February 2002).

Elton, G. R. *The Practice of History* (London: Methuen, 1967).

Evans, R. J. *In Defence of History* (London: Granta Books, 1997).

Factor, J. *Captain Cook Chased a Chook: Children's Folklore in Australia* (Ringwood: Penguin Books, 1988).

Fanon, F. *Black Skin, White Masks* (London: Paladin, 1970).

Faulkner, R. F. 'Improvising on a triad', in J. van Maanen et al. (eds) *Varieties of Qualitative Research* (Beverley Hills: Sage, 1982).

Feuer, J. 'Genre study and television', in Allen (ed.) (1992) pp. 138–60.

Fiske, J. *Introduction to Communication Studies* (London: Methuen, 1982).

Fiske, J. *Television Culture* (London: Methuen, 1987).

Fiske, J. 'Moments of television: "neither the text nor the audience" ', in E. Seiter et al. (eds) *Remote Control: Television, Audiences, and Cultural Power* (London and New York: Routledge, 1989) pp. 56–78.

Fiske, J. *Media Matters: Race and Gender in U.S. Politics* (Minneapolis: University of Minnesota Press, 1996).

Fiske, J. and Hartley, J. *Reading Television* (London: Methuen, 1978).

Flannery, P. 'Internet size and growth', in P. Ensor (ed.) *The Cybrarian's Manual* (Chicago: American Library Association, 1997).

Flitterman-Lewis, S. 'Psycho-analysis, film and television', in Allen (ed.) (1992) pp. 203–46.

Flood, M. and Hamilton, C. 'Youth and pornography in Australia: evidence on the extent of exposure and likely effects. Summary of Australia Institute discussion paper no. 52', (Canberra: Australia Institute, 2003a) www.tai.org.au (visited 3 March 2003).

Flood, M. and Hamilton, C. 'Regulating youth access to pornography' (Canberra: The Australia Institute, 2003b) www.tai.org.au (visited 3 March 2003).

Foerstel, H. N. *Banned in the Media: a Reference Guide to Censorship in the Press, Motion Picture, Broadcasting and the Internet* (Westport: Greenwood Press, 1998).

Fontana, A. and Frey, J. H. 'The interview: from structured questions to negotiated text', in Denzin and Lincoln (eds) (2000) pp. 645–72.

Foster, J. *British Archives: a Guide to Archive Resources in the United Kingdom*, 4th edition (London: Palgrave (now Palgrave Macmillan), 2001).

Foster, H. *Postmodern Culture*, 2nd edition (London: Pluto Press, 1985).

Foucault, M. *The Archaeology of Knowledge* (London: Tavistock, 1972).

Foucault, M. 'Governmentality', *Ideology and Consciousness* VI (1979) 5–21.

Foucault, M. 'What is an Author?', in M. Foucault and P. Rabinow (eds) *The Foucault Reader* (Harmondsworth: Penguin Books, 1986).

Foucault, M. *Ethics: Subjectivity and Truth* (London: Penguin Books, 2000).

Foucault, M. 'Governmentality', in J. D. Faubion (ed.) *Power* (London: Penguin Books, 2002).

Foucault, M. and Gordon, C. *Power/Knowledge: Selected Interviews and Other Writings, 1972–1977* (New York: Pantheon Books, 1980).

Frankenberg, R. *White Women, Race Matters: the Social Construction of Whiteness* (Minneapolis: University of Minnesota Press, 1993).

Franzwa, H. 'The image of women in television: an annotated bibliography', in G. Tuchman et al. *Hearth and Home: Images of Women in the Mass Media* (New York: Oxford University Press, 1978) pp. 272–300.

Friedel, F. *Harvard Guide to American History* (Cambridge, MA: Harvard University Press, 1974).

Frow, J. and Morris, M. 'Cultural studies', in Denzin and Lincoln (eds) (2000) pp. 315–46.

Gadamer, H.-G. *Truth and Method* (New York: Seabury Press, 1973).

Gallagher, M. 'The push and pull of action and research in feminist media studies', *Feminist Media Studies* 1, no. 1 (2000) 11–15.

Galtung, J. and Ruge, M. 'Structuring and selecting news', in S. Cohen and J. Young (eds) *The Manufacture of News* (London: Constable, 1973/1981) pp. 52–63.

Gans, H. J. *Popular Culture and High Culture: an Analysis and Evaluation of Taste* (New York: Basic Books, 1974/1999).

Gans, H. J. *Deciding What's News: a Study of CBS Evening News, NBS Nightly News, 'Newsweek' and 'Time'* (New York: Vantage Books, 1980).

Gauntlett, D. 'Ten things wrong with the media "effects" model', in R. Harindranath and O. Linne (eds) *Approaches to Audiences – a Reader* (London: Arnold, 1998).

Gauntlett, D. *Media, Gender, and Identity : an Introduction* (London and New York: Routledge, 2002).

Gauntlett, D. and Hill, A. *TV Living: Television, Culture and Everyday Life* (London: Routledge, 1999).

Geertz, C. 'Thick description: toward an interpretive theory of culture', in *The Interpretation of Cultures* (New York: Basic Books, 1973) pp. 3–32.

Gelfand, H. and Walker, C. J. *Mastering APA style*. 1st edition (Washington, DC: American Psychological Association, 1991).

Geraghty, C. 'Cinema as social space: understanding cinema-going in Britain, 1947–1963', *Framework* XLII, www.frameworkonline.com/42cg.htm (Summer 2000).

Gerbner, G. 'Dimensions of violence in television drama', in R. K. Baker and S. J. Ball (eds) *Violence in the Media*, Staff Report to the National Commission on the Causes and Prevention of Violence (Washington, DC: US Government Printing Office, 1969) pp. 311–40.

Gerdes, P. 'A content analysis of Australian television news', *Australian Journal of Screen Theory* XI–XII (1982) 58–84.

Gergen, M. M. and Gergen, K. J. 'Qualitative inquiry: tensions and transformation', in Denzin and Lincoln (eds) (2000) pp. 1025–46.

Ghandi, L. *Postcolonial Theory: a Critical Introduction* (St Leonards: Allen and Unwin, 1998).

Ghosh, S. 'The troubled existence of sex and sexuality: feminists engage with censorship', in C. Brosius and M. Butcher (eds) *Image Journeys: Audio-visual Media and Cultural Change in India* (New Delhi and London: Sage, 1999) pp. 233–60.

Gibaldi, J. *The MLA Handbook for Writers of Research Papers*, 5th edition (New York: The Modern Language Association of America, 1999).

Gibson, H. 'Shooting the messenger: a critique of Australia's content regulation regime', *Issue Analysis*, www.cis.org.au/IssueAnalysis/ia10/ia10.pdf (2000, visited 25 April 2003).

Gitlin, T. 'Media sociology: the dominant paradigm', *Theory and Society* VI (1978) 205–53.

Glaser, B. G. *Basics of Grounded Theory Analysis: Emergence v. Forcing* (Mill Valley: Sociology Press, 1992).

Glaser, B. G. (ed.) *More Grounded Theory: a Reader* (Mill Valley: Sociology Press, 1994).

Glaser, B. G. and Strauss, A. L. *The Discovery of Grounded Theory: Strategies for Qualitative Research* (Chicago: Aldine, 1967).

Glasgow Media Group. *Bad News* (London: Routledge and Kegan Paul, 1976).

Glasgow Media Group. *More Bad News* (London: Routledge and Kegan Paul, 1980).

Glossbrenner, A. and Glossbrenner, E. *Search Engines for the World Wide Web* (Berkeley: Peachpit, 1999).

Godwin, M. 'Rimm's fairy tales', *Hotwired*, www.hotwired.lycos.com/special/pornscare/marty.html (1995a: visited 12 February 2002).

Godwin, M. 'The shoddy article: Mike Godwin picks a fight with *Time*, a major perpetrator of the great internet sex panic of 1995', *Hotwired*, www.hotwired.lycos.com/special/pornscare/godwin.html (1995b: visited 12 February 2002).

Gold, R. 'Roles in sociological field observation', *Social Forces* XXXVI, no. 3 (1958) 217–23.

Gordon, C. 'Government rationality: an introduction', in G. Burchell et al. (eds) *The Foucault Effect: Studies in Governmentality* (Chicago: University of Chicago Press, 1991).

Gottschalk, L. *Understanding History: a Primer of Historical Method*, 2nd edition (New York: Alfred A Knopf, 1969).

Graber, D. 'Agenda-setting: are there women's perspectives?', in L. K. Epstein (ed.) *Women and the News* (New York: Communication Arts Books, 1978) pp. 15–37.

Graber, D. *Processing Politics: Learning from Television in the Internet Age* (Chicago: University of Chicago Press, 2001).

Gramsci, A. *Selections from the Prison Notebooks* (London: Lawrence and Wishart, 1971).

Gray, A. *Video Playtime: The Gendering of a Leisure Technology, Comedia* (London and New York: Routledge, 1992).

Gripsrud, J. *The 'Dynasty' Years: Hollywood Television and Critical Media Studies* (London: Routledge, 1995).

Grosof, M. S. and Sardy, H. *A Research Primer for the Social and Behavioural Sciences* (Orlando: Academic Press, 1985).

Gubrium, J. F. and Holstein, J. A. 'Analyzing interpretive practice', in Denzin and Lincoln (eds) (2000) pp. 487–508.

Gunter, B. *Media Research Methods: Measuring Audiences, Reactions and Impact* (London: Sage, 2000).

Habermas, J. *The Theory of Communicative Action, vol. 2, Lifeworld and System: a Critique of Functionalist Reason*, trans. T. McCarthy (Boston: Beacon Press, 1987).

Habermas, J. *The Structural Transformation of the Public Sphere: an Inquiry into a Category of Bourgeois Society*, trans. T. Burger (Cambridge: Polity, 1989).

Hall, S. 'The determinations of newsphotographs', *Cultural Studies* III (Autumn 1972) 53–88.

Hall, S. 'Encoding/decoding', in S. Hall et al. (eds) *Culture, Media, Language* (London: Hutchinson, 1984) pp. 128–38.

Halloran, J. 'The context of mass communications research', in O. Boyd-Barrett and C. Newbold (eds) *Approaches to Media: a Reader* (London: Arnold, 1995) pp. 33–43 (first published 1981).

Hammersley, M. and Atkinson, P. *Ethnography: Principles in Practice* (London: Tavistock, 1983).

Hampton, B. J. *History of the American Film Industry from Its Beginnings to 1931* (New York: Dover Publications, 1970; first published New York: Covici, Friede, 1931).

Haralovich, M. B. 'The proletarian woman's film of the 1930s: contending with censorship and entertainment', *Screen* XXXI, no. 2 (1990) 172–87.

Harley, J. E. *World-wide Influence of the Cinema – a Study of Official Censorship and the International Cultural Aspects of Motion Pictures* (Los Angeles: University of Southern California Press, 1940).

Harper, D. 'Re-imagining visual methods: Galileo to *Neuromancer*', in Denzin and Lincoln (eds) (2000) pp. 717–32.

Harper, S. *Picturing the Past: the Rise and Fall of the British Costume Film* (London: BFI, 1994).

Harper, S. and Porter, V. 'Moved to tears: weeping in the cinema in post-war Britain', *Screen* XXXVII, no. 2 (Summer 1996) 152–73.

Harper, S. and Porter, V. 'Cinema audience tastes in 1950s Britain', *Journal of Popular British Cinema* II (1999) 66–82.

Hartley, J. 'Invisible fictions: television audiences, paedocracy, pleasure', *Textual Practice* I, no. 2 (1987) 121–38.

Hartley, J. *Understanding News* (London: Methuen, 1982).

Hauke, C. and Alister, I. *Jung and Film: Post Jungian Takes on the Moving Image* (Hove: Brunner-Routledge, 2001).

Hawkins, R. H. and Pingree, S. 'Television's influence on social reality', in D. Pearl (ed.) *Television and Behaviour: Ten Years of Scientific Progress and Implications for the Eighties* (New York: US Government Printing Office, 1982).

Hay, J. et al. (eds) *The Audience and its Landscape* (Boulder: Westview Press, 1996).

Hays, W. H. *Memoirs* (New York: Doubleday, 1955).

Helferty, S. and Refauss, R. *Directory of Irish Archives*, 2nd edition (Dublin: Irish Academic Press, 1993).

Hemming, A. 'Soap operas', in *Annual Review of BBC Broadcasting Research Findings*, XV (1989) 27–34.

Heritage, J. 'Conversation analysis and institutional talk: analysing data', in Silverman (ed.) (1997) pp. 161–82.

Herman, E. S. and McChesney, R. W. 'Global media, the internet, and the digital revolution', in E. S. Herman and R. W. McChesney (eds) *The Global Media: the New Missionaries of Corporate Capitalism* (London: Cassell, 1997) pp. 106–35.

Hermes, J. 'Of irritation, texts and men: feminist audience studies and cultural citizenship', *International Journal of Cultural Studies* III, no. 3 (2000) 351–67.

Herzog, H. 'On borrowed experience: an analysis of listening to daytime sketches', *Studies in Philosophy and Social Science* IX, no. 1 (1941) 65–95.

Herzog, H. 'What do we really know about daytime serial listeners?', in P. F. Lazarsfeld and F. Stanton (eds) *Radio Research 1942–3* (New York: Essential Books, 1944) pp. 3–33.

Higginbotham, V. *Spanish Film under Franco* (Austin: University of Texas Press, 1988).

Hill, A. *Shocking Entertainment: Viewer Response to Violent Movies* (Luton: University of Luton Press, 1997).

Hill, A. 'Real TV: audience responses to factual entertainment', Paper prepared for *Visible Evidence X*, December 2002, Marseilles.

Hill, J. and McLoone, M. (eds) *Big Picture, Small Screen – the Relations Between Film and Television* (Luton: University of Luton Press, 1996).

Hill, M. (ed.) *Whiteness: a Critical Reader* (New York: New York University Press, 1997).

Hinton, S. 'Towards a critical theory of the internet', *Media International Australia* (forthcoming).

Hirsch, E. D. Jr *Validity in Interpretation* (New Haven and London: Yale University Press, 1976).

Hobson, D. *'Crossroads': the Drama of a Soap Opera* (London: Methuen, 1982).

Hockley, L. *Cinematic Projections: the Analytical Psychology of C. G. Jung and Film Theory* (Luton: University of Luton Press, 2001).

Hodder, I. 'The interpretation of documents and material culture', in Denzin and Lincoln (eds) (2000) pp. 703–15.

Hoffmann, D. and Novak, T. P. 'A detailed analysis of the conceptual, logical, and methodological flaws in the article: "Marketing pornography on the information superhighway" ', www.ecommerce.vanderbilt.edu/novak/rimm.review.html (updated 2 July 1995a, visited 12 February 2002).

Hoffmann, D. and Novak, T. P. 'A detailed critique of the *Time* article: "On a Screen near You: cyberporn" (Dewitt, 3 July 1995)', *Hotwired*, www.hotwired.lycos.com/special/pornscare/hoffmann.html (1995b, visited 12 February 2002).

Hoffner, C. et al. 'Support for censorship of television violence: the role of the third-person effect and news exposure', *Communication Research* XXVI, no. 6 (Dec. 1999) 726–42.

Höijer, B. 'Social psychological perspectives in reception analysis', in R. Dickinson et al. (eds) *Approaches to Audiences: a Reader* (London: Arnold, 1998) pp. 166–83.

Holland, P. 'When a woman reads the news', in H. Baehr and G. Dyer (eds) *Boxed In: Women and Television* (London: Pandora Press, 1987).

Holstein J. A. and Gubrium, J. F. 'Active interviewing', in Silverman (ed.) (1997) pp. 112–29.

Huaco, G. A. *The Sociology of Film Art* (New York: Basic Books, 1965).

Hughes, H. S. *History as Art and as Science: Twin Vistas on the Past* (New York: Harper Torchbooks, 1964).

Hunnings, N. M. *Film Censors and the Law* (London: Allen and Unwin, 1967).

Iggers, G. G. 'Rationality and history', in H. Kozicki (ed.) *Developments in Modern Historiography* (Basingstoke: Macmillan (now Palgrave Macmillan), 1993) pp. 19–39.

Innis, H. A. *Empire and Communications* (Oxford: Clarendon Press, 1950).

Izod, J. *Myth, Mind and the Screen: Understanding the Heroes of Our Time* (Cambridge: Cambridge University Press, 2001).

Jackson, P. and Penrose, J. *Constructions of Race, Place and Nation* (London: UCL Press, 1993).

Jacobs, L. *The Wages of Sin: Censorship and the Fallen Woman Film, 1928–1942* (Madison: University of Wisconsin Press, 1991).

Jakobson, F. 'Closing statement: linguistics and poetics', in T. Seboek (ed.) *Style and Language* (Cambridge, MA: MIT Press, 1960).

Jameson, F. *The Political Unconscious: Narrative as a Socially Symbolic Act* (London: Methuen, 1981).

Jameson, F. *Postmodernism or The Cultural Logic of Late Capitalism* (Durham: Duke University Press, 1991).

Jary, D. and Jary, J. *Collins Dictionary of Sociology* (London: Collins, 1991/1995).

Jenkins, K. *Rethinking History* (London: Routledge, 1991/2003).

Jenkins, K. *The Postmodern History Reader* (London: Routledge, 1997).

Jensen, K. B. and Rosengren, K. E. 'Five traditions in search of the audience', *European Journal of Communication* V, nos 2–3 (1990) 207–38.

Jensen, K. B. 'The politics of polysemy: television news, everyday consciousness and political action', *Media, Culture and Society* XII, no. 1 (January 1990) 57–77.

Jhally, S. and Livant, B. 'Watching as working: the valorization of audience consciousness', *Journal of Communication* XXXVI, no. 3 (1986) 124–43.

Kaplan, E. A. 'Feminist criticism and television', in Allen (ed.) (1992) pp. 247–83.

Kaplan, E. A. *Looking for the Other: Feminism, Film and the Imperial Gaze* (New York: Routledge, 1997).

Katz, E. and Lazarsfeld, P. F. *Personal Influence: the Part Played by People in the Flow of Mass Communications* (New York: Free Press, 1955).

Kaufman, H. J. 'The appeal of specific daytime serials', in P. F. Lazarsfeld and F. Stanton (eds) *Radio Research 1942–3* (New York: Essential Books, 1944) pp. 86–107.

Kellehear, A. *The Unobtrusive Researcher: a Guide to Methods* (St Leonards: Allen and Unwin, 1993).

Kelson, J. F. (additional material K. R. M. Short) *Catalogue of Forbidden German Feature and Short Film Productions Held in the Zonal Film Archives of Film Section, Information Services Division, Control Commission for Germany* (Wiltshire: Flicks Books, 1996).

Kemmis, S. and McTaggart, R. 'Participatory action research', in Denzin and Lincoln (eds) (2000) pp. 567–606.

Kennedy, V. *Edward Said: a Critical Introduction* (Cambridge: Polity, 2000).

Kerekes, D. and Slater, D. *See No Evil: Banned Films and Video Controversy* (Manchester: Headpress, 2000).

Kim, J. and Rubin, A. M. 'The variable influence of audience activity on media effects', *Communication Research* XXIV, no. 2 (April 1997) 107–35.

Kincheloe, J. E. and McLaren, P. 'Rethinking critical theory and qualitative research', in Denzin and Lincoln (eds) (2000) pp. 279–314.

Kinder, M. 'Review of *Scenes From a Marriage', Film Quarterly* XXVIII, no. 2 (1974–75) 48–53.

Klinger, B. 'Film history terminable and interminable: recovering the past in reception studies', *Screen* XXXVIII, no. 2 (Summer 1997) 107–28.

Kozicki, H. (ed.) *Developments in Modern Historiography* (Basingstoke: Macmillan (now Palgrave Macmillan), 1993).

Kozloff, S. 'Narrative theory and television', in Allen (ed.) (1992) pp. 67–100.

Kracauer, S. *From Caligari to Hitler: a Psychological History of the German Film* (Princeton: Princeton University Press, 1947).

Kramer, K. R. 'Representations of work in the forbidden DEFA films of 1965', in S. Allen and J. Sandford (eds) *DEFA: East German Cinema, 1946–1992* (Oxford and New York: Berghahn Books, 1999) pp. 131–45.

Krippendorf, K. *Content Analysis: an Introduction to Its Methodology* (Beverley Hills: Sage, 1980).

Kruger, C. 'Censoring the internet with pics: an Australian stakeholder analysis' (Online report) www.teloz.latrobe.edu.au/omp (updated 21 October 1998, visited 13 May 2000).

Kubey, R. and Larson, R. 'The use and experience of the new video media among children and young adolescents', *Communication Research* XVII, no. 1 (Feb.1990) 107–30.

Lather, P. *Getting Smart: Feminist Research and Pedagogy with/in the Postmodern* (New York: Routledge, 1991).

Lazarsfeld, P. F. *Radio and the Printed Page: an Introduction to the Story of Radio and Its Role in the Communication of Ideas* (New York: Duell, Sloan and Pearce, 1940).

Lazarsfeld, P. F. 'Remarks on administrative and critical communications research', *Studies in Philosophy and Social Science* IX, no. 1 (1941) 2–16.

Lazarsfeld, P. F. et al. *The People's Choice* (New York: Columbia University Press, 1948).

Leach, E. *Culture and Communication* (Cambridge: Cambridge University Press, 1976).

Lechte, J. (ed.) *Fifty Key Contemporary Thinkers* (London: Routledge, 1994).

Lévi-Strauss, C. 'The structural study of myth', *Journal of American Folklore* LXXVIII, no. 270 (Oct.–Dec.1955) 428–44.

Levin, J. and Fox, J. A. *Elementary Statistics in Social Research*, 7th edition (New York: Longman, 1997).

Lewis, J. 'Decoding television news', in P. Drummond and R. Paterson (eds) *Television in Transition: Papers from the First International Television Studies Conference* (London: BFI, 1985) pp. 205–33.

Lewis, J. *Hollywood v. Hard-Core: How the Struggle over Censorship Saved the Modern Film Industry* (New York: New York University Press, 2000).

Lincoln, Y. S. and Guba, E. G. 'But is it rigorous? Trustworthiness and authenticity in naturalistic evaluation', in D. D.Williams (ed.) *Naturalistic Evaluation* (San Francisco: Jossey-Bass, 1986).

Lincoln Y. S. and Guba, E. G. 'Paradigmatic controversies, contradictions and emerging confluences', in Denzin and Lincoln (eds) (2000) pp. 163–88.

Lindlof, T. (ed.) *Natural Audiences: Qualitative Research of Media Use and Effects* (Norwood: Ablex, 1987).

Lindlof, T. *Qualitative Communication Research Methods* (Thousand Oaks: Sage, 1995).

Lindsay, V. *The Art of the Moving Picture* (New York: Liveright, 1970, first published 1915).

Lipkin, S. 'Technology as ontology: a phenomenological approach to video image resolution', *Quarterly Review of Film and Video* XII, no. 3 (1990) 93–8.

Longford, Lord. *Pornography: the Longford Report* (London: Coronet Books, 1972).

Lopate, C. 'Daytime television: you'll never want to leave home', *Radical America* (Jan. 1977) 32–51.

Lopez, J. (ed.) *After Postmodernism: an Introduction to Critical Realism* (London: Continuum, 2001).

Lotz, A. 'Assessing qualitative television audience research: incorporating feminist and anthropological theoretical innovation', *Communication Theory* X, no. 4 (Nov. 2000) 447–67.

Lull, L. 'The social uses of television', *Human Communication Research* XVI, no. 3 (1980) 197–209.

Lumby, C. *Gotcha: Life in a Tabloid World* (St Leonards: Allen and Unwin, 1999).

Macliammoir, M. *Put Money in Thy Purse* (London: Methuen, 1952).

Macfie, A. L. (ed.) *Orientalism: a Reader* (Edinburgh: Edinburgh University Press, 2000).

MacKenzie, J. M. *Orientalism: History, Theory and the Arts* (Manchester: Manchester University Press, 1995).

Madriz, E. 'Focus groups in feminist research', in Denzin and Lincoln (eds) (2000) pp. 835–50.

Maltby, R. '*Baby Face*, or how Joe Breen made Barbara Stanwyck atone for causing the Wall Street crash', *Screen* XXVII, no. 2 (1986) 22–45.

Maltby, R. ' "To prevent the prevalent type of book": censorship and adaptation in Hollywood, 1924–1934', in F. G. Couvares (ed.) *Movie Censorship and American Culture* (Washington, DC and London: Smithsonian Institution Press, 1996) pp. 97–128.

Maltby, R. and Stokes, M. (eds) *American Movie Audiences: From the Turn of the Century to the Early Sound Era* (London: BFI, 1998).

Marcus, G. E. and Fischer, M. M. J. *Anthropology as Cultural Critique* (Chicago: University of Chicago Press, 1986).

Marwick, A. ' "A fetishism of documents"? The salience of source-based history', in H. Kozicki (ed.) *Developments in Modern Historiography* (Basingstoke: Macmillan (now Palgrave Macmillan), 1993) pp. 107–38.

Mathews, T. D. *Censored* (London: Chatto and Windus, 1994).

McCall, M. M. 'Performance ethnography: a brief history and some advice', in Denzin and Lincoln (eds) (2000) pp. 421–34.

McChesney, R. W. *Telecommunications, Mass Media, and Democracy: the Battle for the Control of U.S. Broadcasting, 1928–1935* (New York: Oxford University Press, 1993).

McChesney, R. W. *The Global Media Giants: the Nine Firms that Dominate the World,* www.fair.org/extra/9711/gmg.html (updated 1997, visited 7 November 2001).

McChesney, R. W. *Rich Media, Poor Democracy: Communication Politics in Dubious Times* (Urbana: University of Illinois Press, 1999).

McChesney, R. W. et al. *Capitalism and the Information Age: the Political Economy of the Global Communication Revolution* (New York: Monthly Review Press, 1998).

McKie, D. 'Exclusion, humour and television news', *Australian Journal of Communication* XX, no. 2 (1993) 68–78.

McQuail, D. *McQuail's Mass Communication Theory*, 4th edition (London: Sage, 2000).

Medick, H. 'The so-called Laichingen Hunger Chronicle: an example of the fiction of the factual, the traps of evidence, and the possibilities of proof in the writing of history', in G. Sider and G. Smith (eds) *Between History and Histories: the Making of Silences and Commemorations* (Toronto: University of Toronto Press,1997) pp. 284–99.

Metz, C. *Film Language: a Semiotics of the Cinema* (New York: Oxford University Press, 1974).

Metz, C. *Psychoanalysis and the Cinema: the Imaginary Signifier* (London: Macmillan (now Palgrave Macmillan), 1983).

Miles, M. B. and Huberman, A. M. *Qualitative Data Analysis: an Expanded Sourcebook*, 2nd edition (Thousand Oaks: Sage, 1994).

Miller, G. 'Building bridges: the possibility of analytic dialogue between ethnography, conversation analysis and Foucault', in Silverman (ed.) (1997) pp. 24–44.

Miller, J. and Glassner, B. 'The "inside" and the "outside": finding realities in interviews', in Silverman (ed.) (1997) pp. 99–129.

Mills, I. 'Pulpit drama: the mythic form of TV news programmes', in P. Edgar (ed.) *The News in Focus: the Journalism of Exception* (South Melbourne: Macmillan (now Palgrave Macmillan), 1980) pp. 44–75.

Modleski, T. 'The search for tomorrow in today's soap operas', in *Loving with a Vengeance* (New York: Methuen, 1982) pp. 85–109.

Modleski, T. 'The rhythms of reception: daytime television and women's work', in E. A. Kaplan (ed.) *Regarding Television* (Frederick: American Film Institute, 1983) pp. 67–75.

Moley, R. *The Hays Office* (Indianapolis: Bobbs-Merrill, 1945).

Mongia, P. (ed.) *Contemporary Postcolonial Theory: a Reader* (London: Arnold, 1996).

Moran, D. and Mooney, T. *The Phenomenology Reader* (London: Routledge, 2002).

Morley, D. *The 'Nationwide' Audience: Structure and Decoding* (London: BFI, 1980).

Morley, D. 'Domestic relations: the framework of family viewing in Great Britain', in J. Lull (ed.) *World Families Watch Television* (Beverley Hills: Sage, 1988) pp. 22–48.

Morley, D. 'Changing paradigms in audience studies', in E. Seiter et al. (eds) *Remote Control: Television, Audiences, and Cultural Power* (London and New York: Routledge, 1989) pp. 16–43.

Morley, D. and Robins, K. 'Spaces of identity: communications technologies and the reconfiguration of Europe', *Screen* XXX, no. 4 (Autumn 1999) 10–35.

Morrison, D. E. *The Search for a Method: Focus Groups and the Development of Mass Communication Research* (Luton: University of Luton Press, 1998).

Mulvey, L. 'Visual pleasure and narrative cinema', *Screen* XVI, no. 3 (Autumn 1975) 6–18.

Mumby, D. and Spitzack, C. 'Ideology and television news: a metaphoric analysis of political stories', *Central States Speech Journal* XXXIV, no. 3 (1985) 162–71.

Nash, R. H. *Ideas of History*, two vols (New York: E. P. Dutton, 1969).

Nightingale, V. 'Shifty characters and shady relations', *Media Information Australia* LXXIII (August 1994) 40–4.

Olesen, V. L. 'Feminisms and qualitative research at and into the millenium', in Denzin and Lincoln (eds) (2000) pp. 645–72.

O'Sullivan, T. et al. *Key Concepts in Communication and Cultural Studies*, 2nd edition (London and New York: Routledge, 1994).

Parkin, F. *Class Inequality and Political Order* (London: Paladin Books, 1973).

Parsons, T. *Social Systems and the Evolution of Action Theory* (New York: Free Press, 1977).

Patton, M. Q. *Qualitative Evaluation and Research Methods*, 2nd edition (Newbury Park: Sage, 1990).

Penley, C. 'Feminism, psychoanalysis, and the study of popular culture', in L. Grossberg et al. (eds) *Cultural Studies* (New York: Routledge, 1992) pp. 479–500.

Peräkylä, A. 'Reliability and validity in research based on tapes and transcripts', in Silverman (ed.) (1997) pp. 201–19.

Pernick, M. S. *The Black Stork: Eugenics and the Death of 'Defective' Babies in American Medicine and Motion Pictures Since 1915* (New York: Oxford University Press, 1996).

Peterson, J. 'Is a cognitive approach to the avant-garde cinema perverse?', in D. Bordwell and N. Carroll (eds) *Post-Theory: Reconstructing Film Studies* (Madison: University of Wisconsin Press, 1996) pp. 108–29.

Phelps, G. *Film Censorship* (London: Gollancz, 1975).

Phillips, J. L. *How to Think About Statistics*, 6th edition (New York: W. H. Freeman, 2000).

Philo, G. et al. *Really Bad News* (London: Writers and Readers, 1982).

Philo, G. and Miller, D. 'Cultural compliance and critical media studies', *Media, Culture and Society* XX (2000) 831–39.

Popper, K. *The Poverty of Historicism* (London: Routledge and Kegan Paul, 1957).

Potter, J. 'Discourse analysis as a way of analysing naturally-occurring talk', in Silverman (ed.) (1997) pp. 144–60.

Potter, W. J. *An Analysis of Thinking and Research about Qualitative Methods* (Mahwah: L. Erlbaum Associates, 1996).

Propp, V. *Morphology of the Folktale* (Austin: University of Texas Press, 1975).

Punch, M. 'Politics and ethics in qualitative research', in Denzin and Lincoln (eds) (2000) pp. 83–97.

Quigley, M. *Decency in Motion Pictures* (New York: Macmillan (now Palgrave Macmillan), 1937).

Radway, J. *Reading the Romance: Women, Patriarchy and Popular Literature* (Chapel Hill: University of North Carolina Press, 1984).

Rakow, L. F. and Kranich, K. 'Woman as sign in television news', *Journal of Communication* XLI, no. 1 (Winter 1991) 8–23.

Randall, M. *Testimonios: a Guide to Oral History* (Toronto: Participatory Research Group, 1985).

Randall, R. *Censorship of the Movies* (Madison: University of Wisconsin Press,1968).

Report of the Enquiry Committee on Film Censorship (New Delhi: Ministry of Information and Broadcasting, 1969).

Report of the [US] *Commission on Obscenity and Pornography* (Toronto: Bantam, 1970).

Report of the Committee on Obscenity and Film Censorship, presented to Parliament by the Secretary of State for the Home Department (London: Her Majesty's Stationery Office, 1980).

Report on the Powers of the Ontario Film Review Board (Toronto: Ontario Law Reform Commission, 1992).

Report on Video and Computer Games and Classification Issues (Canberra: Senate Select Committee on Community Standards Relevant to the Supply of Services Utilising Electronic Technologies, Parliament of the Commonwealth of Australia, 1993).

Reynard, K. W. (ed.) *Aslib Directory of Information Sources in UK*, 11th edition (London: Aslib, 2000).

Richardson, L. 'Writing: a method of enquiry', in Denzin and Lincoln (eds) (2000) pp. 923–48.

Robertson, J. C. *The British Board of Film Censors: Film Censorship in Britain, 1896–1950* (London: Croom Helm, 1985).

Ricoeur, P. *Interpretation Theory: Discourse and the Surplus of Meaning* (Fort Worth: Christian University Press, 1976).

Rimm, M. 'Marketing pornography on the information superhighway: a survey of 917,410 images, descriptions, short stories, and animations downloaded 8.5 million times by consumers in over 2000 cities in forty countries, provinces, and territories', *The Georgetown Law Journal* MDDDIII (1995) 1849–1934.

Robertson, J. C. *The Hidden Cinema: British Film Censorship in Action, 1913–1972* (London: Routledge, 1989).

Robinson, L. S. 'What's my line? Telefiction and women's work', in *Sex, Class and Culture* (Bloomington: Indiana University Press, 1986) pp. 310–44.

Roediger, D. R. *The Wages of Whiteness: Race and the Making of the American Working Class* (London: Verso, 1991).

Roscoe, J. *Documentary in New Zealand: an Immigrant Nation* (Palmerston North: Dunmore Press, 1999).

Rosengren, K. E. et al. (eds) *Media Gratifications Research: Current Perspectives* (Thousand Oaks: Sage, 1985).

Ross, L. *Picture* (New York: Rinehart, 1952).

Rothfield, P. 'Thinking through the phenomenological body', in *'Researching the Self in Postmodernity' Seminar*, La Trobe University (Melbourne, 2003).

Rushing, J. H. and Frentz, T. S. *Projecting the Shadow: the Cyborg Hero in American Film* (Chicago: University of Chicago Press, 1991).

Said, E. W. *Orientalism: Western Conceptions of the Orient* (London: Penguin Books, 1991).

Said, E. W. *Culture and Imperialism* (New York: Random House, 1993).

Sarris, A. *The American Cinema: Directors and Directions 1929–1968* (New York: Dutton, 1968).

Scannell, P. 'For a phenomenology of radio and television', *Journal of Communication* XLV, no. 3 (1995) 4–19.

Scannell, P. *Radio, Television and Modern Life* (Oxford: Blackwell, 1996).

Schaefer, E. *'Bold! Daring! Shocking! True!': a History of Exploitation Films 1919–1959* (Durham: Duke University Press, 1999).

Schlesinger, P. et al., *Women Viewing Violence* (London: BFI, 1992).

Schonlau, M. et al. *Conducting Research Surveys via E-Mail and the Web* (place of publication not given: Rand, 2002).

Schumach, M. *The Face on the Cutting Room Floor: the Story of Movie and Television Censorship* (New York: Morrow, 1964).

Sebstrup, P. 'Methodological developments in content analysis', in K. E. Rosengren (ed.) *Advances in Content Analysis* (Beverley Hills: Sage, 1981) pp. 133–58.

Seiter, E. et al. ' "Don't treat us like we're so stupid and naive": toward an ethnography of soap opera viewers', in E. Seiter et al. (eds) *Remote Control: Television, Audiences, and Cultural Power* (London and New York: Routledge 1989) pp. 223–47.

Seiter, E. 'Making distinctions: case study of a troubling interview', *Cultural Studies* IV, no. 1 (1990) 61–84.

Severin, W. J. and Tankard, J. W. *Communication Theories: Origins, Methods, Uses* (New York: Longman, 1988).

Shanahan, J. and Morgan, M. *Television and its Viewers: Cultivation Theory and Research* (Cambridge: Cambridge University Press, 1999).

Sharot, T. 'Measuring television audiences in the UK', in R. Kent (ed.) *Measuring Media Audiences* (London: Routledge, 1994) pp. 42–87.

Schiller, D. *Digital Capitalism: Networking the Global Market System* (Cambridge, MA: MIT Press, 1999).

Shohat, E. and Stam, R. *Unthinking Eurocentrism: Multiculturalism and the Media* (London: Routledge, 1994).

Sider, G. and Smith, G. (eds) *Between History and Histories: the Making of Silences and Commemorations* (Toronto: University of Toronto Press, 1997).

Signorielli, N. and Morgan, M. (eds) *Cultivation Analysis: New Directions in Media Effects Research* (Newbury Park: Sage, 1990).

Silverman, D. *The Theory of Organisations: a Sociological Framework* (London: Heinemann, 1970).

Silverman, D. (ed.) *Qualitative Research: Theory, Method and Practice* (London: Sage, 1997).

Silverman, D. *Doing Qualitative Research: a Practical Handbook* (Thousand Oaks: Sage, 2000).

Silverstone, R. *Television and Everyday Life* (London: Routledge, 1994).

Silverstone, R. 'Convergence is a dangerous word', *Convergence* 1, no. 1 (1995) 11–13.

Skinner, J. M. *The Cross and the Cinema: the Legion of Decency and the National Catholic Office for Motion Pictures 1933–1970* (Westport: Praeger, 1993).

Smith, J. K. and Deemer, D. K. 'The problem of criteria in the age of relativism', in Denzin and Lincoln (eds) (2000) pp. 877–97.

Sobchack, V. *The Address of the Eye: a Phenomenology of the Film Experience* (Princeton: Princeton University Press, 1992).

Sobchack, V. 'Phenomenology and the film experience', in L. Williams (ed.) *Viewing Positions: Ways of Seeing Film* (New Brunswick: Rutgers University Press, 1995).

Sobchack, V. 'The scene of the screen: envisioning cinematic and electronic "presence" ', in J. T. Caldwell (ed.) *Electronic Media and Technoculture* (Piscataway: Rutgers University Press, 2000).

Sperry, S. 'Television news as narrative', in R. P. Adler (ed.) *Understanding Television* (New York: Praeger, 1981) pp. 245–312.

Spivak, G. C. 'Can the subaltern speak?', in C. Nelson and L. Grossberg (eds) *Marxist Interpretations of Culture* (Urbana: University of Illinois Press, 1988).

Spoto, D. *The Art of Alfred Hitchcock: Fifty Years of His Motion Pictures*, 2nd edition (New York: Doubleday, 1992).

Spradley, J. P. *The Ethnographic Interview* (New York: Holt, Rinehart and Winston, 1979).

Stadler, H. A. 'Film as experience: phenomenological concepts of cinema and television studies', *Quarterly Review of Film and Video* XII, no. 3 (1990) 37–50.

Staiger, J. and Barker, M. 'Traces of interpretations: Janet Staiger and Martin Barker in conversation', *Framework* XLII, www.frameworkonline.com/42jsmb.htm (Summer 2000).

Stake, R. E. 'Case studies', in Denzin and Lincoln (eds) (2000) pp. 435–54.

Startt, J. D. and Sloan, W. D. *Historical Methods in Mass Communication* (Hillsdale: L. Erlbaum Associates, 1989).

St John-Stevas, N. *Obscenity and the Law* (London: Secker and Warburg, 1956).

Stokes, M. and Maltby, R. (eds) *Identifying Hollywood's Audiences: Cultural Identity and the Movies* (London: BFI, 1999).

Storr, A. *Freud: a Very Short Introduction* (Oxford: Oxford University Press, 2001).

Strauss, A. *Qualitative Analysis for Social Scientists* (Cambridge: Cambridge University Press, 1987).

Strauss, A. L. and Corbin, J. *Basics of Qualitative Research: Grounded Theory Procedures and Techniques* (Newbury Park: Sage, 1990).

Strauss, A. L. and Corbin, J. *Basics of Qualitative Research: Techniques and Procedures for Developing Grounded Theory* (Thousand Oaks: Sage, 1998).

Street, S. *British Cinema in Documents* (London: Routledge, 2000).

Strunk, William and White, E. B. *The Elements of Style*, 4th edition (Boston: Allyn and Bacon, 2000).

Studlar, G. 'Masochism and the perverse pleasures of the cinema', in B. Nichols (ed.) *Movies and Methods*, vol. 2 (Berkeley: University of California Press, 1984) pp. 602–21.

Sweeney, K. W. 'The persistence of vision: the re-emergence of phenomenological theories of film', *Film and Philosophy* 1, no. 1 (1994) 29–38.

Tedlock, B. 'Ethnography and ethnographic representation', in Denzin and Lincoln (eds) (2000) pp. 455–86.

ten Have, P. *Doing Conversation Analysis: a Practical Guide* (London: Sage, 1998).

Thornham, S. ' "A Good Body": the case of/for feminist media studies', *European Journal of Cultural Studies* VI, no. 1 (2003) 75–94.

Tierney, W. G. 'Undaunted courage: life history and the postmodern challenge', in Denzin and Lincoln (eds) (2000) pp. 537–53.

Todorov, T. *The Poetics of Prose* (Oxford: Blackwell, 1977).

Todorov, T. *Introduction to Poetics*, trans. R. Howard (Minneapolis: University of Minnesota Press, 1981).

Trevelyan, J. *What the Censor Saw* (London: Michael Joseph, 1973).

Tuchman, G. 'The symbolic annihilation of women by the mass media', in S. Cohen and J. Young (eds) *The Manufacture of News* (London: Constable, 1973/1981).

Tuchman, G. *Making News: a Study in the Construction of Reality* (New York: Free Press, 1978).

Tulloch, J. *Watching Television Audiences: Cultural Theories and Methods* (London: Arnold, 2000).

Tulloch, J. and Moran, A. *A Country Practice: Quality Soap* (Sydney: Allen and Unwin, 1986).

Turabian, K. L. *A Manual for Writers of Term Papers, Theses and Dissertations*, 6th edition (Chicago: University of Chicago Press, 1996).

Turner, G. *National Fictions: Literature, Film and the Construction of Australian Narrative*, 2nd edition (St Leonards: Allen and Unwin, 1993).

University of Chicago Press. *The Chicago Manual of Style: for Authors, Editors, and Copywriters*, 14th edition (Chicago: University of Chicago Press, 1996).

U.S. Commission on Civil Rights. *Window Dressing on the Set: Women and Minorities in Television* (New York: U.S. Commission on Civil Rights, 1977).

Vaillancourt, P. M. *When Marxists Do Research* (New York: Greenwood Press,1986).

Van Dijk, T. A. *Discourse and Communication: New Approaches to the Analysis of Mass Media Discourse and Communication* (Berlin and New York: Walter de Gruyter, 1985).

van Maanen, J. (ed.) *Qualitative Studies of Organizations* (Thousand Oaks: Sage, 1998).

Vansina, J. *Oral Tradition* (London: Routledge and Kegan Paul, 1965).

van Zoonen, L. 'Rethinking women and the news', *European Journal of Communication* III (1988) 35–53.

van Zoonen, L. *Feminist Media Studies* (Thousand Oaks: Sage, 1994).

Vieira, M. *Sin in Soft Focus: Pre-code Hollywood* (New York: Harry Abrams, 1999).

Walkerdine, V. 'Video replay: families, films and fantasy', in V. Burgin et al. (eds) *Formations of Fantasy* (London: Methuen, 1986) pp. 167–99.

Watson, C. and Shuker, R. *In the Public Good? Censorship in New Zealand* (Palmerston North: Dunmore Press, 1998).

Watson, R. 'Ethnomethodology and textual analysis', in Silverman (ed.) (1997) pp. 81–98.

Webb, E. J. et al. *Unobtrusive Measures: Non-reactive Research in the Social Sciences* (Chicago: Rand McNally, 1966).

Webb, E. J. et al. *Non-reactive Measures in the Social Sciences*, 2nd edition (Boston: Houghton Miflin, 1981).

Weitzman, E. A. 'Software and qualitative research', in Denzin and Lincoln (eds) (2000) pp. 803–20.

Wentland, E. J. *Survey Responses: an Evaluation of Their Validity* (San Diego: Academic Press, 1993).

Wetherell, M. et al. (eds) *Discourse Theory and Practice: a Reader* (London: Sage, 2001).

White, H. *Metahistory: the Historical Imagination in Nineteenth Century Europe* (Baltimore: Johns Hopkins University Press, 1973).

White, H. *The Content of the Form: Narrative Discourse and Historical Representation* (Baltimore: John Hopkins University Press, 1987).

White, M. 'Ideological analysis and television', in Allen (ed.) (1992) pp. 161–202.

White, R. *Inventing Australia: Images and Identity 1688–1980* (Sydney: George Allen and Unwin, 1981).

Wilkin, R. 'Textu(r)al engagement: a conaesthetics of contemporary freeways', *IO* 1, no. 4, www.lpt.fi/io/io2000/wilken.html (2000, visited 10 December 2002).

Williams, R. *Television: Technology and Cultural Form* (London, Fontana, 1974).

Williams, R. 'A lecture on realism', *Screen* XVIII, no. 1 (Spring 1977) 61–74.

Williams, R. *Keywords: a Vocabulary of Culture and Society* (London: Fontana Press, 1988).

Wilson, T. *Watching Television: Hermeneutics, Reception and Popular Culture* (Cambridge: Polity, 1993).

Wise, G. *American Historical Explanations: a Strategy for Grounded Inquiry,* 2nd edition (Minneapolis: University of Minnesota Press, 1980).

Wober, J. M. and Fazal, S. '*Neighbours* at *Home and Away*: British viewers' perceptions of Australian soap operas', *Media Information Australia* LXXI (February 1994) 78–87.

Wober, J. M. 'Cultural Indicators: European reflections on a research paradigm', in R. Dickinson et al. (eds) *Approaches to Audiences: a Reader* (London: Arnold, 1998) pp. 61–73.

Wollen, T. 'Perspectives of belonging', *Metro* LXXXVII (Spring 1991) 31–7.

Wood, E. M. and Foster, J. B. (eds) *In Defense of History: Marxism and the Postmodern Agenda* (New York: Monthly Review Press, 1997).

Wood, R. E. 'Toward an ontology of film, a phenomenological approach', *Film Philosophy* V, no. 24, www.film-philosophy.com/vol5-2001/n24wood (2001, visited 19 August 2001).

Wright, W. *Six-guns and Society: a Structural Study of the Western* (Berkeley: University of California Press, 1975).

Wyndham, D. 'Advertisers' woman, 80s woman: which twin is the phoney', *Media Information Australia* XXXI (1984) 26–33.

Index